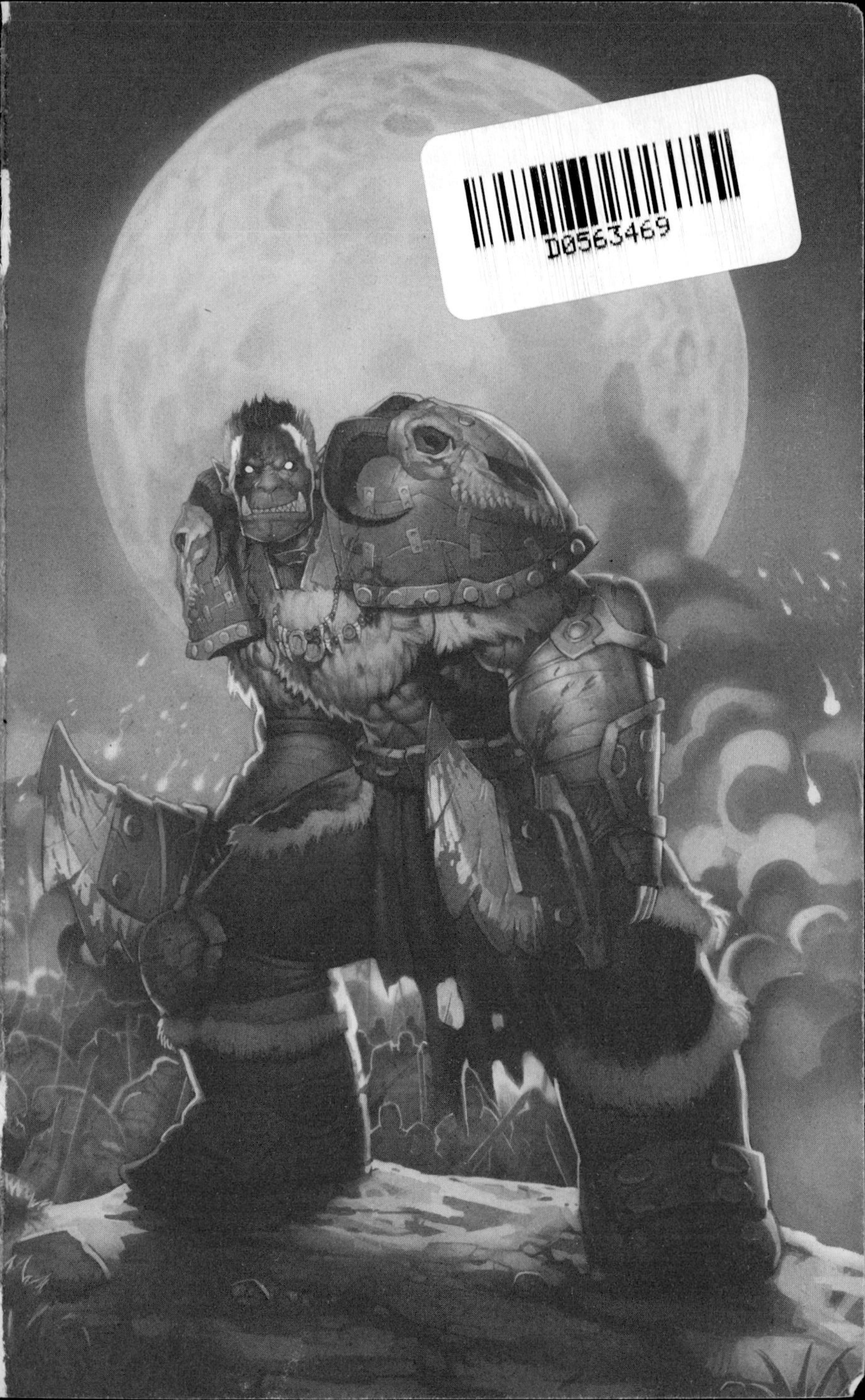

Warcraft: Legends Vol. 1

Contributing Editors - Rob Tokar, Luis Reyes and Hyun Joo Kim
Associate Editor - Shannon Watters
Layout and Lettering - Michael Paolilli and Lucas Rivera
Creative Consultant - Michael Paolilli
Graphic Designer - James Lee
Cover Artist - UDON with Saejin Oh

Editors - Tim Beedle and Troy Lewter
Digital Imaging Manager - Chris Buford
Pre-Production Supervisor - Vince Rivera
Art Director - Al-Insan Lashley
Managing Editor - Vy Nguyen
Editor-in-Chief - Rob Tokar
Publisher - Mike Kiley
President and C.O.O. - John Parker
C.E.O. and Chief Creative Officer - Stu Levy

BLIZZARD ENTERTAINMENT

Senior Vice President, Creative Development - Chris Metzen
Manager, Creative Development - Shawn Carnes
Story Consultation and Development - Micky Neilson
Art Director - Glenn Rane
Director, Global Business
Development and Licensing - Cory Jones
Associate Licensing Manager - Jason Bischoff
Additional Development - Samwise Didier, Evelyn Fredericksen,
Ben Brode, Sean Wang
Blizzard Special Thanks - Brian Hsieh, Gina Pippin

A **TOKYOPOP** Manga

TOKYOPOP and ⓣ are trademarks or registered trademarks of TOKYOPOP Inc.

TOKYOPOP Inc.
5900 Wilshire Blvd. Suite 2000
Los Angeles, CA 90036

E-mail: info@TOKYOPOP.com
Come visit us online at www.TOKYOPOP.com

ISBN: 978-1-4278-0722-9

First TOKYOPOP printing: August 2008
10 9 8 7 6 5 4 3 2 1
Printed in the USA

LEGENDS

VOLUME ONE

HAMBURG // LONDON // LOS ANGELES // TOKYO

WARCRAFT
LEGENDS
VOLUME ONE

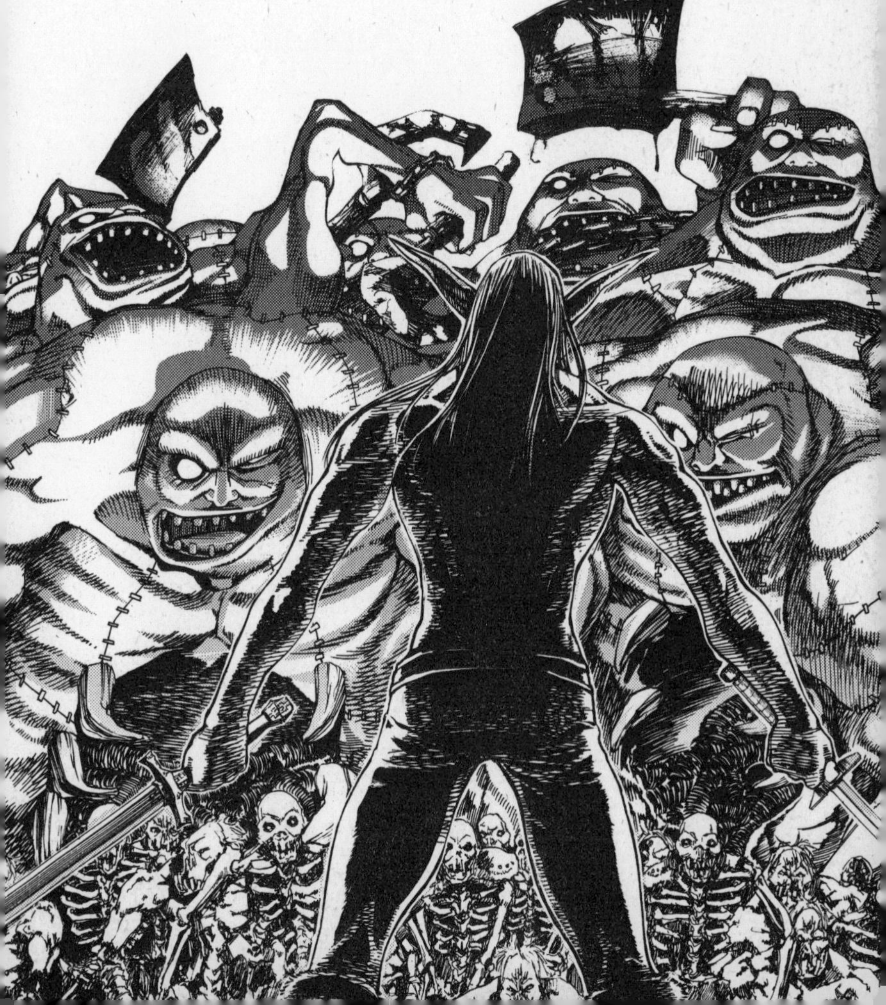

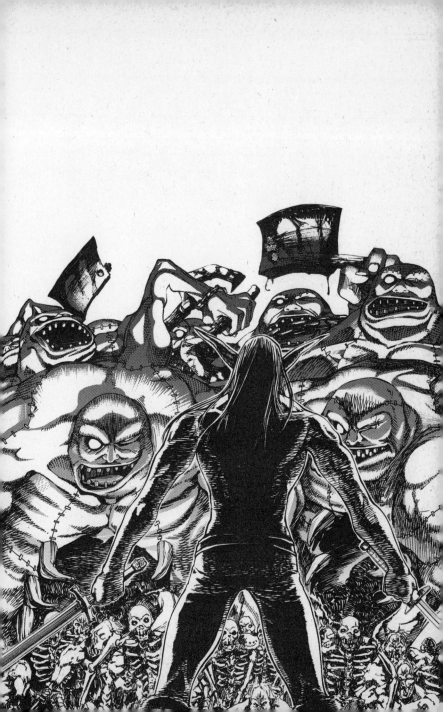

WARCRAFT®

LEGENDS™

VOLUME ONE

FALLEN

WRITTEN BY RICHARD A. KNAAK

ART BY JAE-HWAN KIM

Editor: Tim Beedle
Contributing Editor: Hyun Joo Kim
Associate Editor: Shannon Watters
Letterer: Michael Paolilli

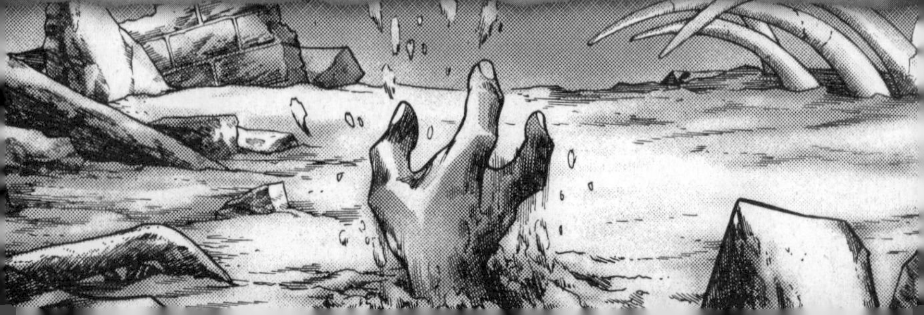

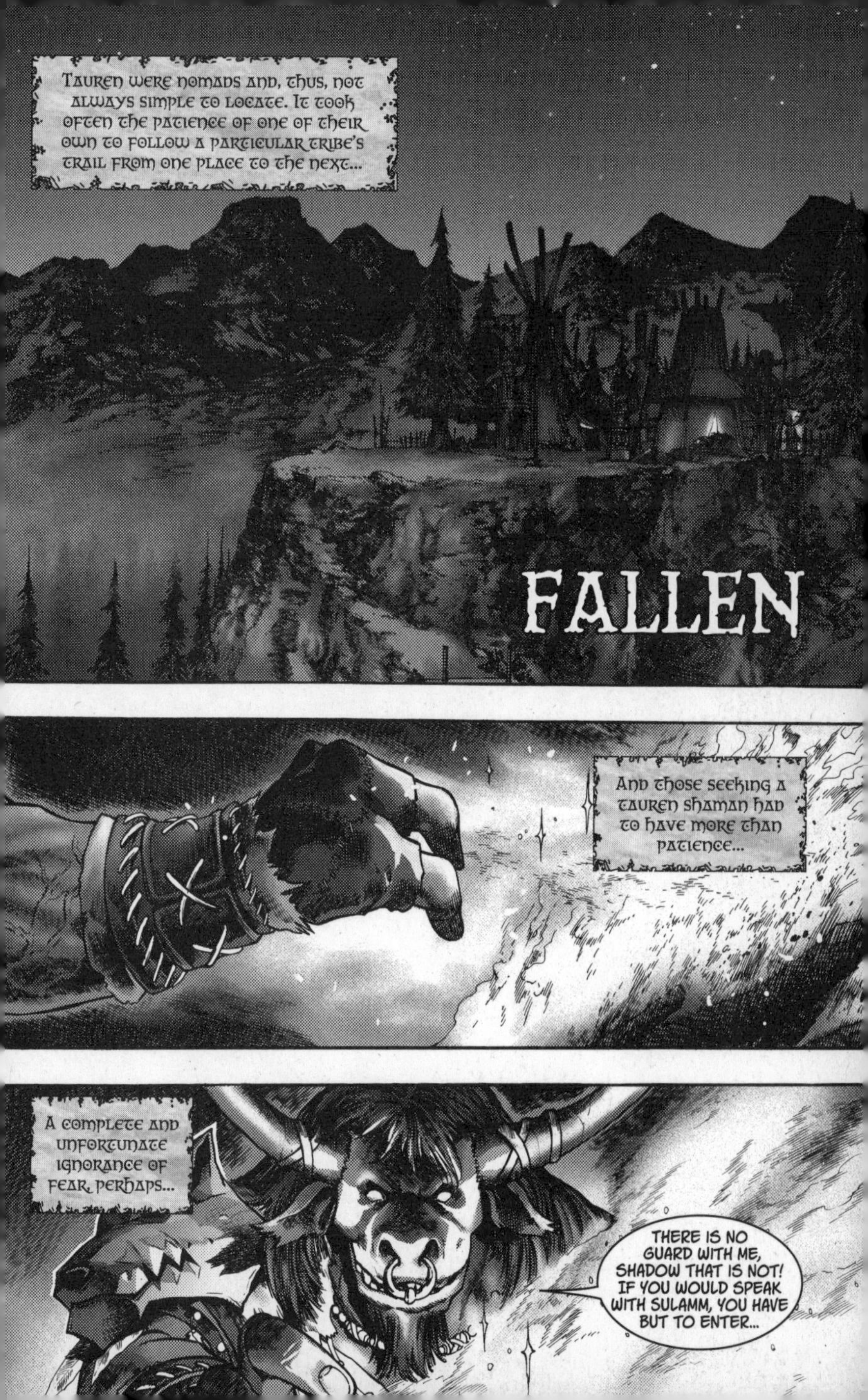
Tauren were nomads and, thus, not always simple to locate. It took often the patience of one of their own to follow a particular tribe's trail from one place to the next...
FALLEN
And those seeking a tauren shaman had to have more than patience...
A complete and unfortunate ignorance of fear, perhaps...
THERE IS NO GUARD WITH ME, SHADOW THAT IS NOT! IF YOU WOULD SPEAK WITH SULAMM, YOU HAVE BUT TO ENTER...

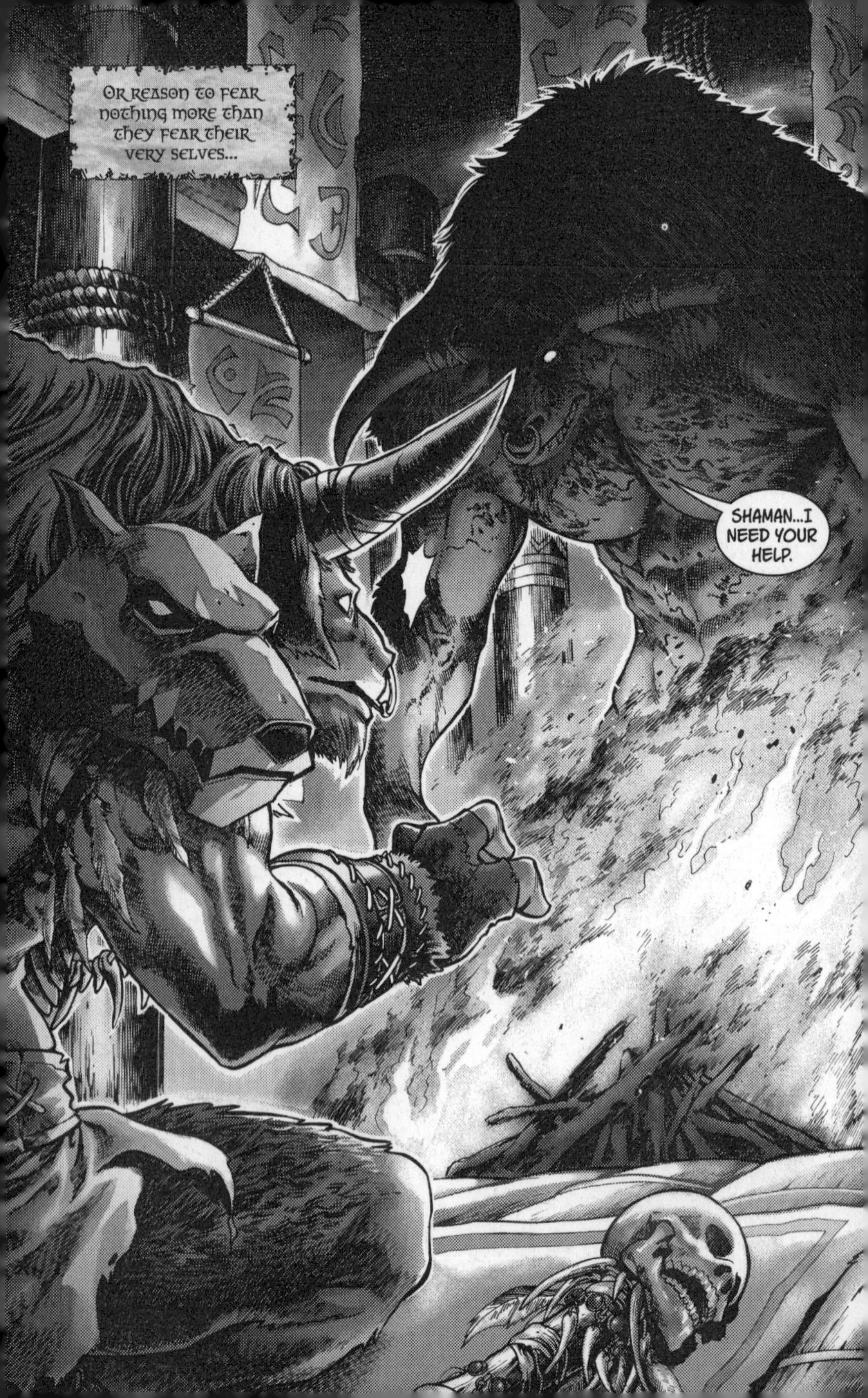
OR REASON TO FEAR NOTHING MORE THAN THEY FEAR THEIR VERY SELVES...
SHAMAN...I NEED YOUR HELP.

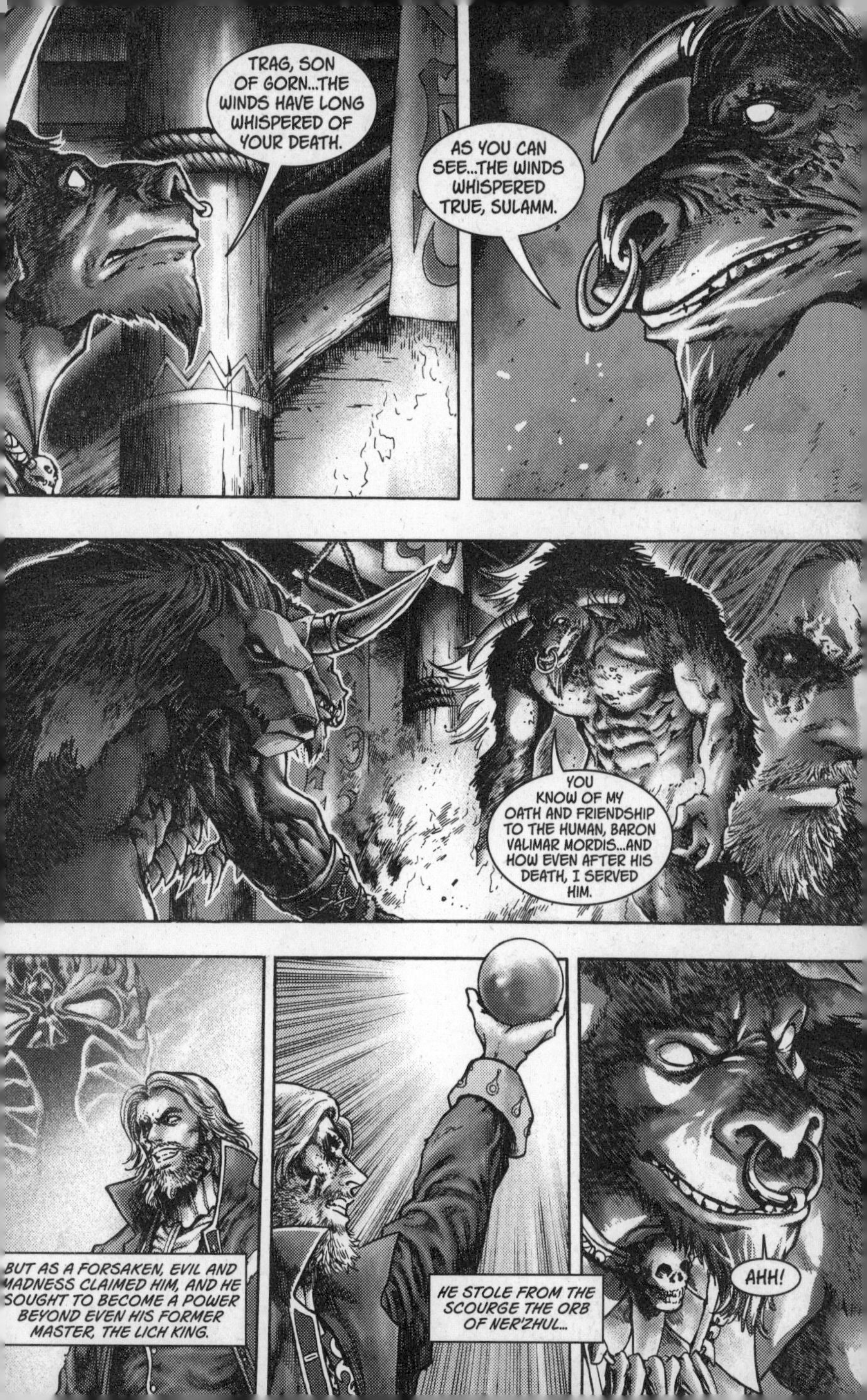
TRAG, SON OF GORN...THE WINDS HAVE LONG WHISPERED OF YOUR DEATH.
AS YOU CAN SEE...THE WINDS WHISPERED TRUE, SULAMM.
YOU KNOW OF MY OATH AND FRIENDSHIP TO THE HUMAN, BARON VALIMAR MORDIS...AND HOW EVEN AFTER HIS DEATH, I SERVED HIM.
BUT AS A FORSAKEN, EVIL AND MADNESS CLAIMED HIM, AND HE SOUGHT TO BECOME A POWER BEYOND EVEN HIS FORMER MASTER, THE LICH KING.
HE STOLE FROM THE SCOURGE THE ORB OF NER'ZHUL...
AHH!

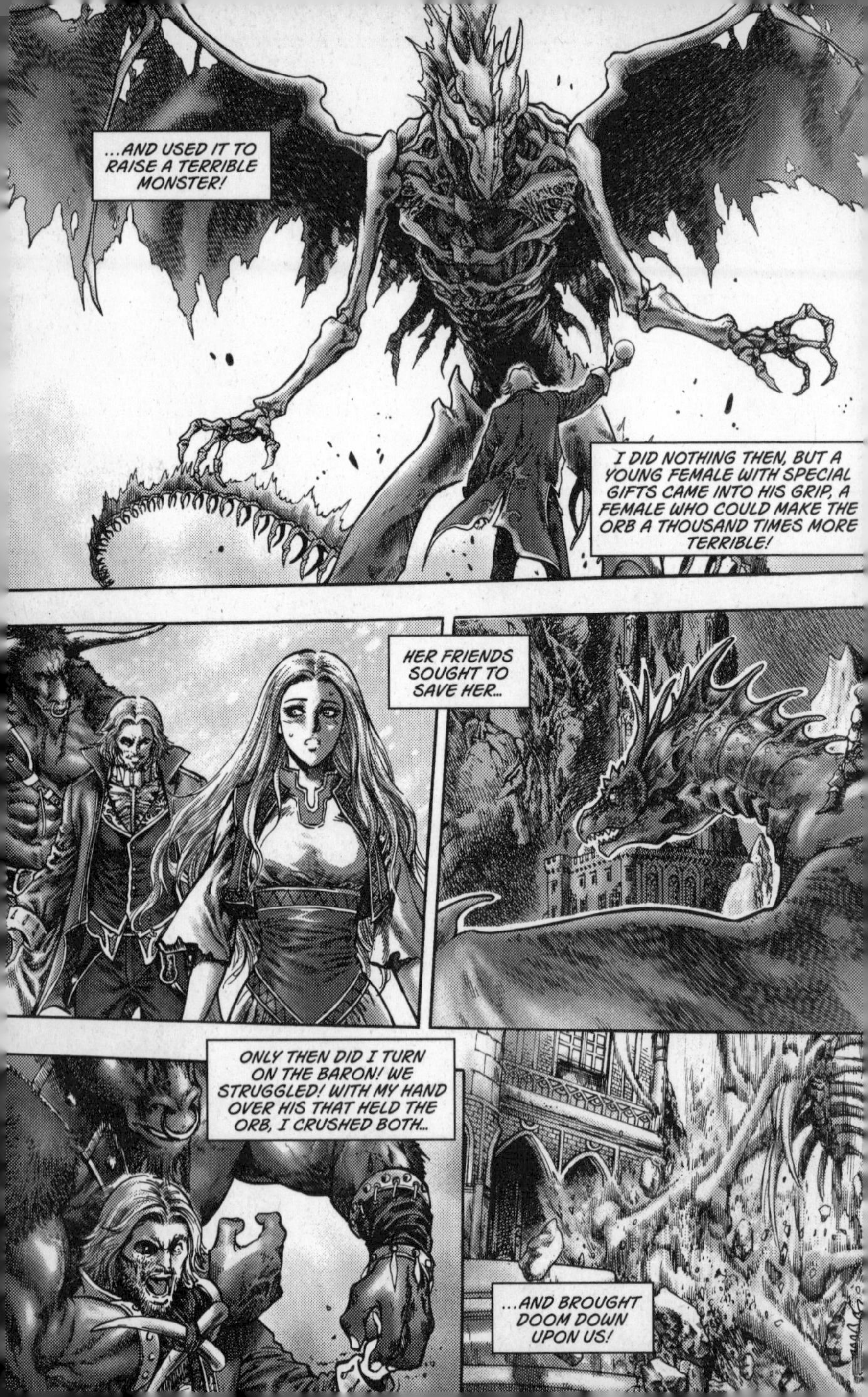
...AND USED IT TO RAISE A TERRIBLE MONSTER!
I DID NOTHING THEN, BUT A YOUNG FEMALE WITH SPECIAL GIFTS CAME INTO HIS GRIP, A FEMALE WHO COULD MAKE THE ORB A THOUSAND TIMES MORE TERRIBLE!
HER FRIENDS SOUGHT TO SAVE HER...
ONLY THEN DID I TURN ON THE BARON! WE STRUGGLED! WITH MY HAND OVER HIS THAT HELD THE ORB, I CRUSHED BOTH...
...AND BROUGHT DOOM DOWN UPON US!

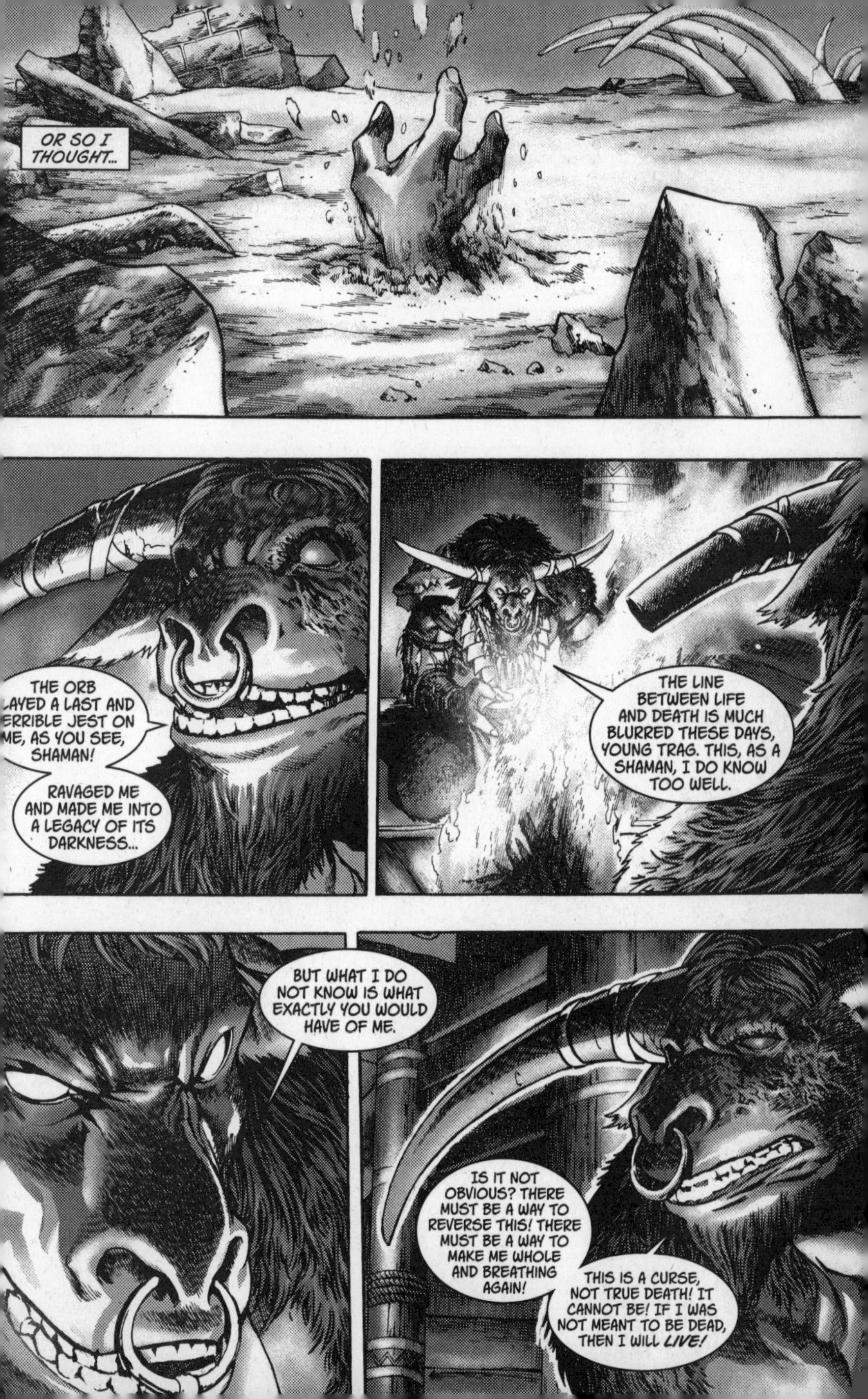
OR SO I THOUGHT...
THE ORB LAYED A LAST AND ERRIBLE JEST ON ME, AS YOU SEE, SHAMAN!
RAVAGED ME AND MADE ME INTO A LEGACY OF ITS DARKNESS...
THE LINE BETWEEN LIFE AND DEATH IS MUCH BLURRED THESE DAYS, YOUNG TRAG. THIS, AS A SHAMAN, I DO KNOW TOO WELL.
BUT WHAT I DO NOT KNOW IS WHAT EXACTLY YOU WOULD HAVE OF ME.
IS IT NOT OBVIOUS? THERE MUST BE A WAY TO REVERSE THIS! THERE MUST BE A WAY TO MAKE ME WHOLE AND BREATHING AGAIN!
THIS IS A CURSE, NOT TRUE DEATH! IT CANNOT BE! IF I WAS NOT MEANT TO BE DEAD, THEN I WILL *LIVE!*

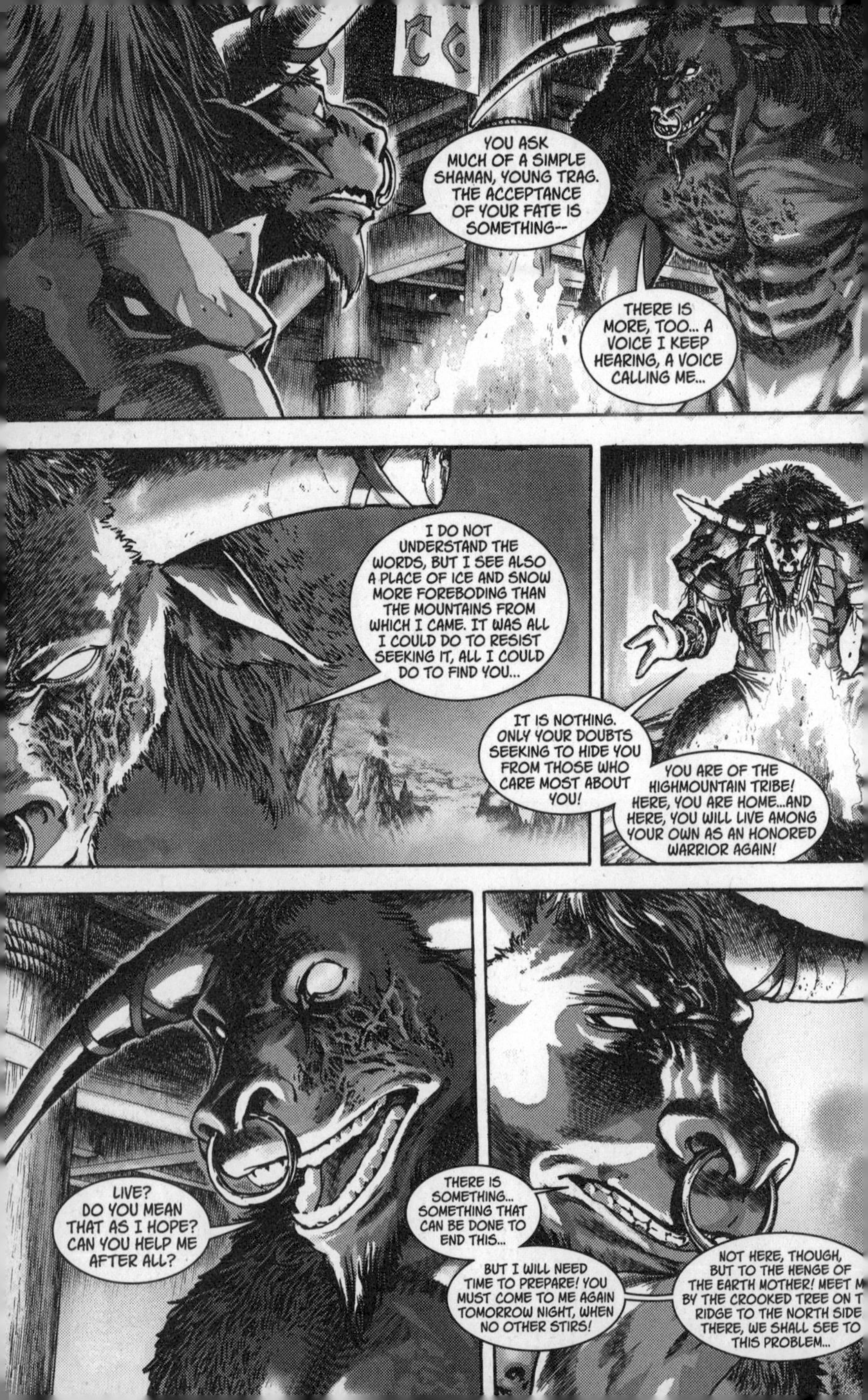
YOU ASK MUCH OF A SIMPLE SHAMAN, YOUNG TRAG. THE ACCEPTANCE OF YOUR FATE IS SOMETHING--
THERE IS MORE, TOO... A VOICE I KEEP HEARING, A VOICE CALLING ME...
I DO NOT UNDERSTAND THE WORDS, BUT I SEE ALSO A PLACE OF ICE AND SNOW MORE FOREBODING THAN THE MOUNTAINS FROM WHICH I CAME. IT WAS ALL I COULD DO TO RESIST SEEKING IT, ALL I COULD DO TO FIND YOU...
IT IS NOTHING. ONLY YOUR DOUBTS SEEKING TO HIDE YOU FROM THOSE WHO CARE MOST ABOUT YOU!
YOU ARE OF THE HIGHMOUNTAIN TRIBE! HERE, YOU ARE HOME...AND HERE, YOU WILL LIVE AMONG YOUR OWN AS AN HONORED WARRIOR AGAIN!
LIVE? DO YOU MEAN THAT AS I HOPE? CAN YOU HELP ME AFTER ALL?
THERE IS SOMETHING... SOMETHING THAT CAN BE DONE TO END THIS...
BUT I WILL NEED TIME TO PREPARE! YOU MUST COME TO ME AGAIN TOMORROW NIGHT, WHEN NO OTHER STIRS!
NOT HERE, THOUGH, BUT TO THE HENGE OF THE EARTH MOTHER! MEET M BY THE CROOKED TREE ON T RIDGE TO THE NORTH SIDE THERE, WE SHALL SEE TO THIS PROBLEM...

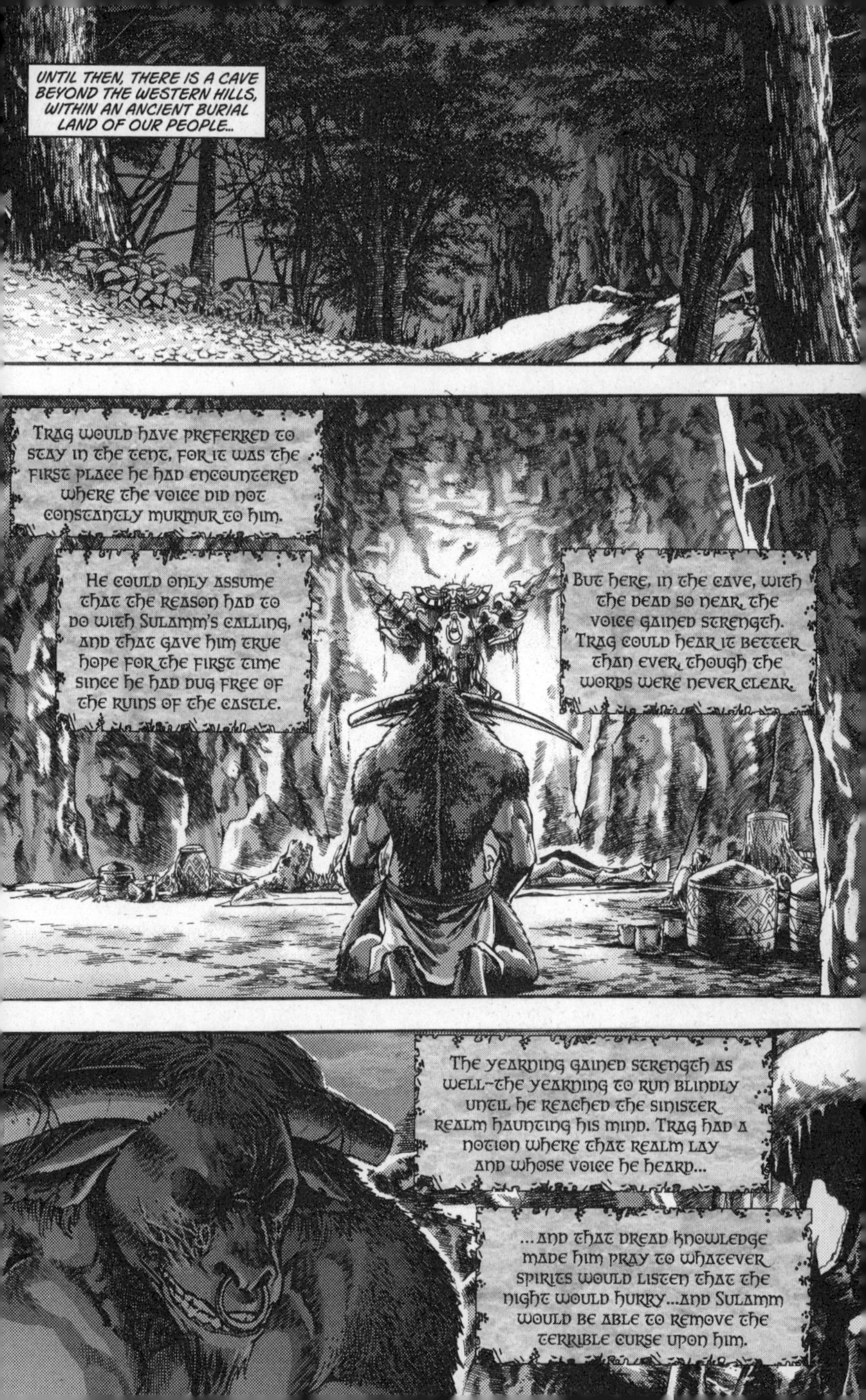
UNTIL THEN, THERE IS A CAVE BEYOND THE WESTERN HILLS, WITHIN AN ANCIENT BURIAL LAND OF OUR PEOPLE...
Trag would have preferred to stay in the tent, for it was the first place he had encountered where the voice did not constantly murmur to him.
He could only assume that the reason had to do with Sulamm's calling, and that gave him true hope for the first time since he had dug free of the ruins of the castle.
But here, in the cave, with the dead so near, the voice gained strength. Trag could hear it better than ever, though the words were never clear.
The yearning gained strength as well–the yearning to run blindly until he reached the sinister realm haunting his mind. Trag had a notion where that realm lay and whose voice he heard...
...and that dread knowledge made him pray to whatever spirits would listen that the night would hurry...and Sulamm would be able to remove the terrible curse upon him.

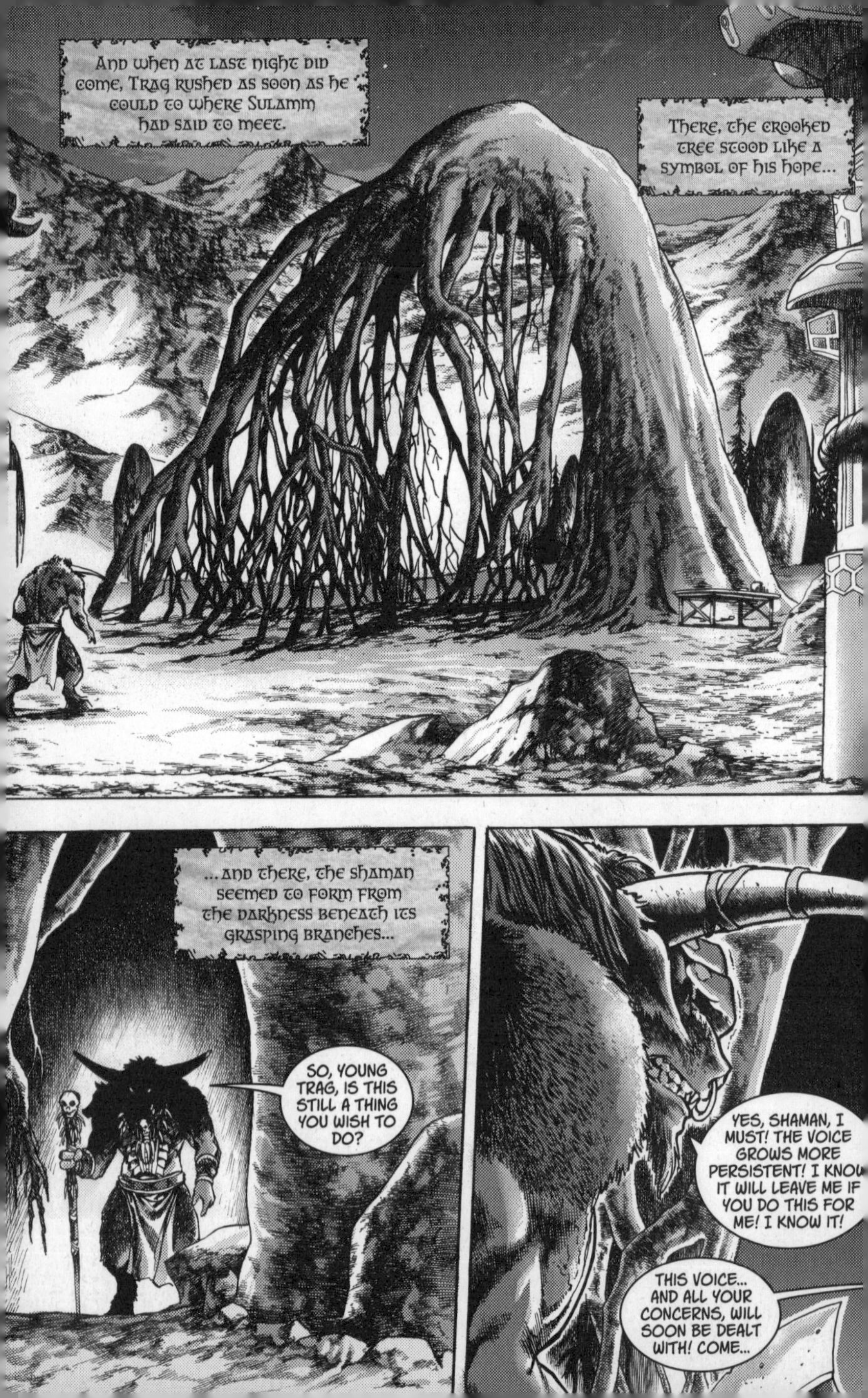
And when at last night did come, Trag rushed as soon as he could to where Sulamm had said to meet.
There, the crooked tree stood like a symbol of his hope...
...and there, the shaman seemed to form from the darkness beneath its grasping branches...
SO, YOUNG TRAG, IS THIS STILL A THING YOU WISH TO DO?
YES, SHAMAN, I MUST! THE VOICE GROWS MORE PERSISTENT! I KNOW IT WILL LEAVE ME IF YOU DO THIS FOR ME! I KNOW IT!
THIS VOICE... AND ALL YOUR CONCERNS, WILL SOON BE DEALT WITH! COME...

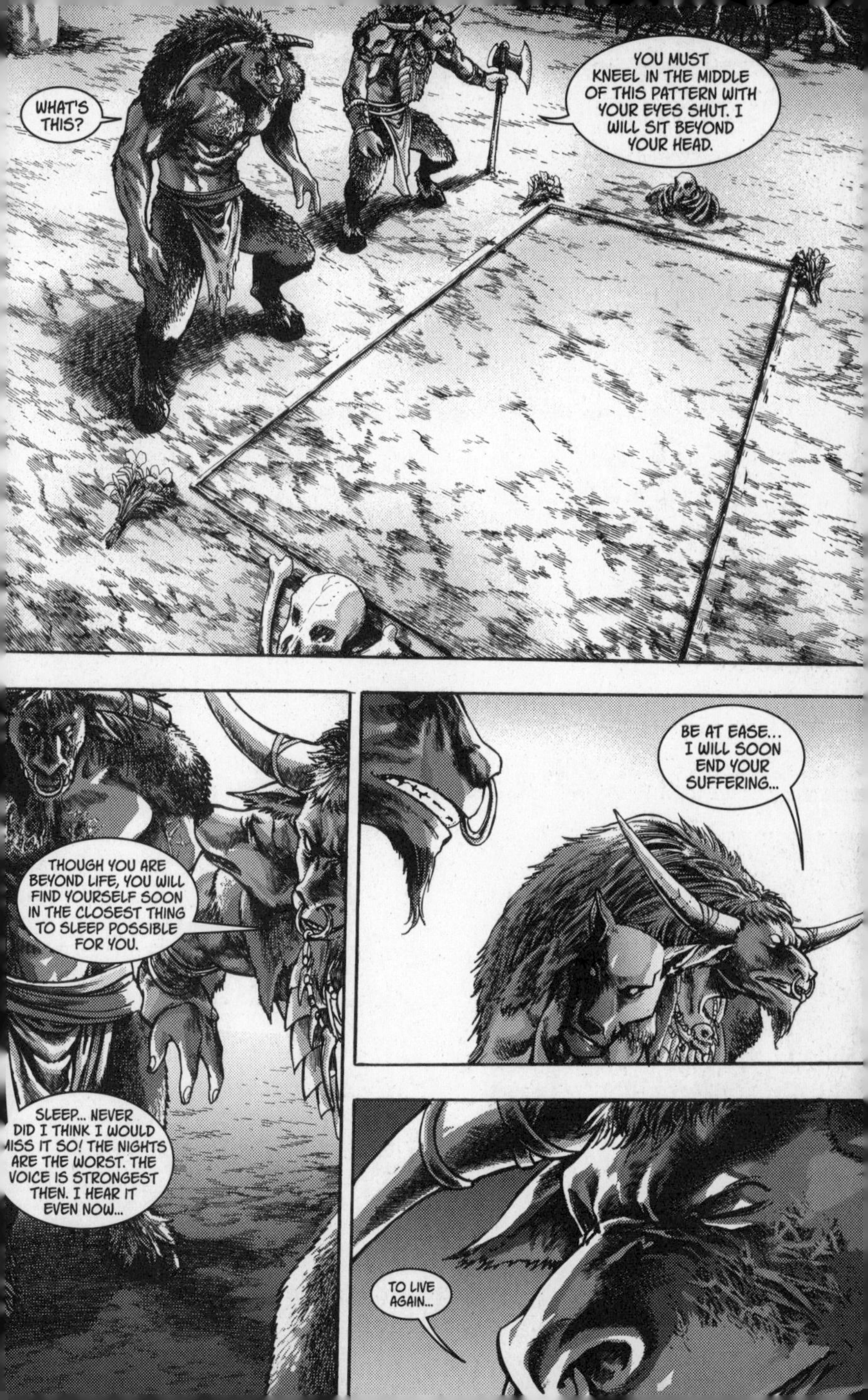
WHAT'S THIS?
YOU MUST KNEEL IN THE MIDDLE OF THIS PATTERN WITH YOUR EYES SHUT. I WILL SIT BEYOND YOUR HEAD.
THOUGH YOU ARE BEYOND LIFE, YOU WILL FIND YOURSELF SOON IN THE CLOSEST THING TO SLEEP POSSIBLE FOR YOU.
SLEEP... NEVER DID I THINK I WOULD MISS IT SO! THE NIGHTS ARE THE WORST. THE VOICE IS STRONGEST THEN. I HEAR IT EVEN NOW...
BE AT EASE... I WILL SOON END YOUR SUFFERING...
TO LIVE AGAIN...

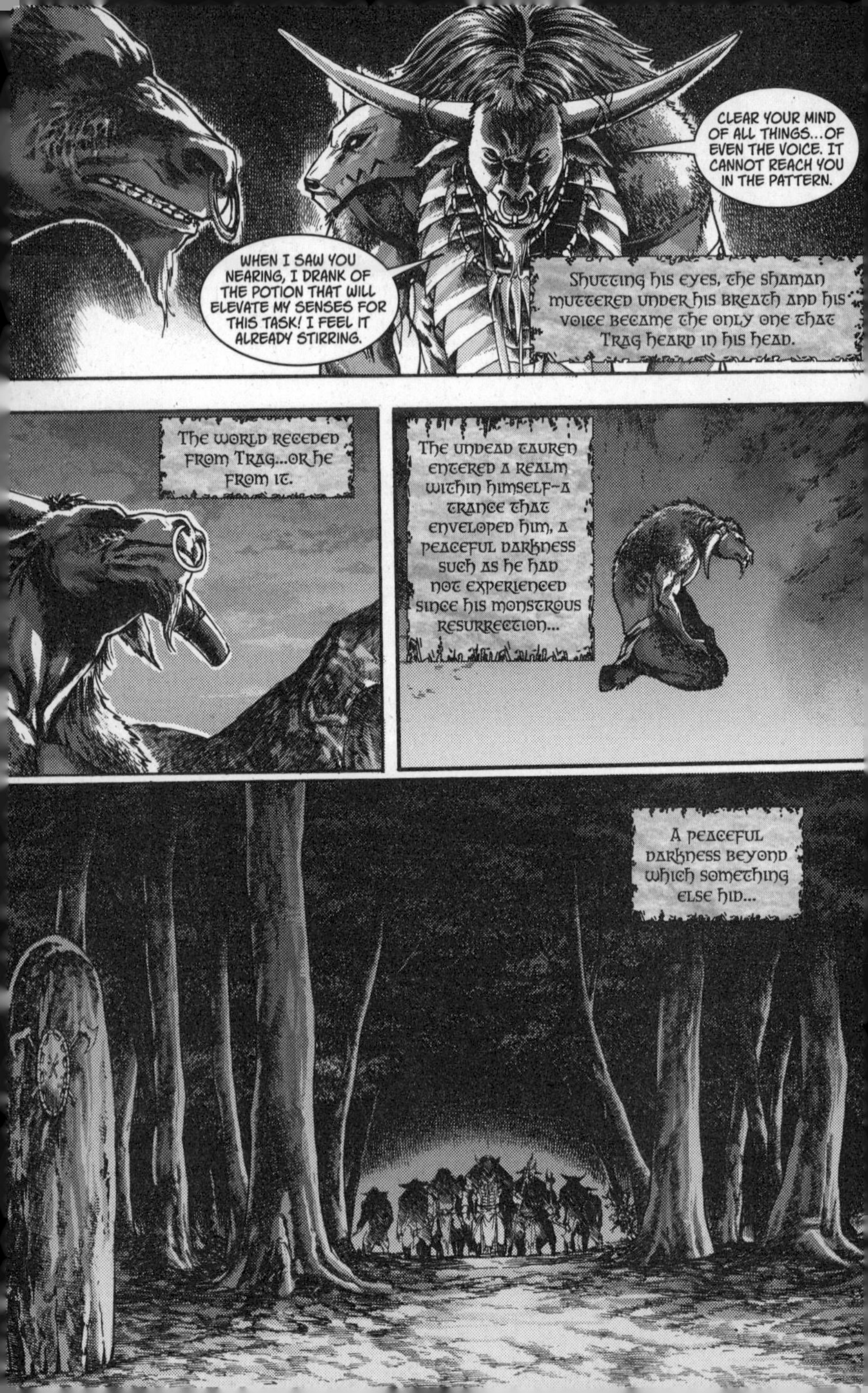
CLEAR YOUR MIND OF ALL THINGS...OF EVEN THE VOICE. IT CANNOT REACH YOU IN THE PATTERN.
WHEN I SAW YOU NEARING, I DRANK OF THE POTION THAT WILL ELEVATE MY SENSES FOR THIS TASK! I FEEL IT ALREADY STIRRING.
Shutting his eyes, the shaman muttered under his breath and his voice became the only one that Trag heard in his head.
The world receded from Trag...or he from it.
The undead tauren entered a realm within himself–a trance that enveloped him, a peaceful darkness such as he had not experienced since his monstrous resurrection...
A peaceful darkness beyond which something else hid...

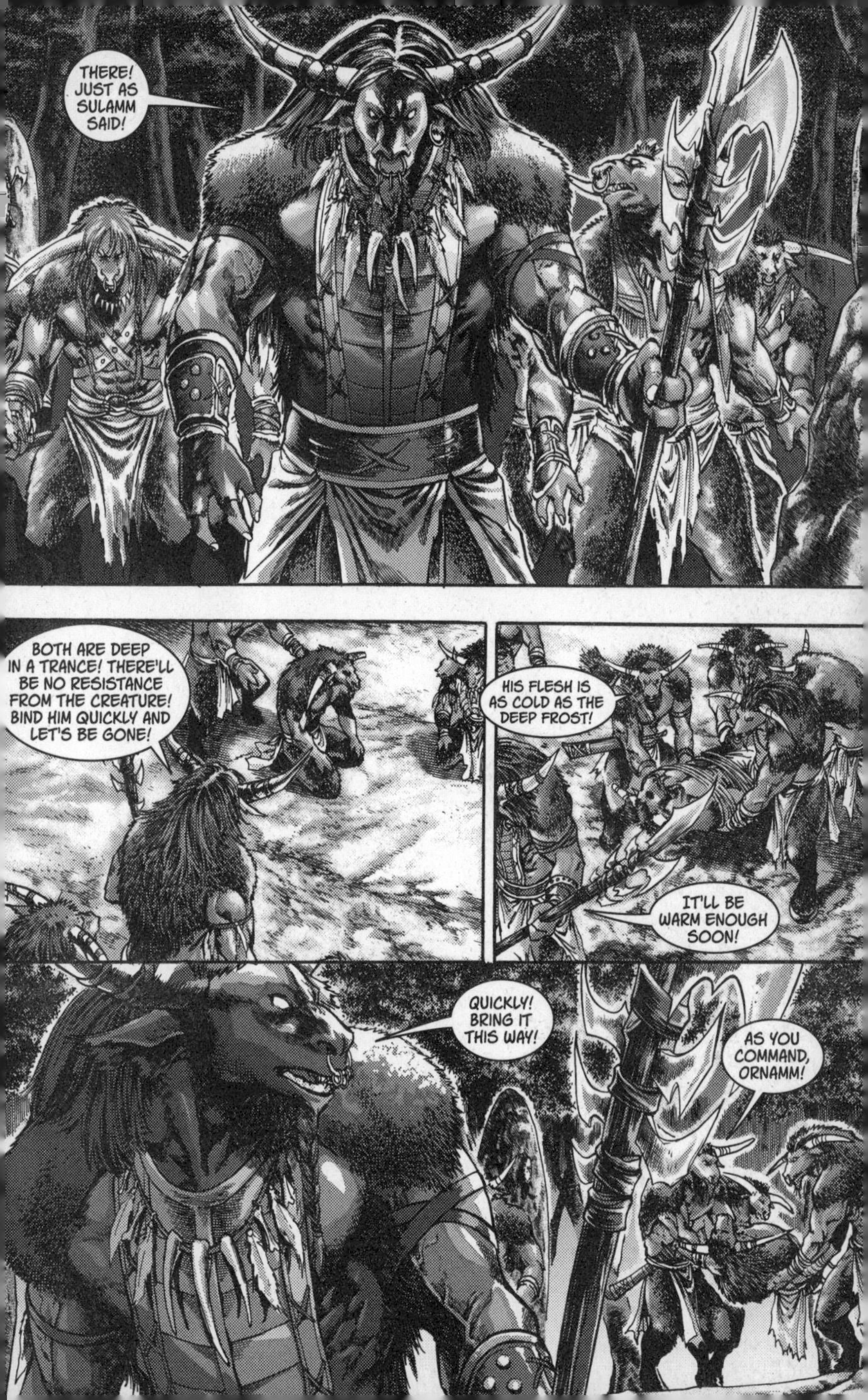
THERE! JUST AS SULAMM SAID!
BOTH ARE DEEP IN A TRANCE! THERE'LL BE NO RESISTANCE FROM THE CREATURE! BIND HIM QUICKLY AND LET'S BE GONE!
HIS FLESH IS AS COLD AS THE DEEP FROST!
IT'LL BE WARM ENOUGH SOON!
QUICKLY! BRING IT THIS WAY!
AS YOU COMMAND, ORNAMM!

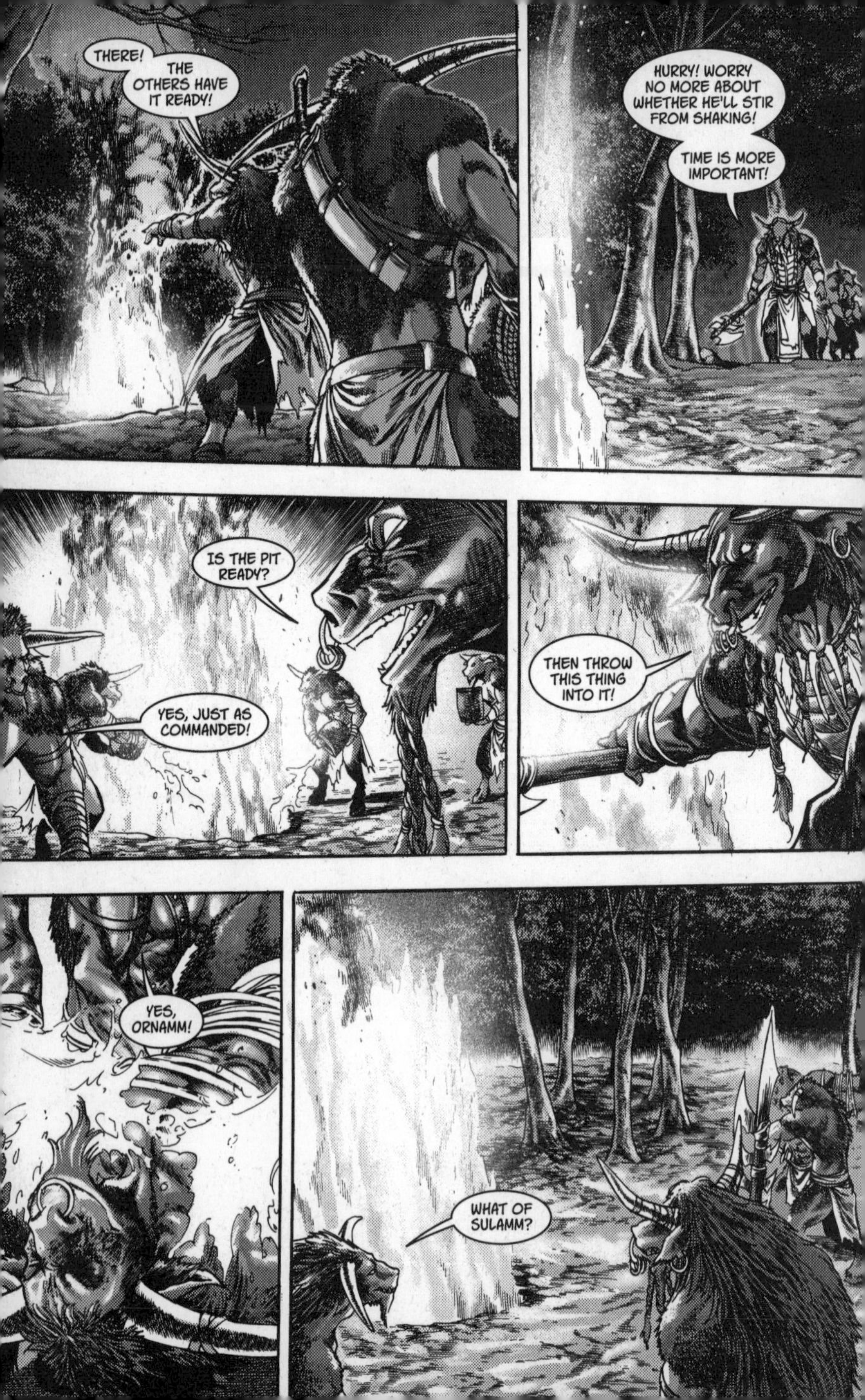
THERE!
THE OTHERS HAVE IT READY!
HURRY! WORRY NO MORE ABOUT WHETHER HE'LL STIR FROM SHAKING!
TIME IS MORE IMPORTANT!
IS THE PIT READY?
YES, JUST AS COMMANDED!
THEN THROW THIS THING INTO IT!
YES, ORNAMM!
WHAT OF SULAMM?

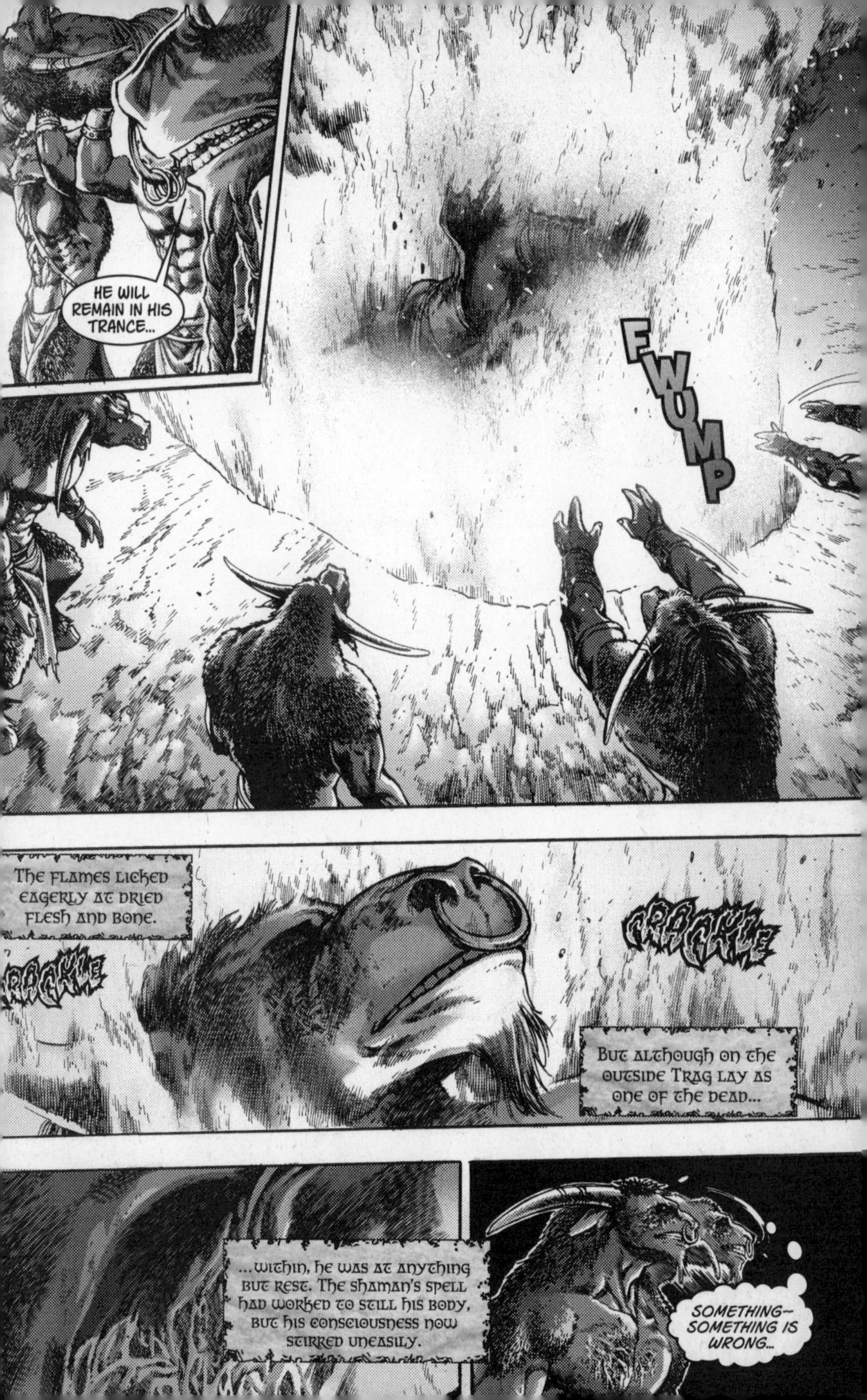

HE WILL REMAIN IN HIS TRANCE...
FWUMP
The flames licked eagerly at dried flesh and bone.
RACKLE
CRACKLE
But although on the outside Trag lay as one of the dead...
...within, he was at anything but rest. The shaman's spell had worked to still his body, but his consciousness now stirred uneasily.
SOMETHING— SOMETHING IS WRONG...

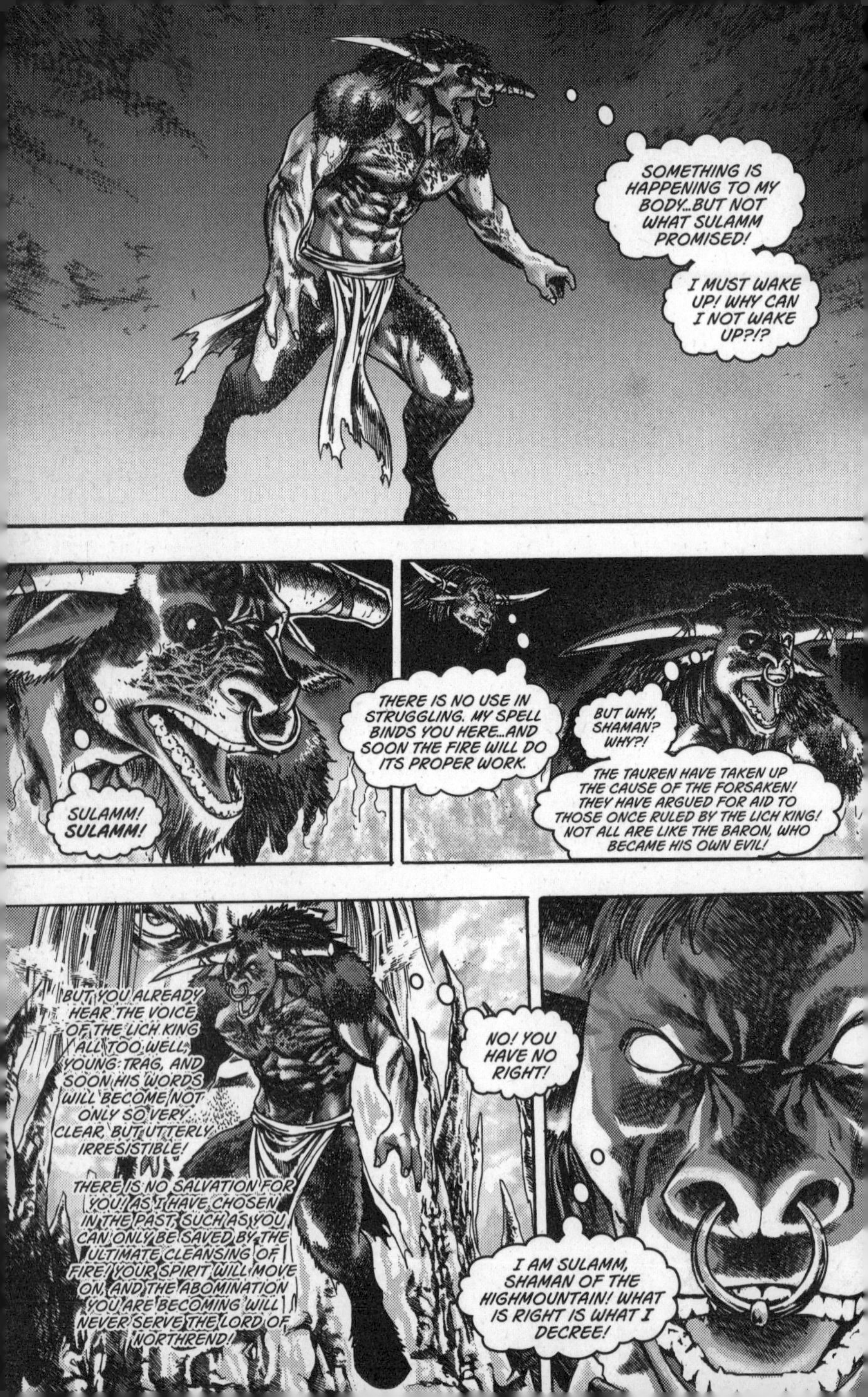
SOMETHING IS HAPPENING TO MY BODY...BUT NOT WHAT SULAMM PROMISED!
I MUST WAKE UP! WHY CAN I NOT WAKE UP?!?
SULAMM! SULAMM!
THERE IS NO USE IN STRUGGLING. MY SPELL BINDS YOU HERE...AND SOON THE FIRE WILL DO ITS PROPER WORK.
BUT WHY, SHAMAN? WHY?!
THE TAUREN HAVE TAKEN UP THE CAUSE OF THE FORSAKEN! THEY HAVE ARGUED FOR AID TO THOSE ONCE RULED BY THE LICH KING! NOT ALL ARE LIKE THE BARON, WHO BECAME HIS OWN EVIL!
BUT YOU ALREADY HEAR THE VOICE OF THE LICH KING ALL TOO WELL, YOUNG TRAG, AND SOON HIS WORDS WILL BECOME NOT ONLY SO VERY CLEAR, BUT UTTERLY IRRESISTIBLE!
THERE IS NO SALVATION FOR YOU! AS I HAVE CHOSEN IN THE PAST, SUCH AS YOU CAN ONLY BE SAVED BY THE ULTIMATE CLEANSING OF FIRE! YOUR SPIRIT WILL MOVE ON, AND THE ABOMINATION YOU ARE BECOMING WILL NEVER SERVE THE LORD OF NORTHREND!
NO! YOU HAVE NO RIGHT!
I AM SULAMM, SHAMAN OF THE HIGHMOUNTAIN! WHAT IS RIGHT IS WHAT I DECREE!

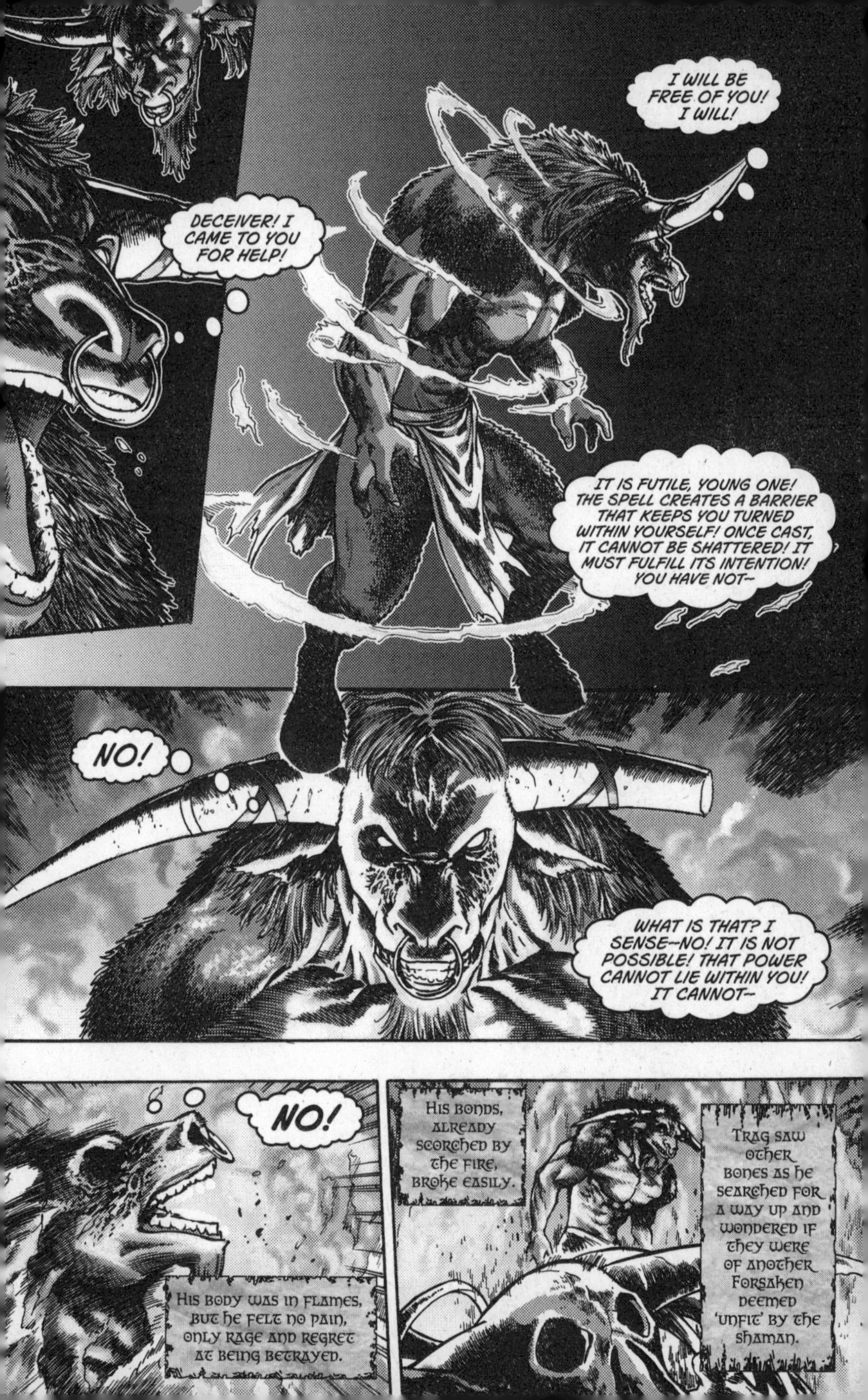
DECEIVER! I CAME TO YOU FOR HELP!
I WILL BE FREE OF YOU! I WILL!
IT IS FUTILE, YOUNG ONE! THE SPELL CREATES A BARRIER THAT KEEPS YOU TURNED WITHIN YOURSELF! ONCE CAST, IT CANNOT BE SHATTERED! IT MUST FULFILL ITS INTENTION! YOU HAVE NOT--
NO!
WHAT IS THAT? I SENSE--NO! IT IS NOT POSSIBLE! THAT POWER CANNOT LIE WITHIN YOU! IT CANNOT--
NO!
His body was in flames, but he felt no pain, only rage and regret at being betrayed.
His bonds, already scorched by the fire, broke easily.
Trag saw other bones as he searched for a way up and wondered if they were of another Forsaken deemed 'unfit' by the shaman.

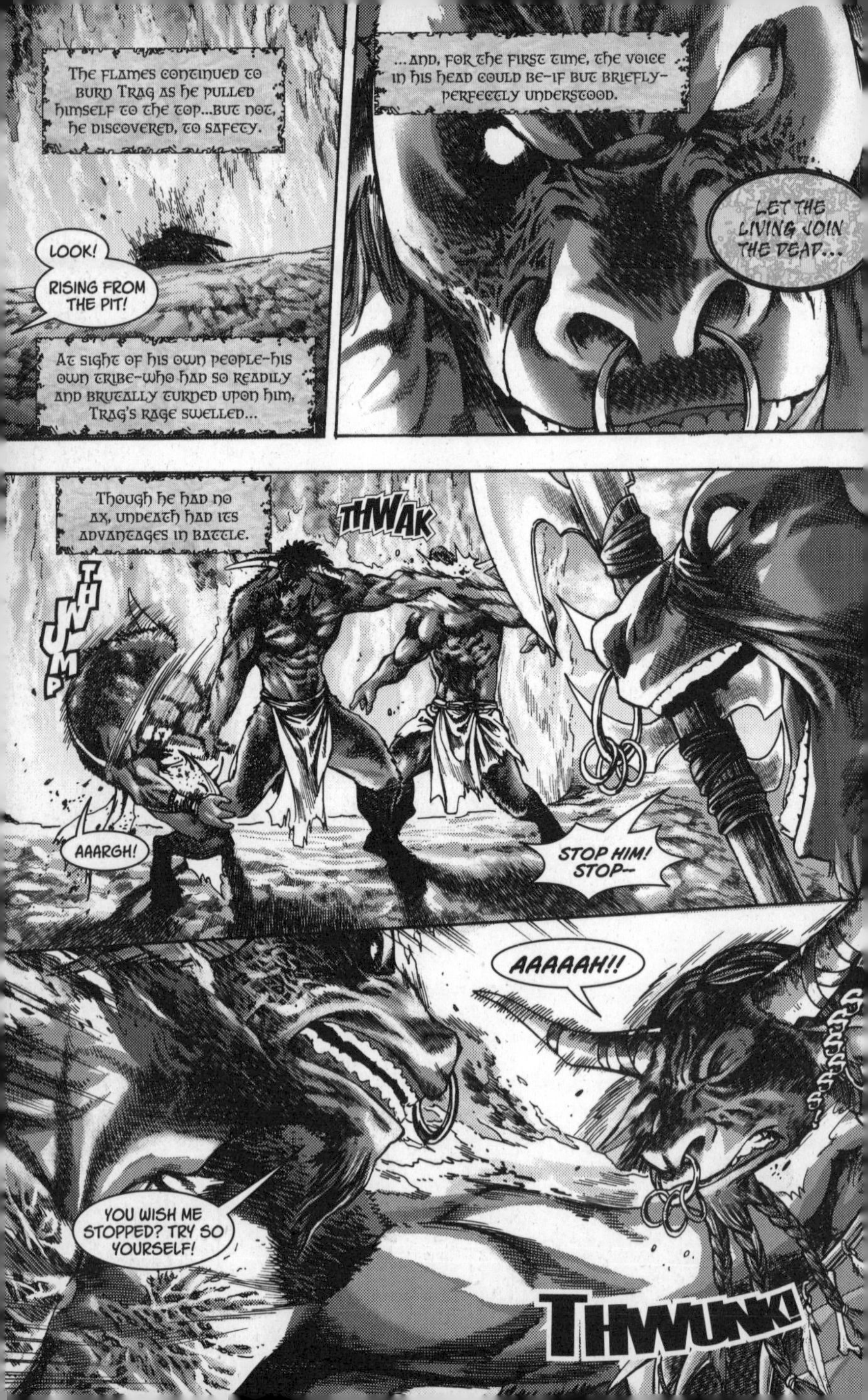
The flames continued to burn Trag as he pulled himself to the top...but not, he discovered, to safety.
LOOK!
RISING FROM THE PIT!
At sight of his own people–his own tribe–who had so readily and brutally turned upon him, Trag's rage swelled...
...and, for the first time, the voice in his head could be–if but briefly–perfectly understood.
LET THE LIVING JOIN THE DEAD...
Though he had no ax, undeath had its advantages in battle.
THWAK
THWUMP
AAARGH!
STOP HIM! STOP--
AAAAAH!!
YOU WISH ME STOPPED? TRY SO YOURSELF!
THWUNK!

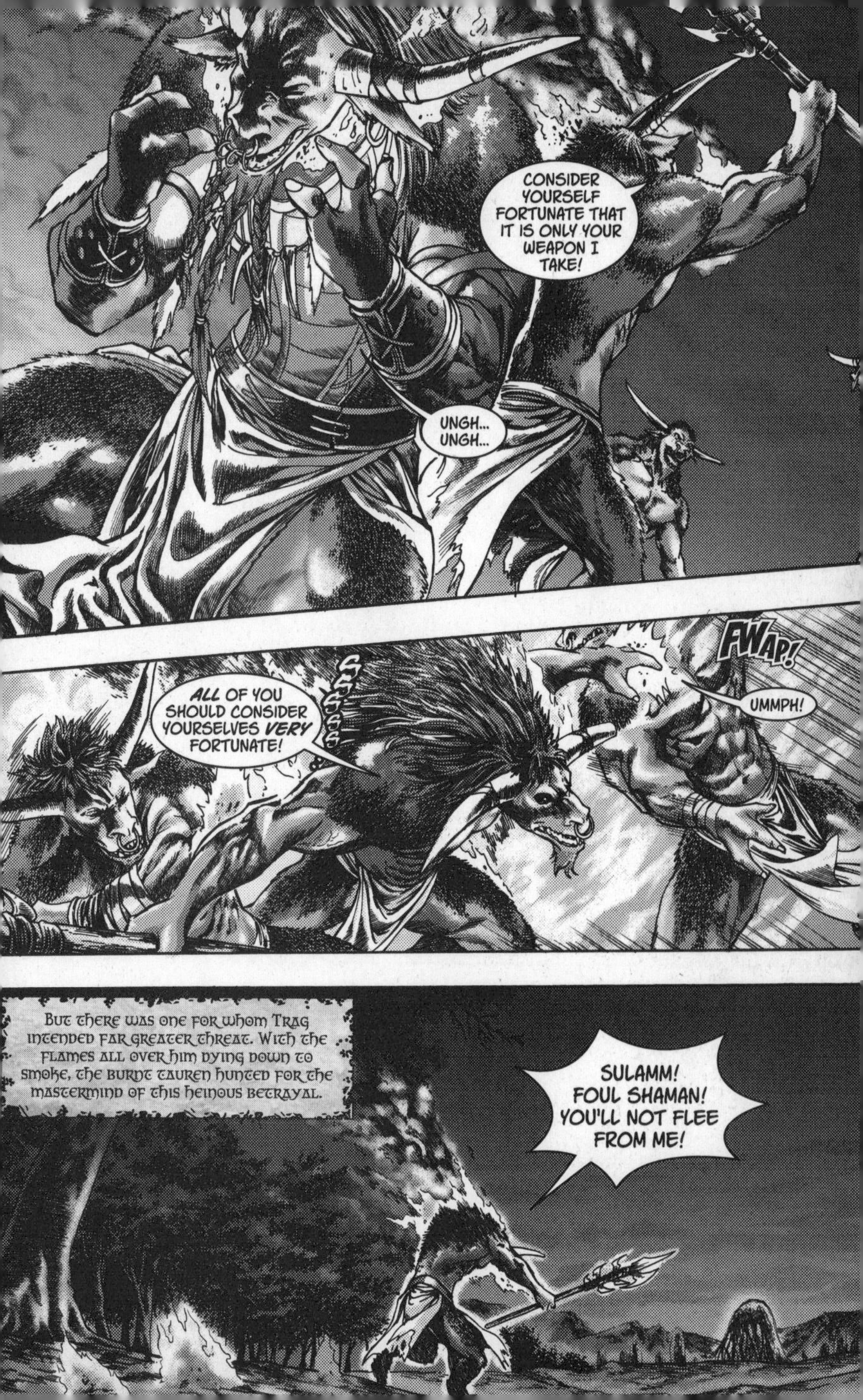
CONSIDER YOURSELF FORTUNATE THAT IT IS ONLY YOUR WEAPON I TAKE!
UNGH... UNGH...
ALL OF YOU SHOULD CONSIDER YOURSELVES VERY FORTUNATE!
FWAP!
UMMPH!
But there was one for whom Trag intended far greater threat. With the flames all over him dying down to smoke, the burnt tauren hunted for the mastermind of this heinous betrayal.
SULAMM! FOUL SHAMAN! YOU'LL NOT FLEE FROM ME!

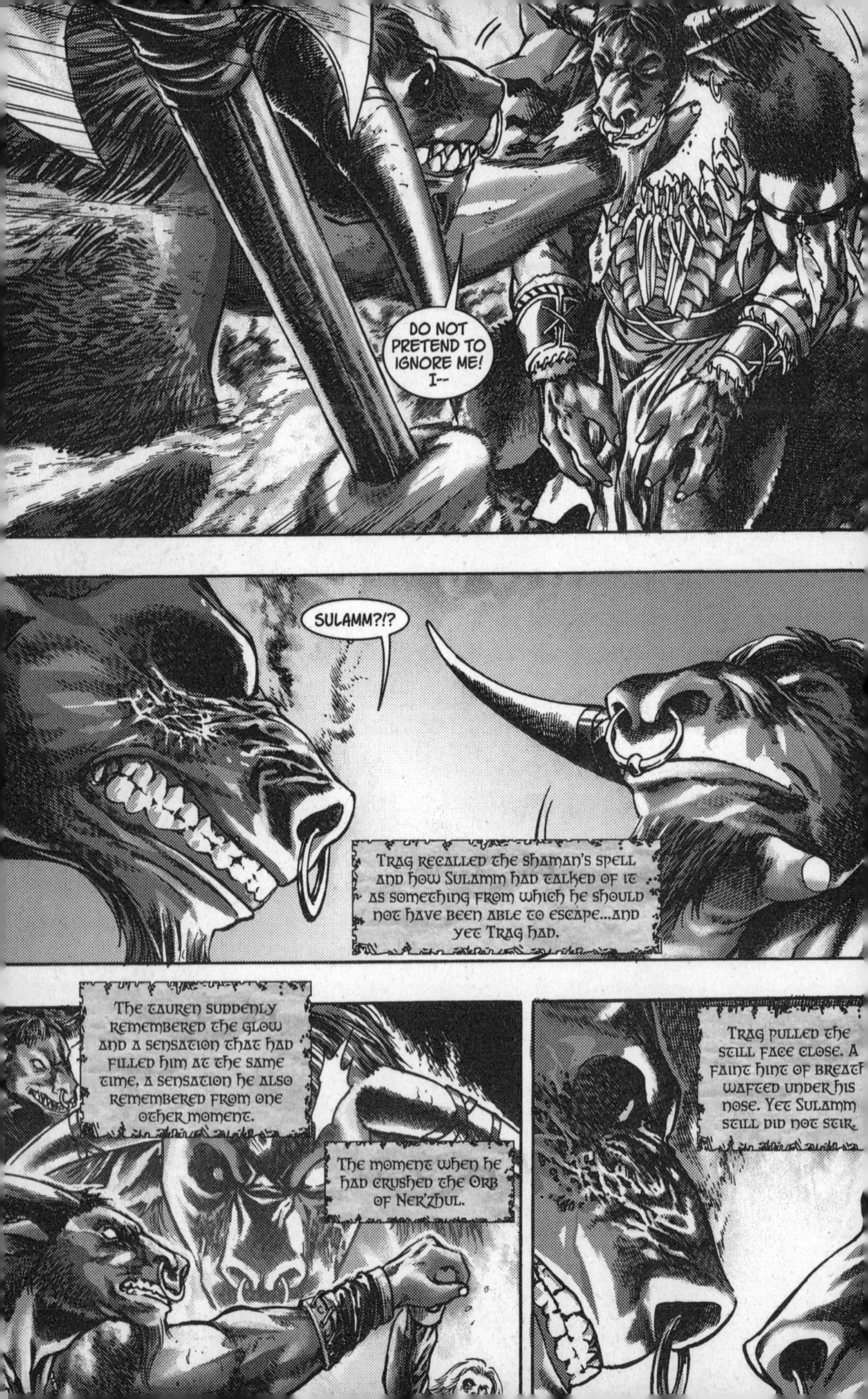
DO NOT PRETEND TO IGNORE ME! I--
SULAMM?!?
Trag recalled the shaman's spell and how Sulamm had talked of it as something from which he should not have been able to escape...and yet Trag had.
The tauren suddenly remembered the glow and a sensation that had filled him at the same time, a sensation he also remembered from one other moment.
The moment when he had crushed the Orb of Ner'zhul.
Trag pulled the still face close. A faint hint of breat wafted under his nose. Yet Sulamm still did not stir.

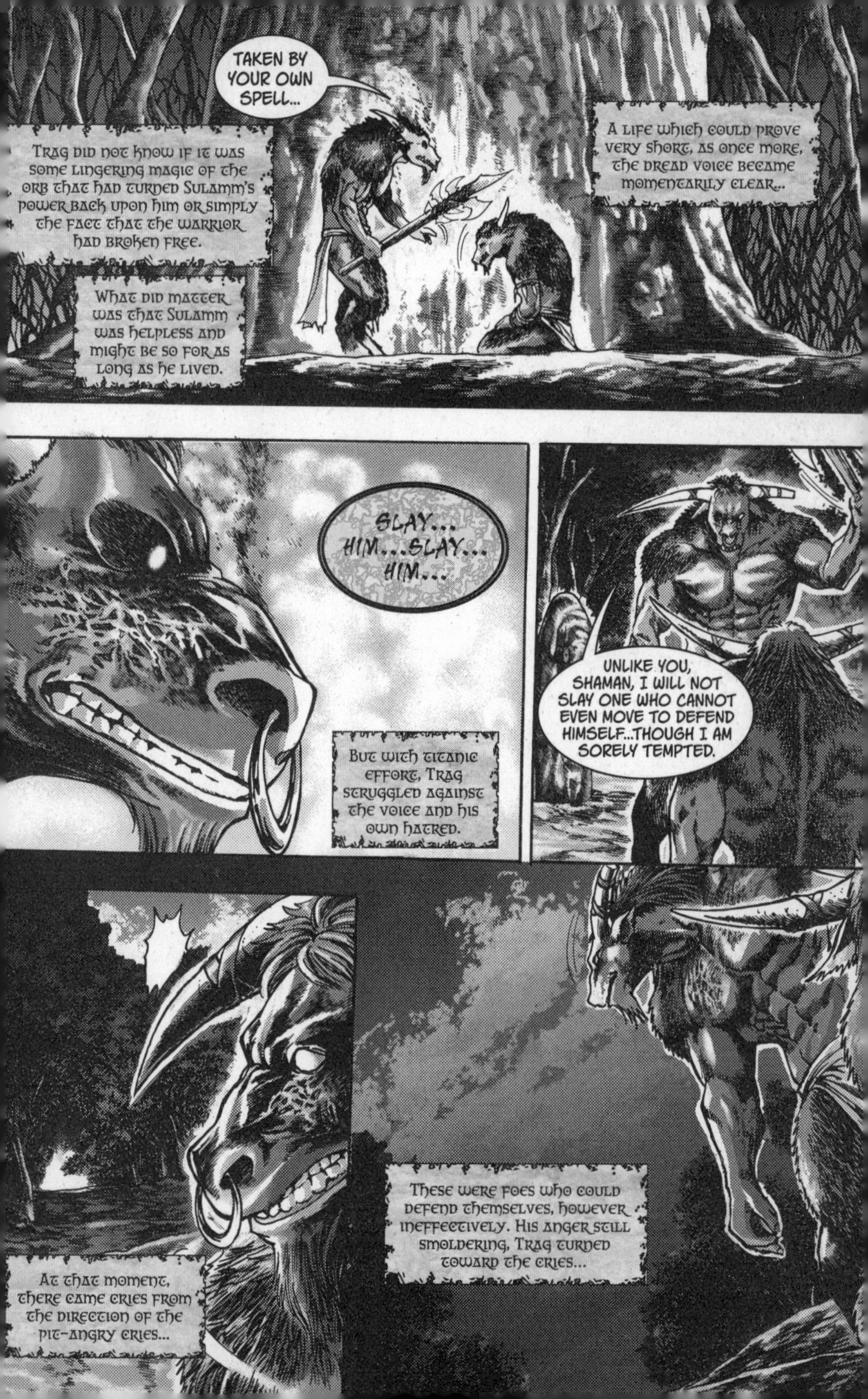
TAKEN BY YOUR OWN SPELL...
Trag did not know if it was some lingering magic of the orb that had turned Sulamm's power back upon him or simply the fact that the warrior had broken free.
What did matter was that Sulamm was helpless and might be so for as long as he lived.
A life which could prove very short, as once more, the dread voice became momentarily clear...
SLAY... HIM...SLAY... HIM...
But with titanic effort, Trag struggled against the voice and his own hatred.
UNLIKE YOU, SHAMAN, I WILL NOT SLAY ONE WHO CANNOT EVEN MOVE TO DEFEND HIMSELF...THOUGH I AM SORELY TEMPTED.
At that moment, there came cries from the direction of the pit-angry cries...
These were foes who could defend themselves, however ineffectively. His anger still smoldering, Trag turned toward the cries...

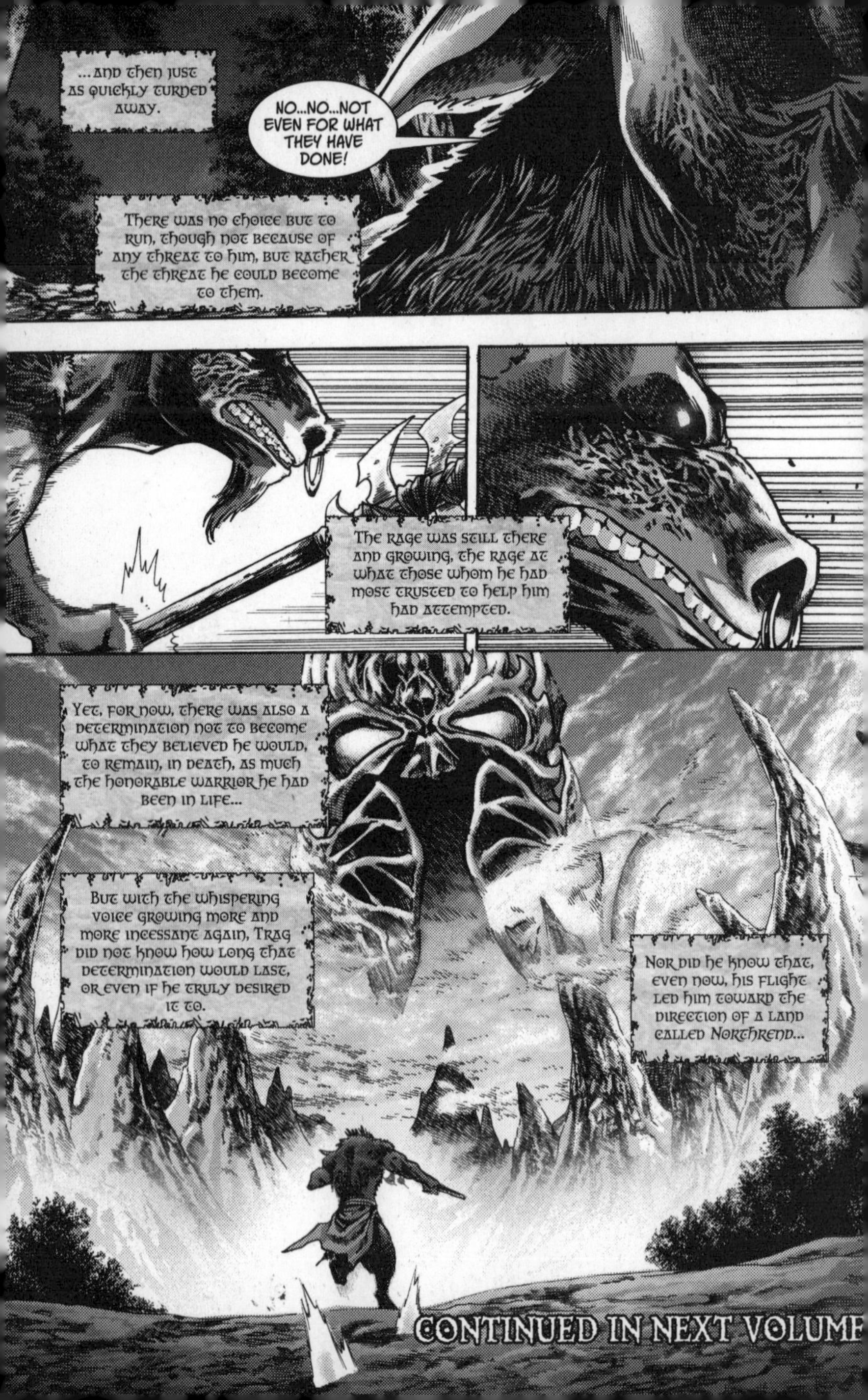

...AND THEN JUST AS QUICKLY TURNED AWAY.
NO...NO...NOT EVEN FOR WHAT THEY HAVE DONE!
THERE WAS NO CHOICE BUT TO RUN, THOUGH NOT BECAUSE OF ANY THREAT TO HIM, BUT RATHER THE THREAT HE COULD BECOME TO THEM.
THE RAGE WAS STILL THERE AND GROWING, THE RAGE AT WHAT THOSE WHOM HE HAD MOST TRUSTED TO HELP HIM HAD ATTEMPTED.
YET, FOR NOW, THERE WAS ALSO A DETERMINATION NOT TO BECOME WHAT THEY BELIEVED HE WOULD, TO REMAIN, IN DEATH, AS MUCH THE HONORABLE WARRIOR HE HAD BEEN IN LIFE...
BUT WITH THE WHISPERING VOICE GROWING MORE AND MORE INCESSANT AGAIN, TRAG DID NOT KNOW HOW LONG THAT DETERMINATION WOULD LAST, OR EVEN IF HE TRULY DESIRED IT TO.
NOR DID HE KNOW THAT, EVEN NOW, HIS FLIGHT LED HIM TOWARD THE DIRECTION OF A LAND CALLED NORTHREND...
CONTINUED IN NEXT VOLUME

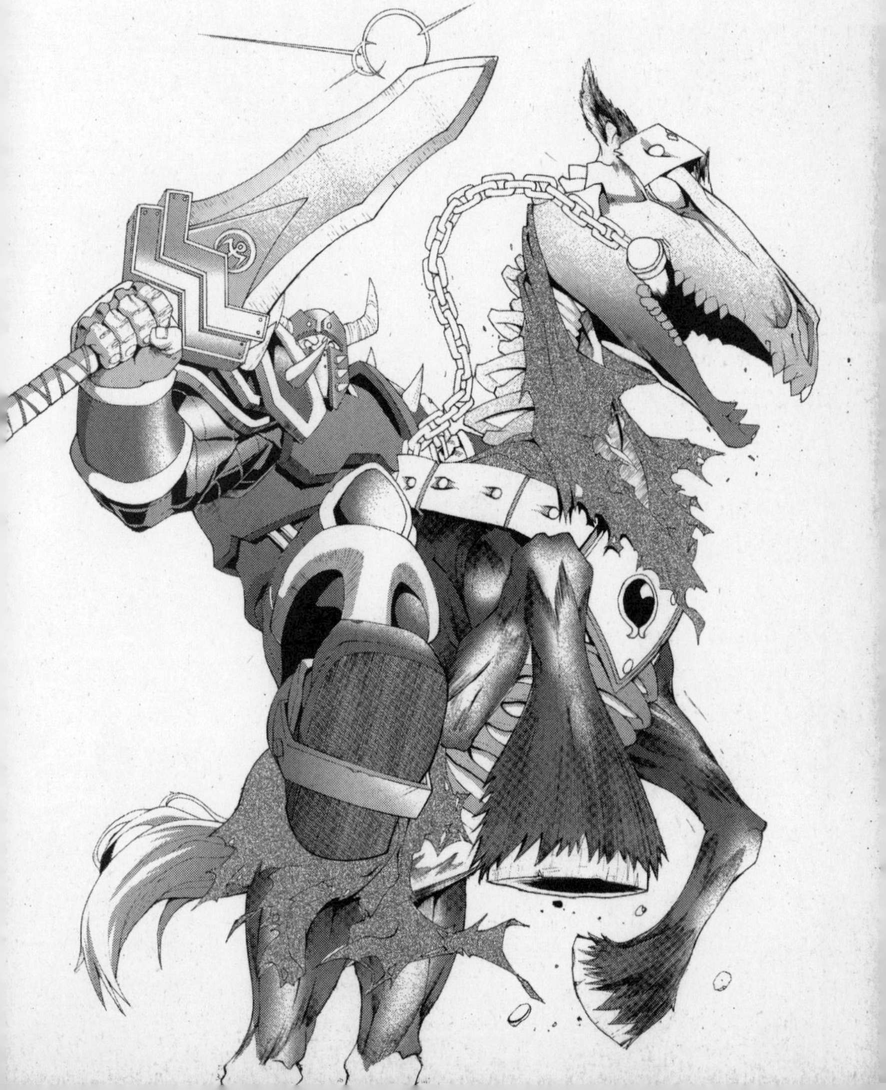

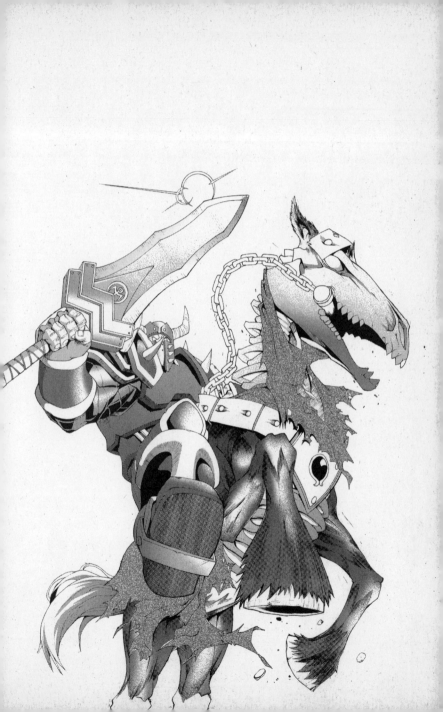

WARCRAFT®

LEGENDS™

VOLUME ONE

THE JOURNEY

STORY BY TROY LEWTER & MIKE WELLMAN
WRITTEN BY TROY LEWTER

PENCILS BY MI-YOUNG NO
BACKGROUNDS BY MI-JUNG KANG
INKS BY MI-YOUNG NO & MI-JUNG KANG
TONES BY HYUN-HONG-YOOK & SOON-SHIK HONG

Editor: Troy Lewter
Contributing Editor: Hyun Joo Kim
Associate Editor: Shannon Watters
Letterer: Michael Paolilli

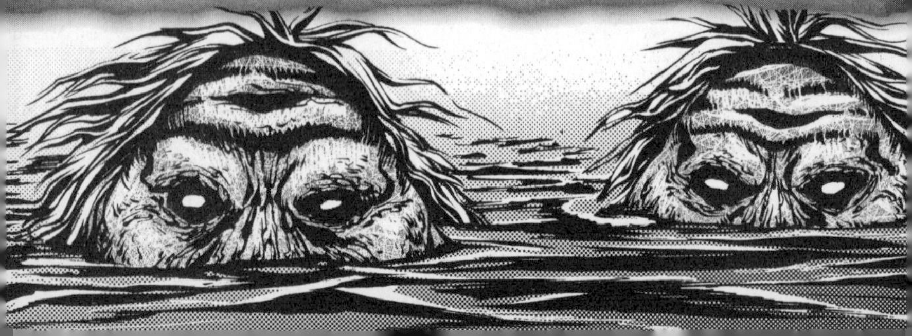

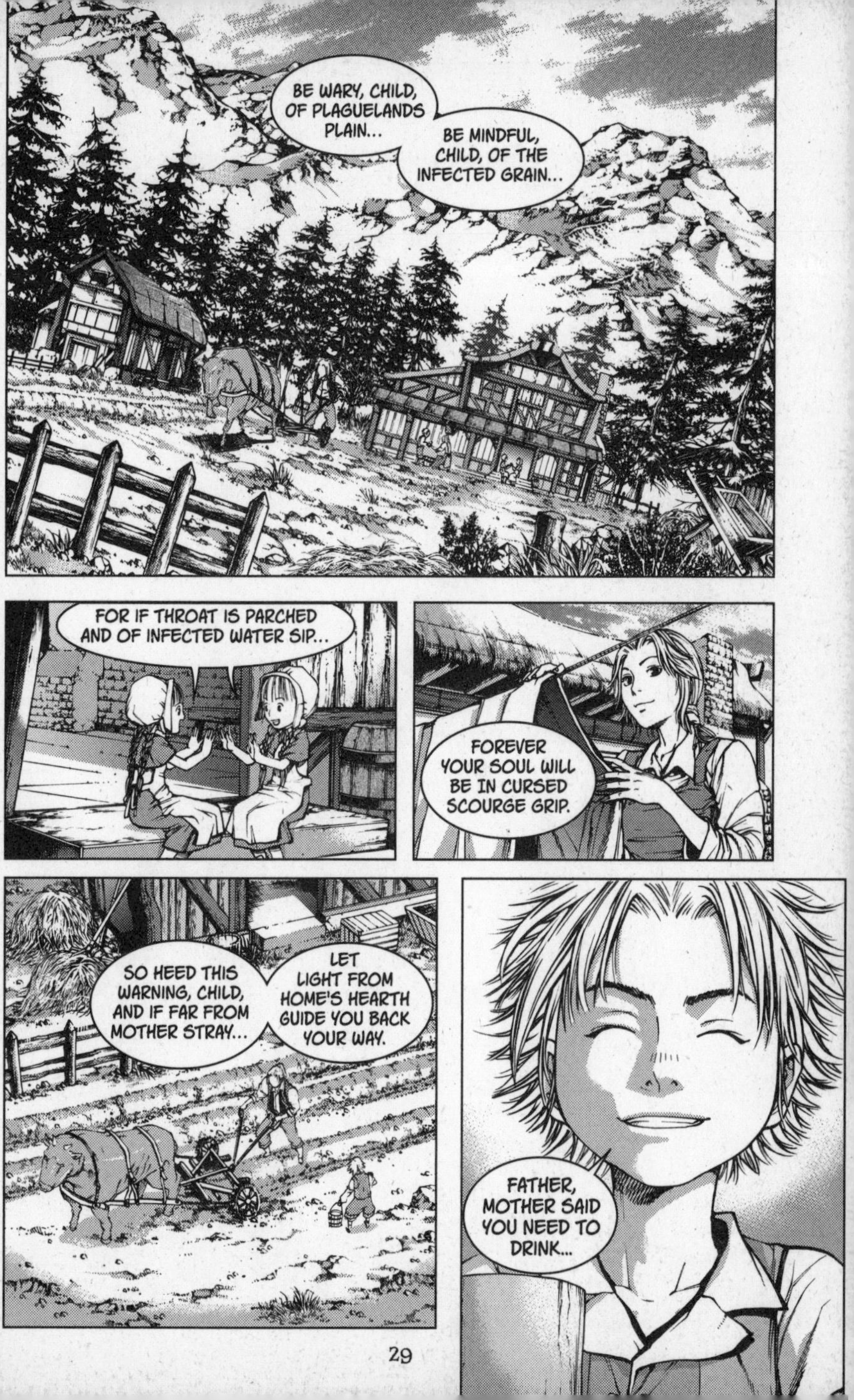
BE WARY, CHILD, OF PLAGUELANDS PLAIN...
BE MINDFUL, CHILD, OF THE INFECTED GRAIN...
FOR IF THROAT IS PARCHED AND OF INFECTED WATER SIP...
FOREVER YOUR SOUL WILL BE IN CURSED SCOURGE GRIP.
SO HEED THIS WARNING, CHILD, AND IF FAR FROM MOTHER STRAY...
LET LIGHT FROM HOME'S HEARTH GUIDE YOU BACK YOUR WAY.
FATHER, MOTHER SAID YOU NEED TO DRINK...

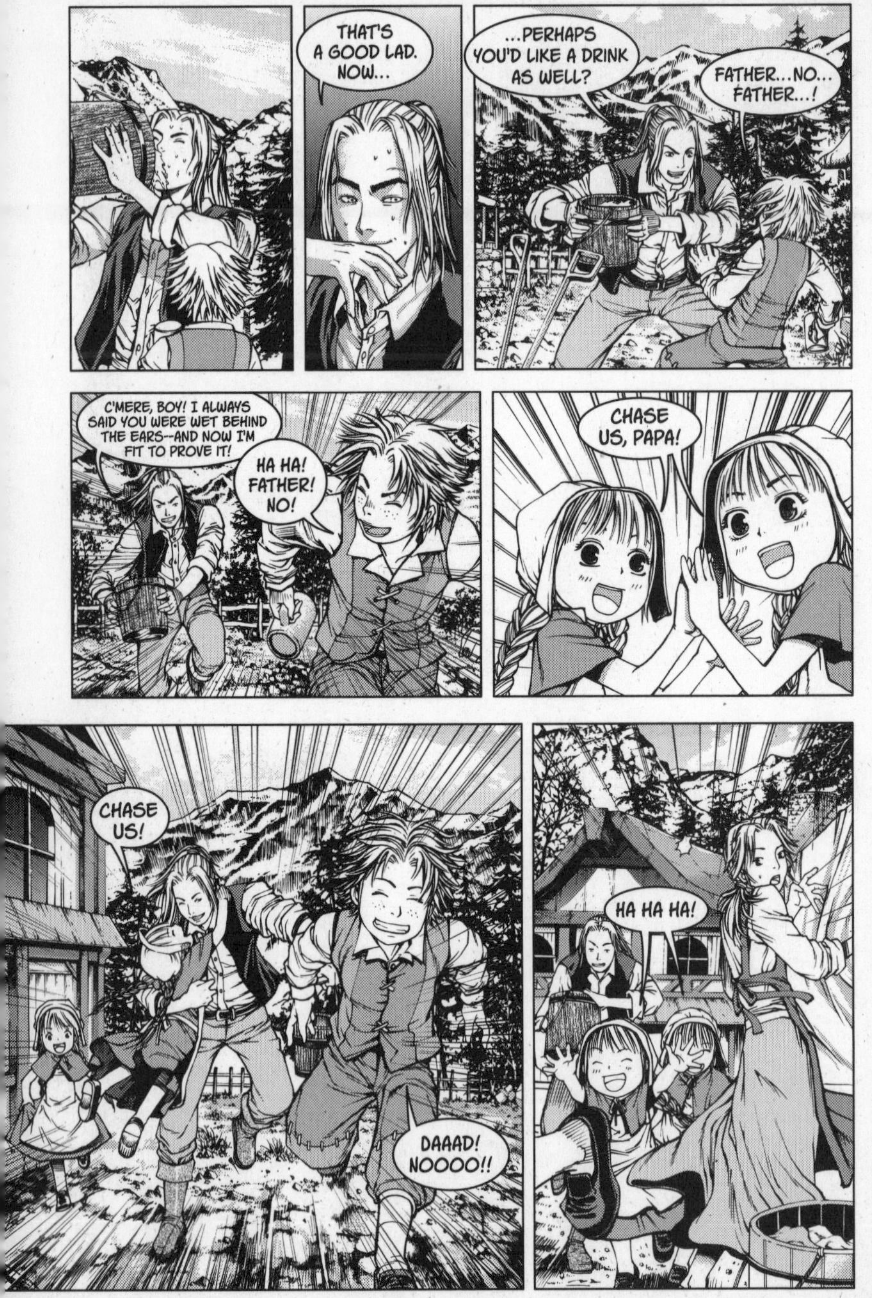
THAT'S A GOOD LAD. NOW...
...PERHAPS YOU'D LIKE A DRINK AS WELL?
FATHER...NO... FATHER...!
C'MERE, BOY! I ALWAYS SAID YOU WERE WET BEHIND THE EARS--AND NOW I'M FIT TO PROVE IT!
HA HA! FATHER! NO!
CHASE US, PAPA!
CHASE US!
DAAAD! NOOOO!!
HA HA HA!

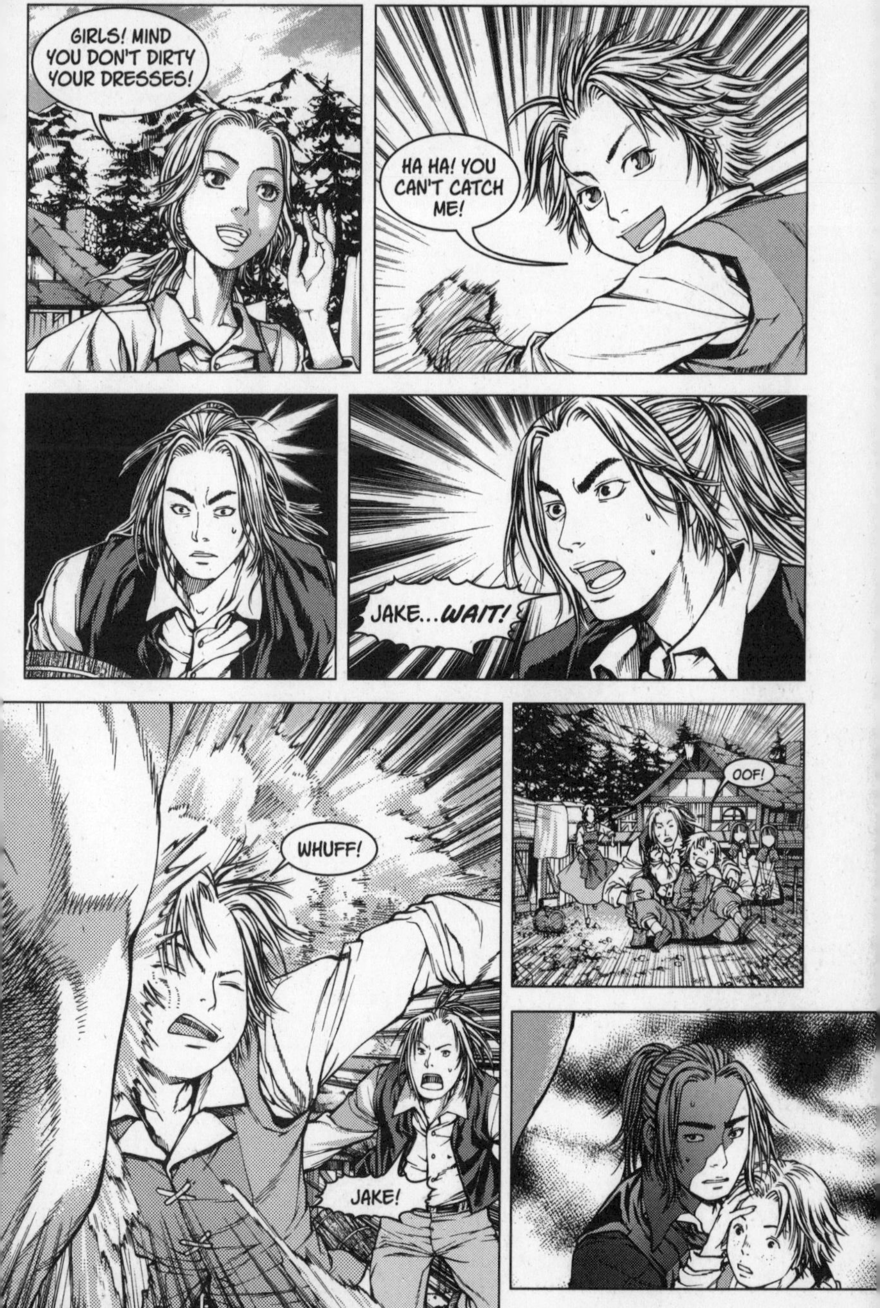
GIRLS! MIND YOU DON'T DIRTY YOUR DRESSES!
HA HA! YOU CAN'T CATCH ME!
JAKE...WAIT!
WHUFF!
JAKE!
OOF!

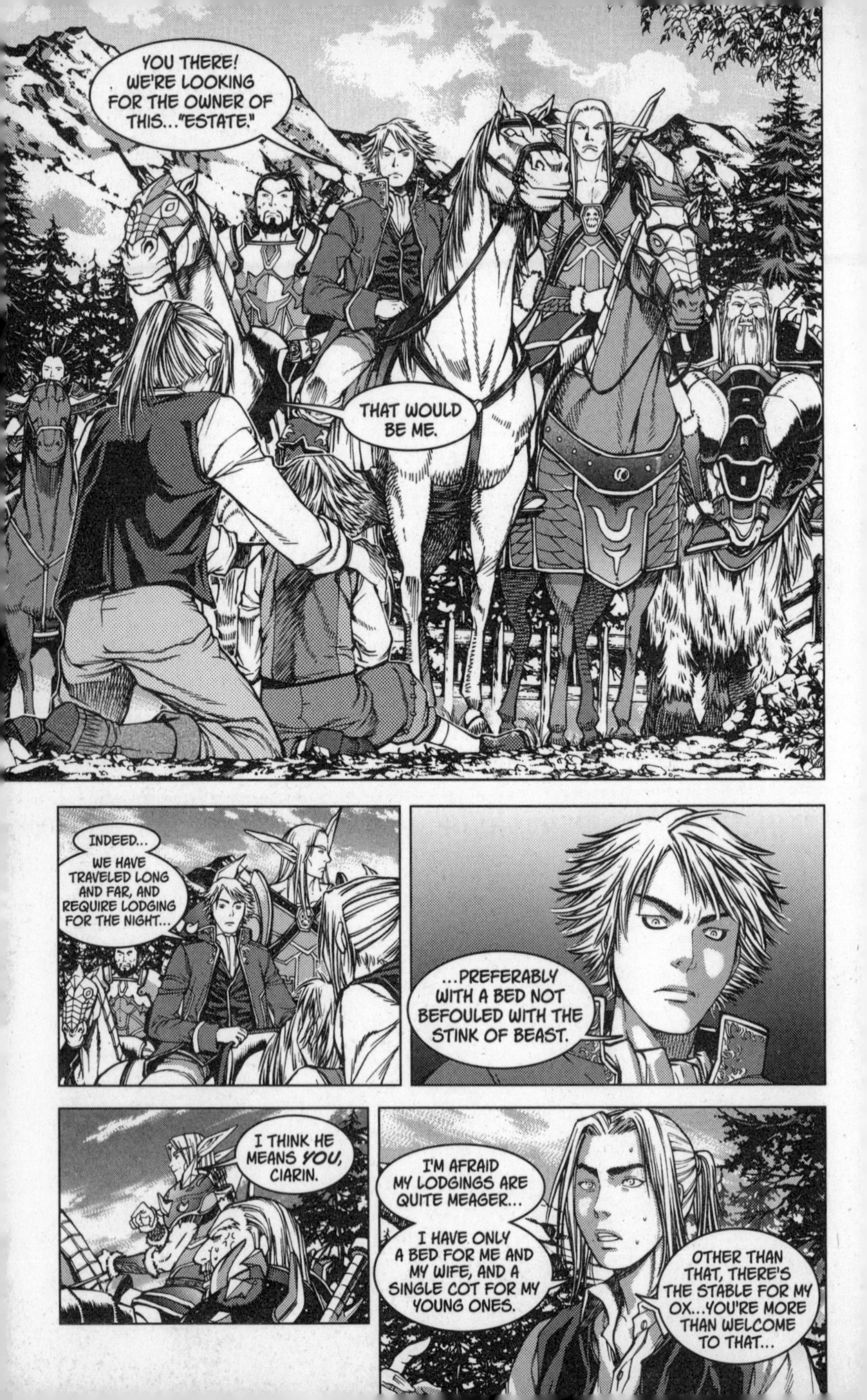
YOU THERE! WE'RE LOOKING FOR THE OWNER OF THIS..."ESTATE."
THAT WOULD BE ME.
INDEED...
WE HAVE TRAVELED LONG AND FAR, AND REQUIRE LODGING FOR THE NIGHT...
...PREFERABLY WITH A BED NOT BEFOULED WITH THE STINK OF BEAST.
I THINK HE MEANS YOU, CIARIN.
I'M AFRAID MY LODGINGS ARE QUITE MEAGER...
I HAVE ONLY A BED FOR ME AND MY WIFE, AND A SINGLE COT FOR MY YOUNG ONES.
OTHER THAN THAT, THERE'S THE STABLE FOR MY OX...YOU'RE MORE THAN WELCOME TO THAT...

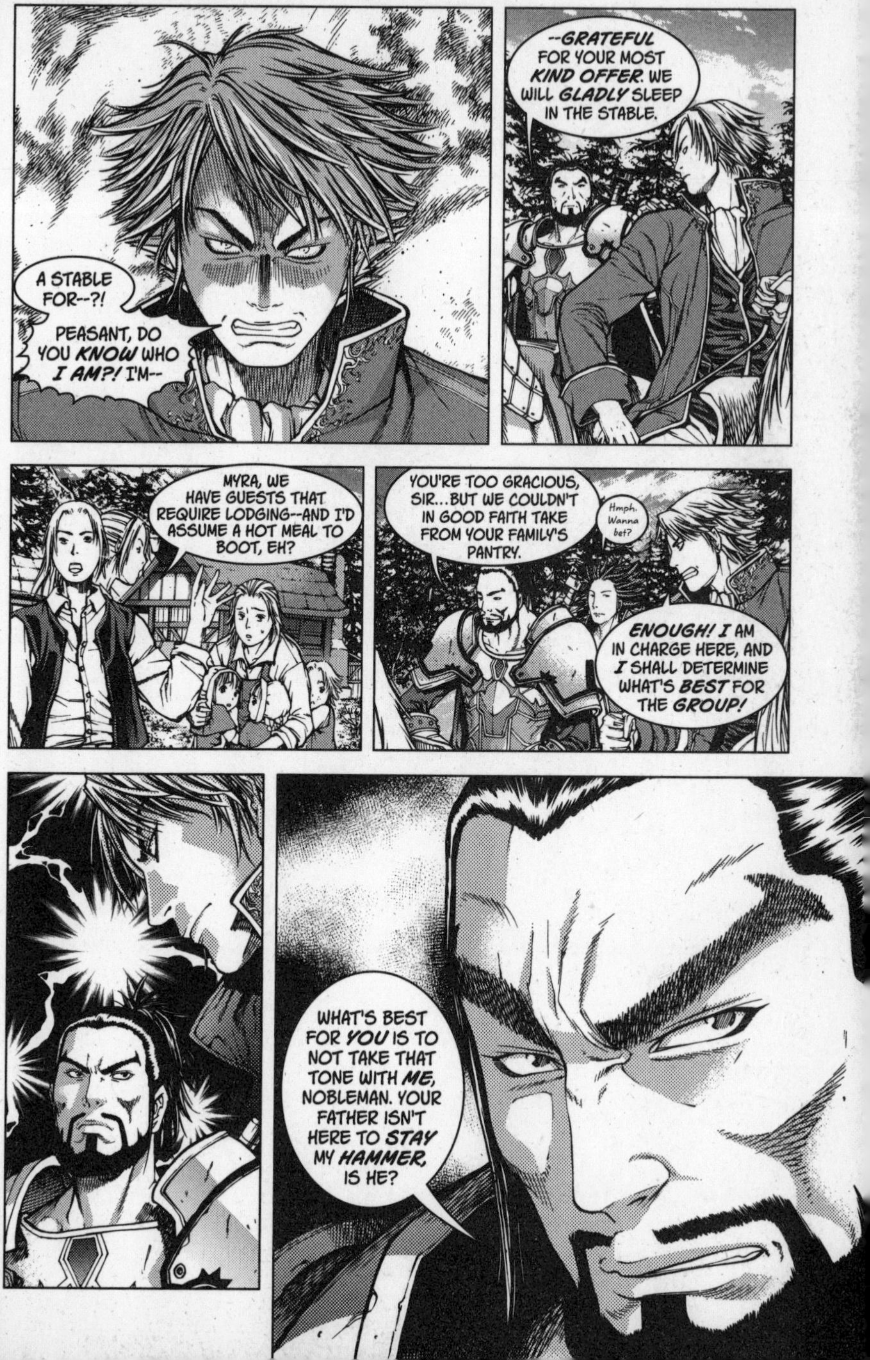

A STABLE FOR--?!
PEASANT, DO YOU KNOW WHO I AM?! I'M--
--GRATEFUL FOR YOUR MOST KIND OFFER. WE WILL GLADLY SLEEP IN THE STABLE.
MYRA, WE HAVE GUESTS THAT REQUIRE LODGING--AND I'D ASSUME A HOT MEAL TO BOOT, EH?
YOU'RE TOO GRACIOUS, SIR...BUT WE COULDN'T IN GOOD FAITH TAKE FROM YOUR FAMILY'S PANTRY.
Hmph. Wanna bet?
ENOUGH! I AM IN CHARGE HERE, AND I SHALL DETERMINE WHAT'S BEST FOR THE GROUP!
WHAT'S BEST FOR YOU IS TO NOT TAKE THAT TONE WITH ME, NOBLEMAN. YOUR FATHER ISN'T HERE TO STAY MY HAMMER, IS HE?

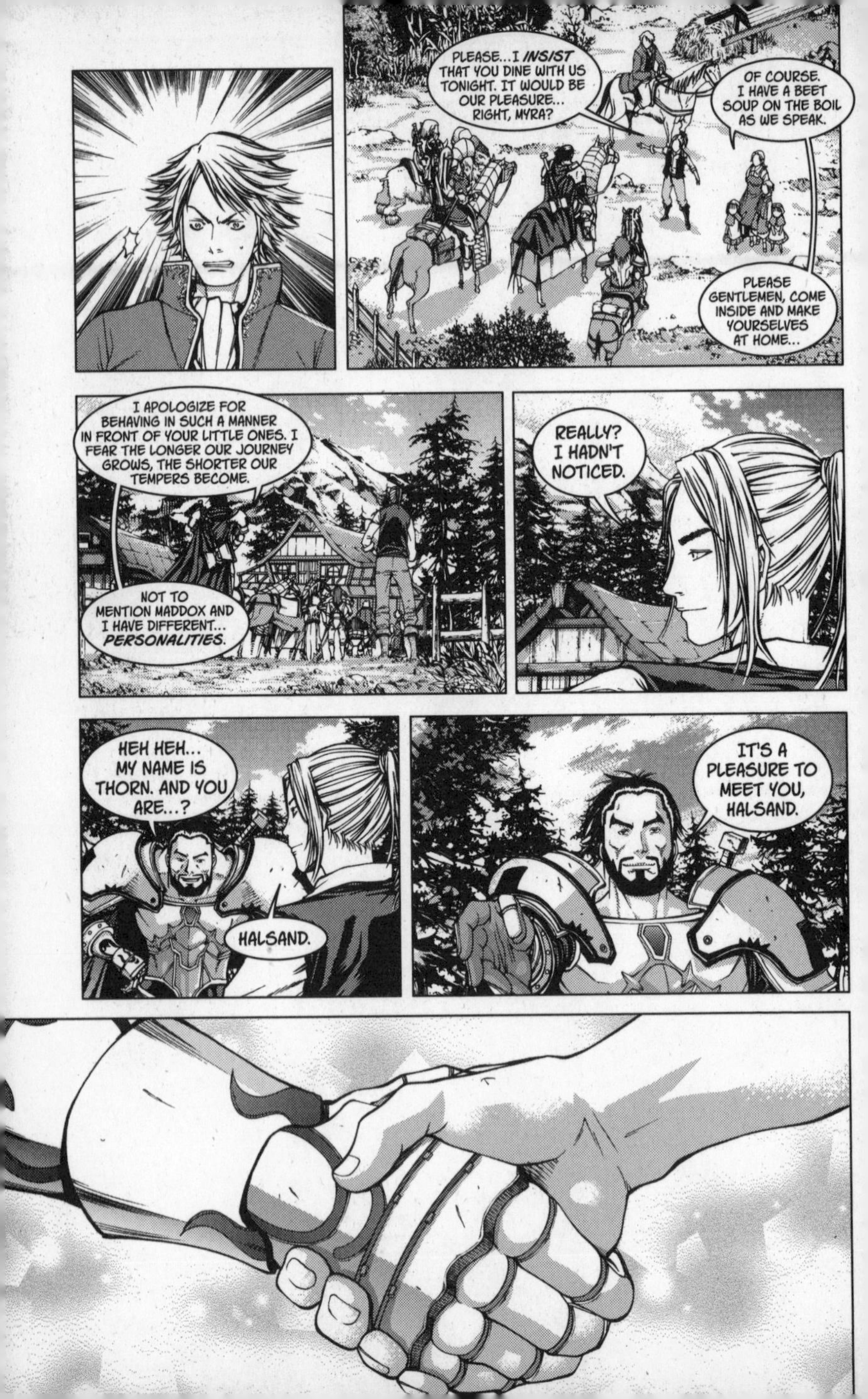
PLEASE...I *INSIST* THAT YOU DINE WITH US TONIGHT. IT WOULD BE OUR PLEASURE... RIGHT, MYRA?
OF COURSE. I HAVE A BEET SOUP ON THE BOIL AS WE SPEAK.
PLEASE GENTLEMEN, COME INSIDE AND MAKE YOURSELVES AT HOME...
I APOLOGIZE FOR BEHAVING IN SUCH A MANNER IN FRONT OF YOUR LITTLE ONES. I FEAR THE LONGER OUR JOURNEY GROWS, THE SHORTER OUR TEMPERS BECOME.
NOT TO MENTION MADDOX AND I HAVE DIFFERENT... *PERSONALITIES*.
REALLY? I HADN'T NOTICED.
HEH HEH... MY NAME IS THORN. AND YOU ARE...?
HALSAND.
IT'S A PLEASURE TO MEET YOU, HALSAND.

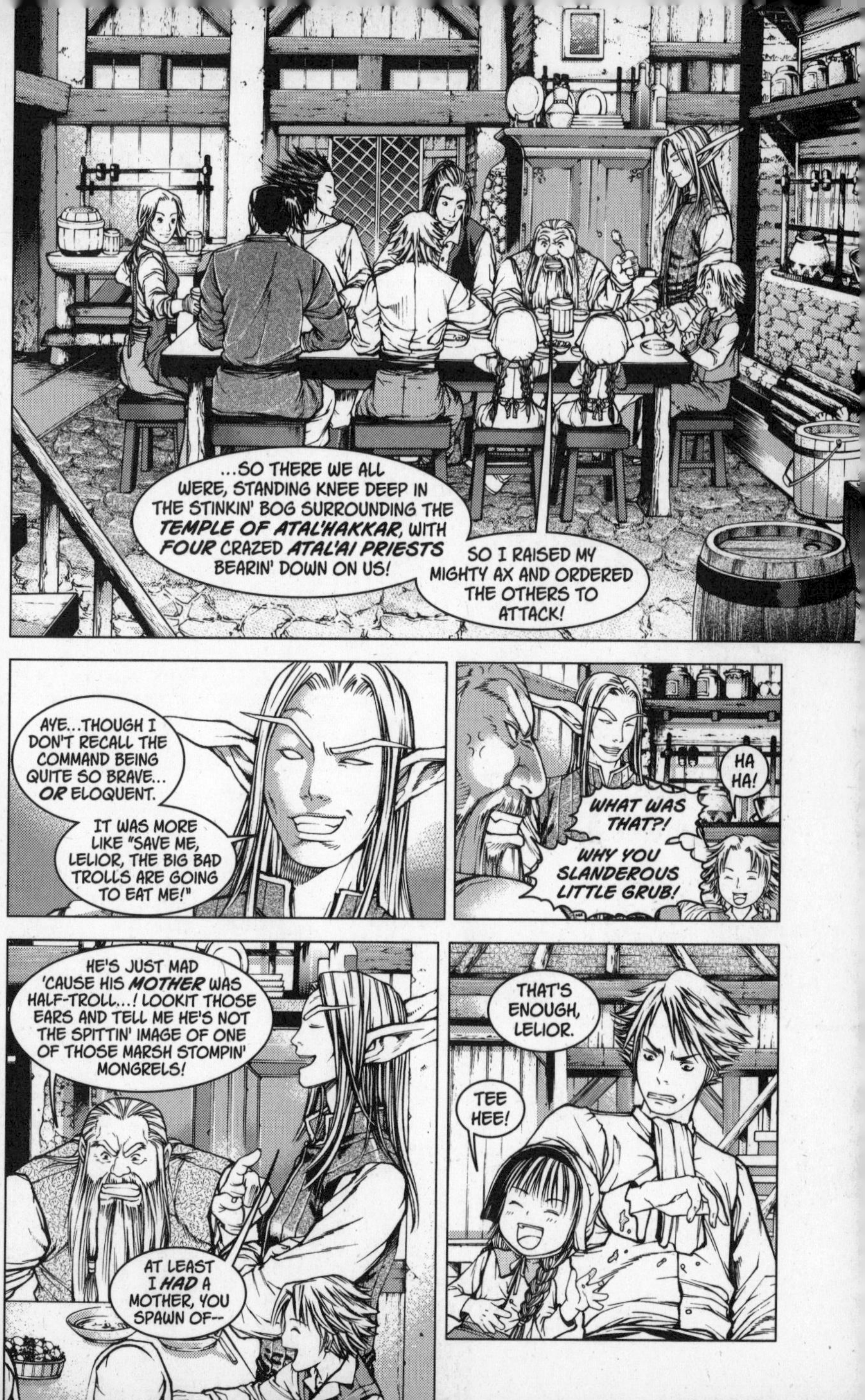
...SO THERE WE ALL WERE, STANDING KNEE DEEP IN THE STINKIN' BOG SURROUNDING THE *TEMPLE OF ATAL'HAKKAR*, WITH *FOUR* CRAZED *ATAL'AI PRIESTS* BEARIN' DOWN ON US!
SO I RAISED MY MIGHTY AX AND ORDERED THE OTHERS TO ATTACK!
AYE...THOUGH I DON'T RECALL THE COMMAND BEING QUITE SO BRAVE... *OR* ELOQUENT.
IT WAS MORE LIKE "SAVE ME, LELIOR, THE BIG BAD TROLLS ARE GOING TO EAT ME!"
HA HA!
WHAT WAS THAT?!
WHY YOU SLANDEROUS LITTLE GRUB!
HE'S JUST MAD 'CAUSE HIS *MOTHER* WAS HALF-TROLL...! LOOKIT THOSE EARS AND TELL ME HE'S NOT THE SPITTIN' IMAGE OF ONE OF THOSE MARSH STOMPIN' MONGRELS!
AT LEAST I *HAD* A MOTHER, YOU SPAWN OF--
THAT'S ENOUGH, LELIOR.
TEE HEE!

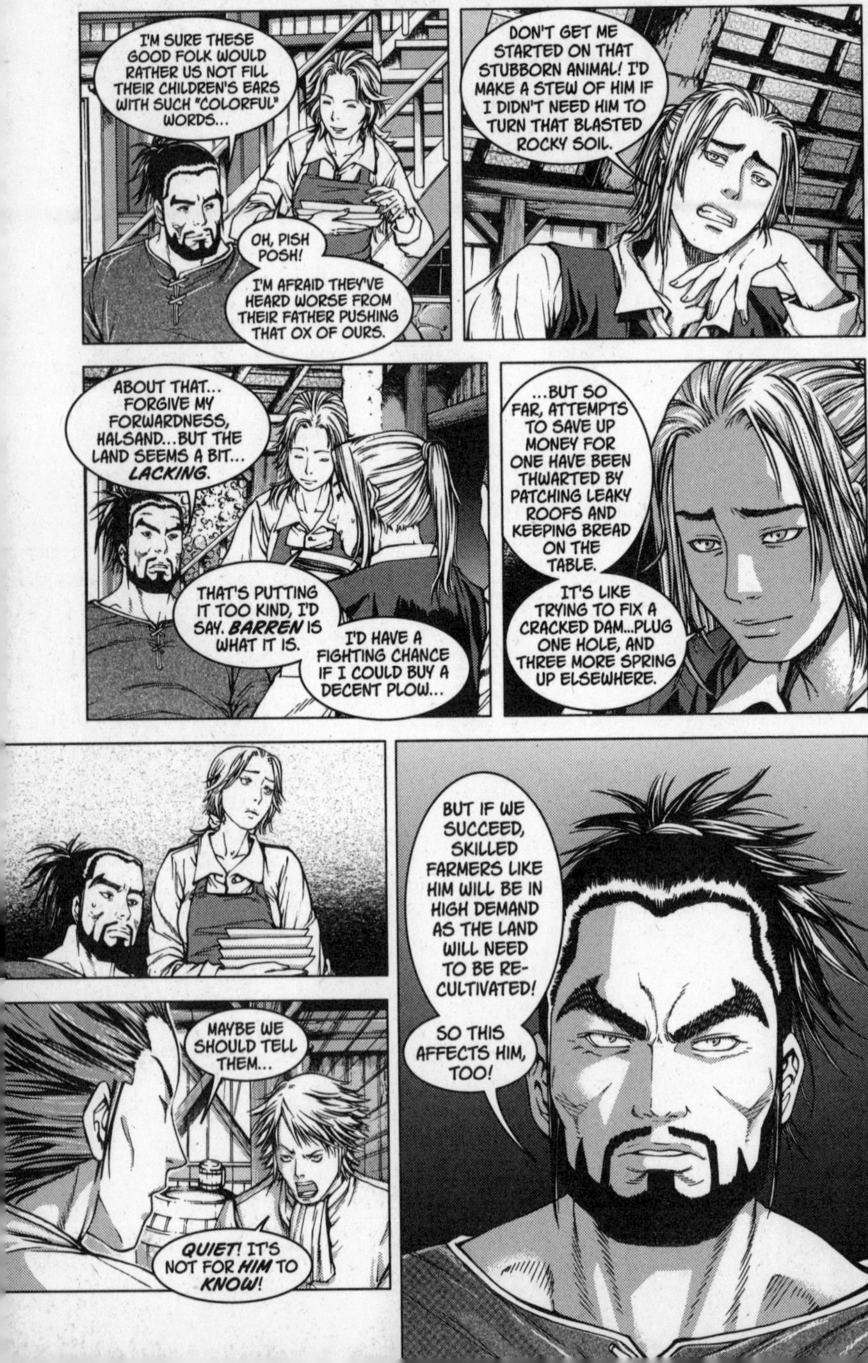
I'M SURE THESE GOOD FOLK WOULD RATHER US NOT FILL THEIR CHILDREN'S EARS WITH SUCH "COLORFUL" WORDS...
OH, PISH POSH!
I'M AFRAID THEY'VE HEARD WORSE FROM THEIR FATHER PUSHING THAT OX OF OURS.
DON'T GET ME STARTED ON THAT STUBBORN ANIMAL! I'D MAKE A STEW OF HIM IF I DIDN'T NEED HIM TO TURN THAT BLASTED ROCKY SOIL.
ABOUT THAT... FORGIVE MY FORWARDNESS, HALSAND...BUT THE LAND SEEMS A BIT... LACKING.
THAT'S PUTTING IT TOO KIND, I'D SAY. BARREN IS WHAT IT IS.
I'D HAVE A FIGHTING CHANCE IF I COULD BUY A DECENT PLOW...
...BUT SO FAR, ATTEMPTS TO SAVE UP MONEY FOR ONE HAVE BEEN THWARTED BY PATCHING LEAKY ROOFS AND KEEPING BREAD ON THE TABLE.
IT'S LIKE TRYING TO FIX A CRACKED DAM...PLUG ONE HOLE, AND THREE MORE SPRING UP ELSEWHERE.
MAYBE WE SHOULD TELL THEM...
QUIET! IT'S NOT FOR HIM TO KNOW!
BUT IF WE SUCCEED, SKILLED FARMERS LIKE HIM WILL BE IN HIGH DEMAND AS THE LAND WILL NEED TO BE RE-CULTIVATED!
SO THIS AFFECTS HIM, TOO!

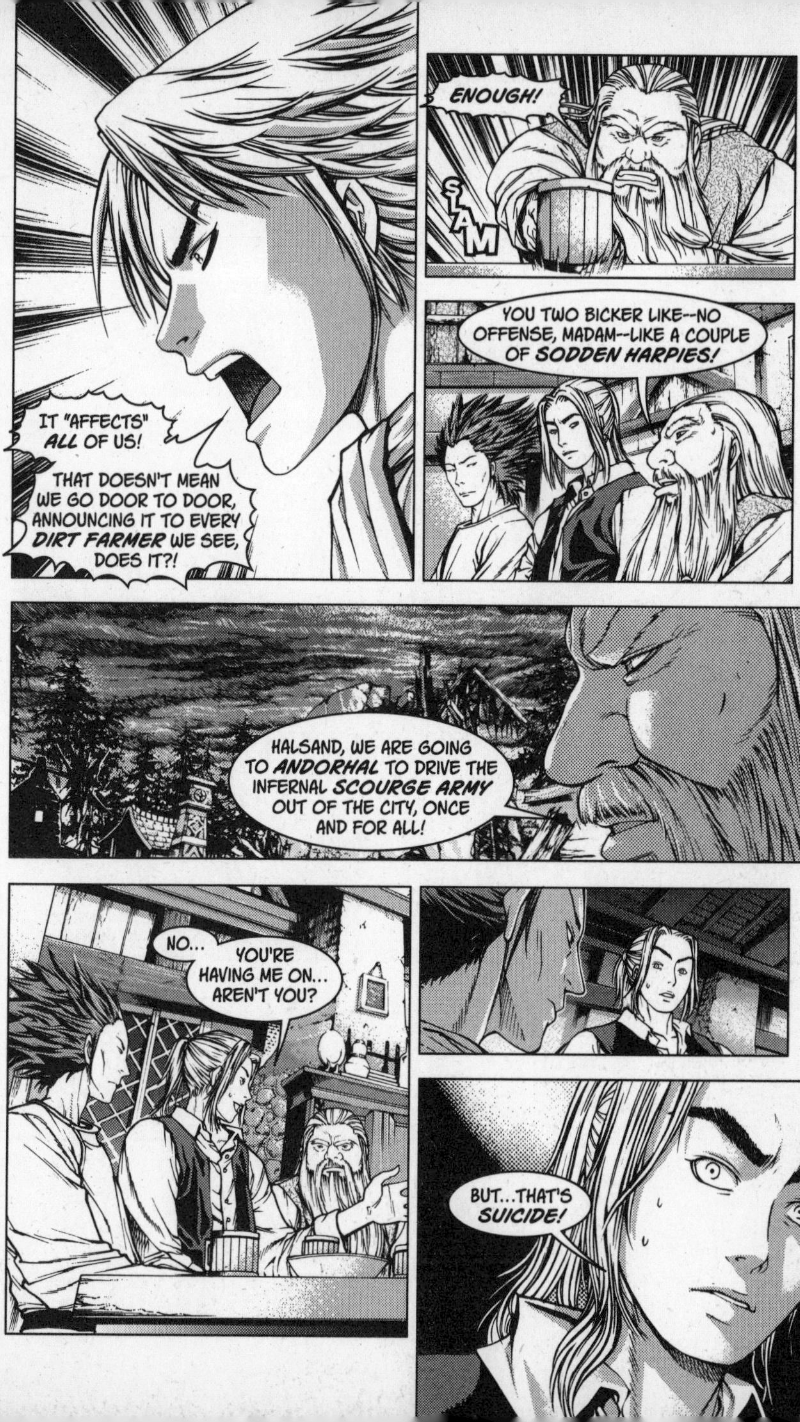
IT "AFFECTS" ALL OF US!
THAT DOESN'T MEAN WE GO DOOR TO DOOR, ANNOUNCING IT TO EVERY DIRT FARMER WE SEE, DOES IT?!
ENOUGH!
SLAM
YOU TWO BICKER LIKE--NO OFFENSE, MADAM--LIKE A COUPLE OF SODDEN HARPIES!
HALSAND, WE ARE GOING TO ANDORHAL TO DRIVE THE INFERNAL SCOURGE ARMY OUT OF THE CITY, ONCE AND FOR ALL!
NO...
YOU'RE HAVING ME ON... AREN'T YOU?
BUT...THAT'S SUICIDE!

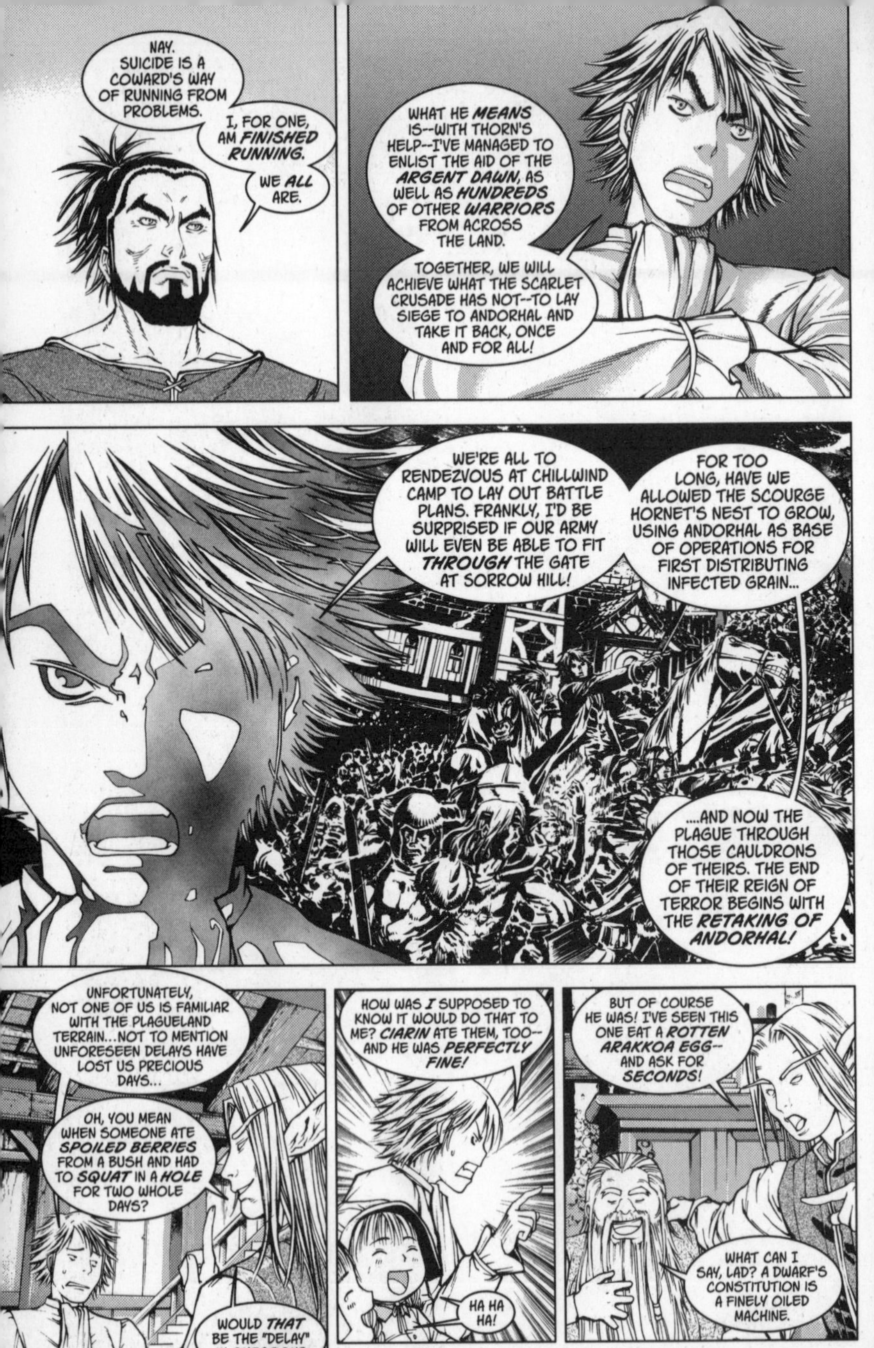
NAY. SUICIDE IS A COWARD'S WAY OF RUNNING FROM PROBLEMS.
I, FOR ONE, AM *FINISHED RUNNING.*
WE *ALL* ARE.
WHAT HE *MEANS* IS--WITH THORN'S HELP--I'VE MANAGED TO ENLIST THE AID OF THE *ARGENT DAWN,* AS WELL AS *HUNDREDS* OF OTHER *WARRIORS* FROM ACROSS THE LAND.
TOGETHER, WE WILL ACHIEVE WHAT THE SCARLET CRUSADE HAS NOT--TO LAY SIEGE TO ANDORHAL AND TAKE IT BACK, ONCE AND FOR ALL!
WE'RE ALL TO RENDEZVOUS AT CHILLWIND CAMP TO LAY OUT BATTLE PLANS. FRANKLY, I'D BE SURPRISED IF OUR ARMY WILL EVEN BE ABLE TO FIT *THROUGH* THE GATE AT SORROW HILL!
FOR TOO LONG, HAVE WE ALLOWED THE SCOURGE HORNET'S NEST TO GROW, USING ANDORHAL AS BASE OF OPERATIONS FOR FIRST DISTRIBUTING INFECTED GRAIN...
....AND NOW THE PLAGUE THROUGH THOSE CAULDRONS OF THEIRS. THE END OF THEIR REIGN OF TERROR BEGINS WITH THE *RETAKING OF ANDORHAL!*
UNFORTUNATELY, NOT ONE OF US IS FAMILIAR WITH THE PLAGUELAND TERRAIN...NOT TO MENTION UNFORESEEN DELAYS HAVE LOST US PRECIOUS DAYS...
OH, YOU MEAN WHEN SOMEONE ATE *SPOILED BERRIES* FROM A BUSH AND HAD TO *SQUAT* IN A *HOLE* FOR TWO WHOLE DAYS?
WOULD *THAT* BE THE "DELAY" IN QUESTION?
HOW WAS *I* SUPPOSED TO KNOW IT WOULD DO THAT TO ME? *CIARIN* ATE THEM, TOO--AND HE WAS *PERFECTLY FINE!*
HA HA HA!
BUT OF COURSE HE WAS! I'VE SEEN THIS ONE EAT A *ROTTEN ARAKKOA EGG*--AND ASK FOR *SECONDS!*
WHAT CAN I SAY, LAD? A DWARF'S CONSTITUTION IS A FINELY OILED MACHINE.

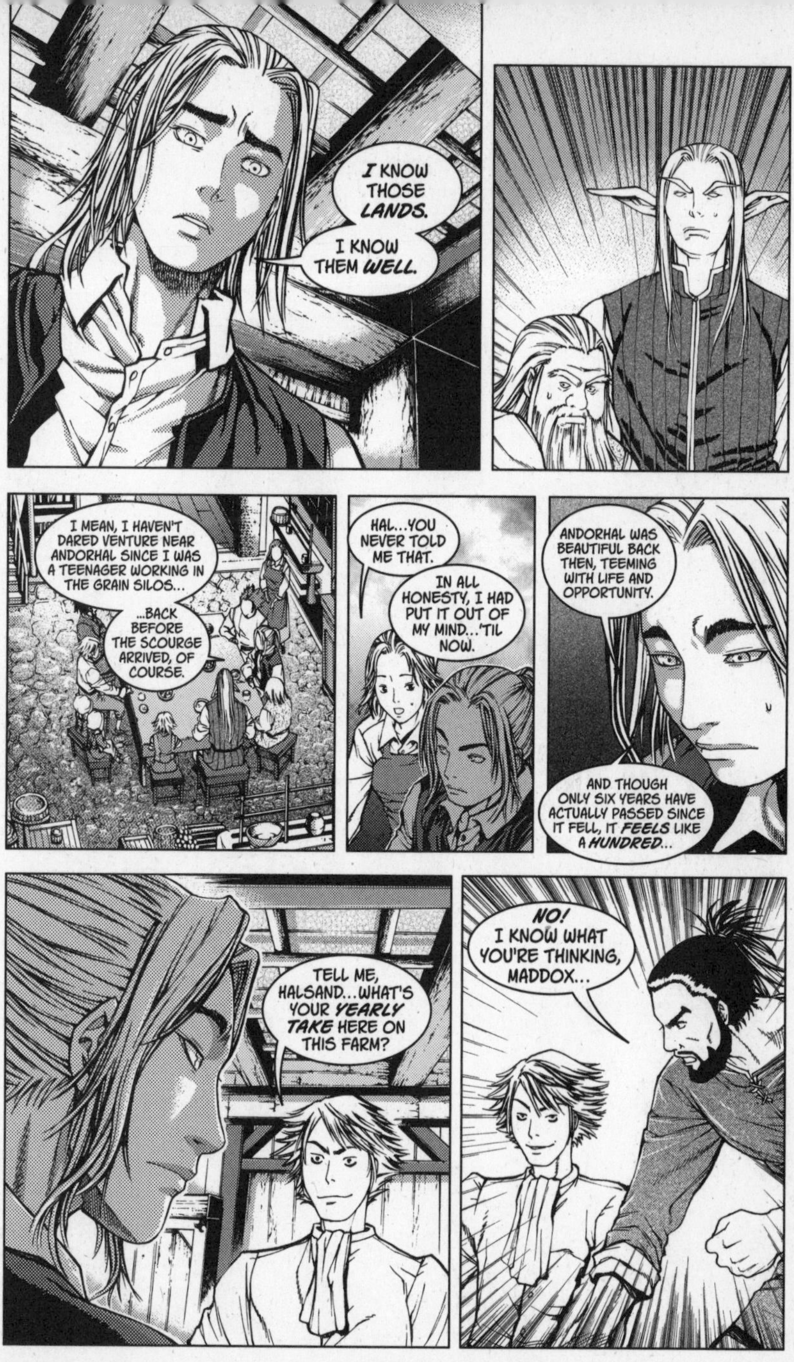
I KNOW THOSE LANDS.
I KNOW THEM WELL.
I MEAN, I HAVEN'T DARED VENTURE NEAR ANDORHAL SINCE I WAS A TEENAGER WORKING IN THE GRAIN SILOS...
...BACK BEFORE THE SCOURGE ARRIVED, OF COURSE.
HAL...YOU NEVER TOLD ME THAT.
IN ALL HONESTY, I HAD PUT IT OUT OF MY MIND...'TIL NOW.
ANDORHAL WAS BEAUTIFUL BACK THEN, TEEMING WITH LIFE AND OPPORTUNITY.
AND THOUGH ONLY SIX YEARS HAVE ACTUALLY PASSED SINCE IT FELL, IT FEELS LIKE A HUNDRED...
TELL ME, HALSAND...WHAT'S YOUR YEARLY TAKE HERE ON THIS FARM?
NO! I KNOW WHAT YOU'RE THINKING, MADDOX...

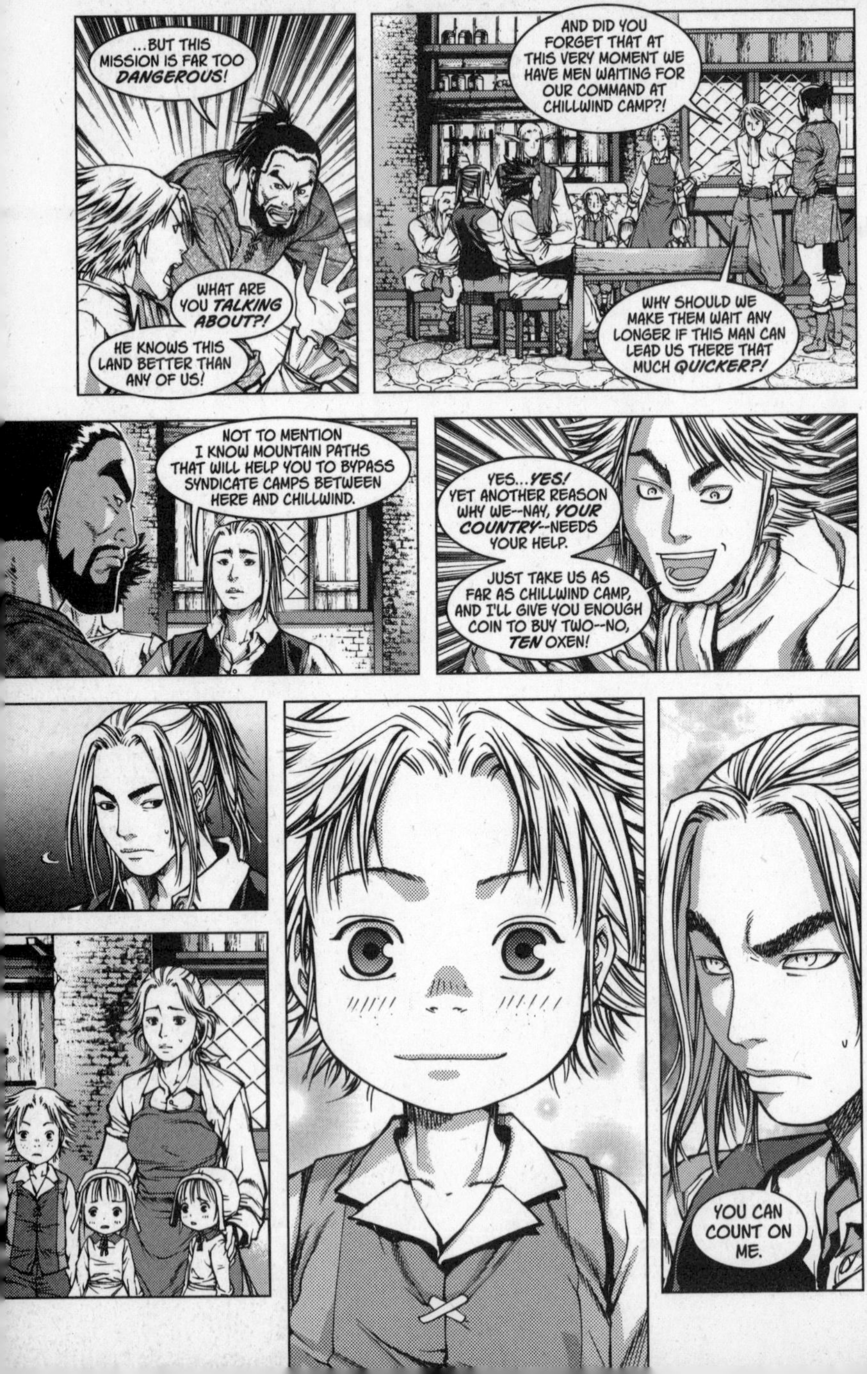
...BUT THIS MISSION IS FAR TOO *DANGEROUS*!
WHAT ARE YOU *TALKING ABOUT?!*
HE KNOWS THIS LAND BETTER THAN ANY OF US!
AND DID YOU FORGET THAT AT THIS VERY MOMENT WE HAVE MEN WAITING FOR OUR COMMAND AT CHILLWIND CAMP?!
WHY SHOULD WE MAKE THEM WAIT ANY LONGER IF THIS MAN CAN LEAD US THERE THAT MUCH *QUICKER?!*
NOT TO MENTION I KNOW MOUNTAIN PATHS THAT WILL HELP YOU TO BYPASS SYNDICATE CAMPS BETWEEN HERE AND CHILLWIND.
YES...*YES!* YET ANOTHER REASON WHY WE--NAY, *YOUR COUNTRY*--NEEDS YOUR HELP.
JUST TAKE US AS FAR AS CHILLWIND CAMP, AND I'LL GIVE YOU ENOUGH COIN TO BUY TWO--NO, *TEN* OXEN!
YOU CAN COUNT ON ME.

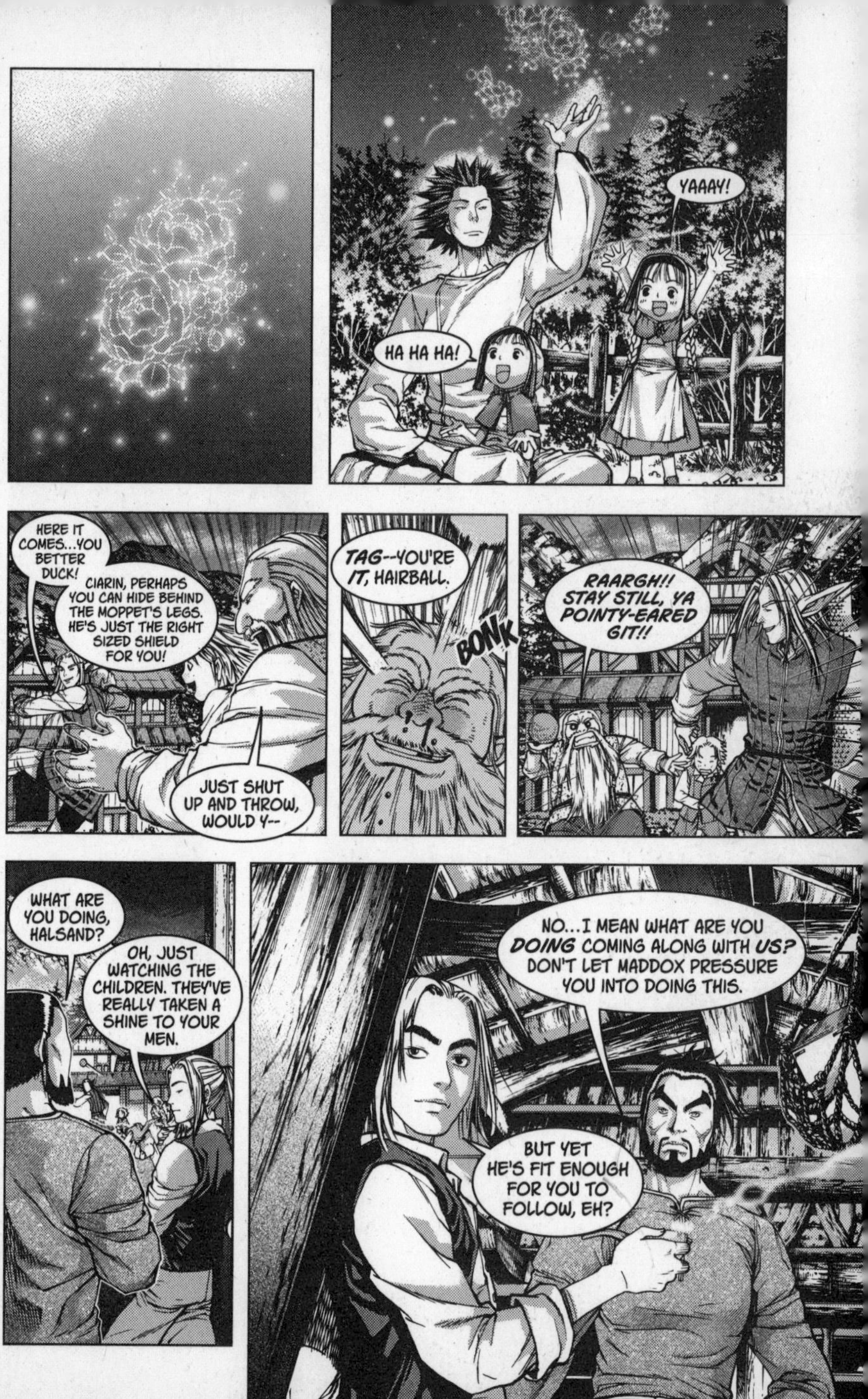
YAAAY!
HA HA HA!
HERE IT COMES...YOU BETTER DUCK!
CIARIN, PERHAPS YOU CAN HIDE BEHIND THE MOPPET'S LEGS. HE'S JUST THE RIGHT SIZED SHIELD FOR YOU!
JUST SHUT UP AND THROW, WOULD Y--
TAG--YOU'RE IT, HAIRBALL.
BONK
RAARGH!! STAY STILL, YA POINTY-EARED GIT!!
WHAT ARE YOU DOING, HALSAND?
OH, JUST WATCHING THE CHILDREN. THEY'VE REALLY TAKEN A SHINE TO YOUR MEN.
NO...I MEAN WHAT ARE YOU DOING COMING ALONG WITH US? DON'T LET MADDOX PRESSURE YOU INTO DOING THIS.
BUT YET HE'S FIT ENOUGH FOR YOU TO FOLLOW, EH?

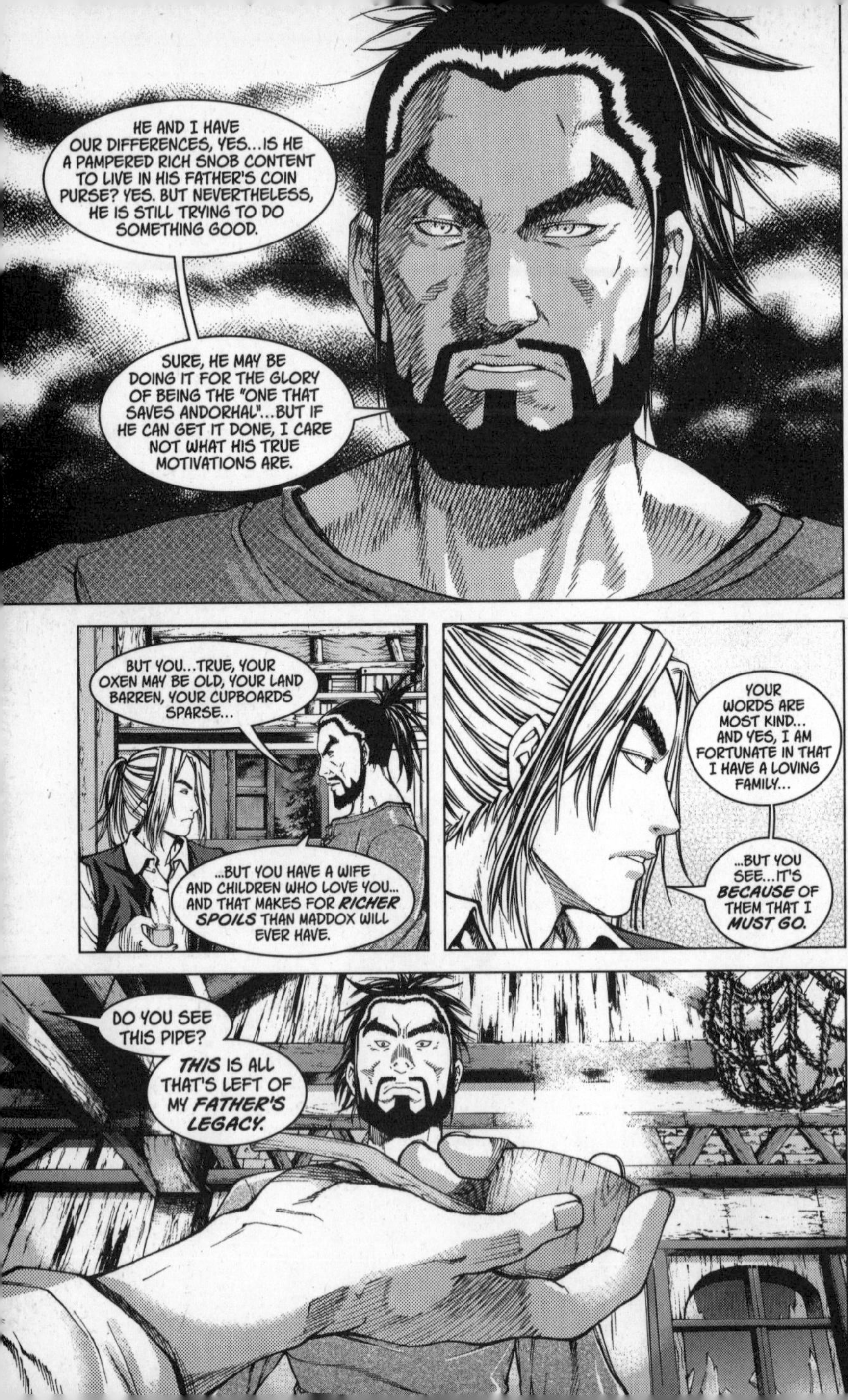
HE AND I HAVE OUR DIFFERENCES, YES...IS HE A PAMPERED RICH SNOB CONTENT TO LIVE IN HIS FATHER'S COIN PURSE? YES. BUT NEVERTHELESS, HE IS STILL TRYING TO DO SOMETHING GOOD.
SURE, HE MAY BE DOING IT FOR THE GLORY OF BEING THE "ONE THAT SAVES ANDORHAL"...BUT IF HE CAN GET IT DONE, I CARE NOT WHAT HIS TRUE MOTIVATIONS ARE.
BUT YOU...TRUE, YOUR OXEN MAY BE OLD, YOUR LAND BARREN, YOUR CUPBOARDS SPARSE...
...BUT YOU HAVE A WIFE AND CHILDREN WHO LOVE YOU... AND THAT MAKES FOR *RICHER SPOILS* THAN MADDOX WILL EVER HAVE.
YOUR WORDS ARE MOST KIND... AND YES, I AM FORTUNATE IN THAT I HAVE A LOVING FAMILY...
...BUT YOU SEE...IT'S *BECAUSE* OF THEM THAT I *MUST GO.*
DO YOU SEE THIS PIPE?
THIS IS ALL THAT'S LEFT OF MY *FATHER'S LEGACY.*

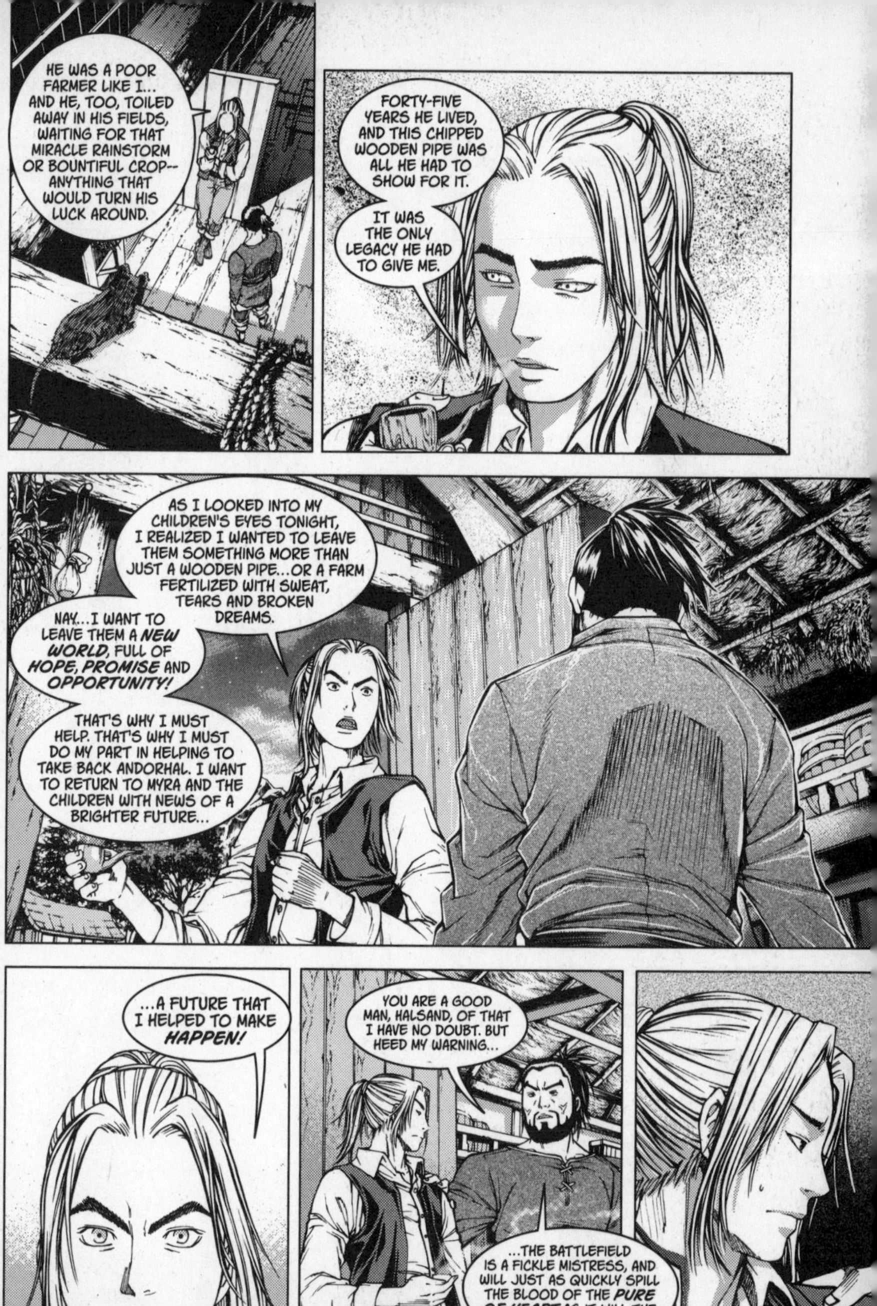
HE WAS A POOR FARMER LIKE I... AND HE, TOO, TOILED AWAY IN HIS FIELDS, WAITING FOR THAT MIRACLE RAINSTORM OR BOUNTIFUL CROP-- ANYTHING THAT WOULD TURN HIS LUCK AROUND.
FORTY-FIVE YEARS HE LIVED, AND THIS CHIPPED WOODEN PIPE WAS ALL HE HAD TO SHOW FOR IT.
IT WAS THE ONLY LEGACY HE HAD TO GIVE ME.
AS I LOOKED INTO MY CHILDREN'S EYES TONIGHT, I REALIZED I WANTED TO LEAVE THEM SOMETHING MORE THAN JUST A WOODEN PIPE...OR A FARM FERTILIZED WITH SWEAT, TEARS AND BROKEN DREAMS.
NAY...I WANT TO LEAVE THEM A *NEW WORLD*, FULL OF *HOPE, PROMISE* AND *OPPORTUNITY!*
THAT'S WHY I MUST HELP. THAT'S WHY I MUST DO MY PART IN HELPING TO TAKE BACK ANDORHAL. I WANT TO RETURN TO MYRA AND THE CHILDREN WITH NEWS OF A BRIGHTER FUTURE...
...A FUTURE THAT I HELPED TO MAKE *HAPPEN!*
YOU ARE A GOOD MAN, HALSAND, OF THAT I HAVE NO DOUBT. BUT HEED MY WARNING...
...THE BATTLEFIELD IS A FICKLE MISTRESS, AND WILL JUST AS QUICKLY SPILL THE BLOOD OF THE *PURE OF HEART* AS IT WILL THE *SOUR OF SOUL.*

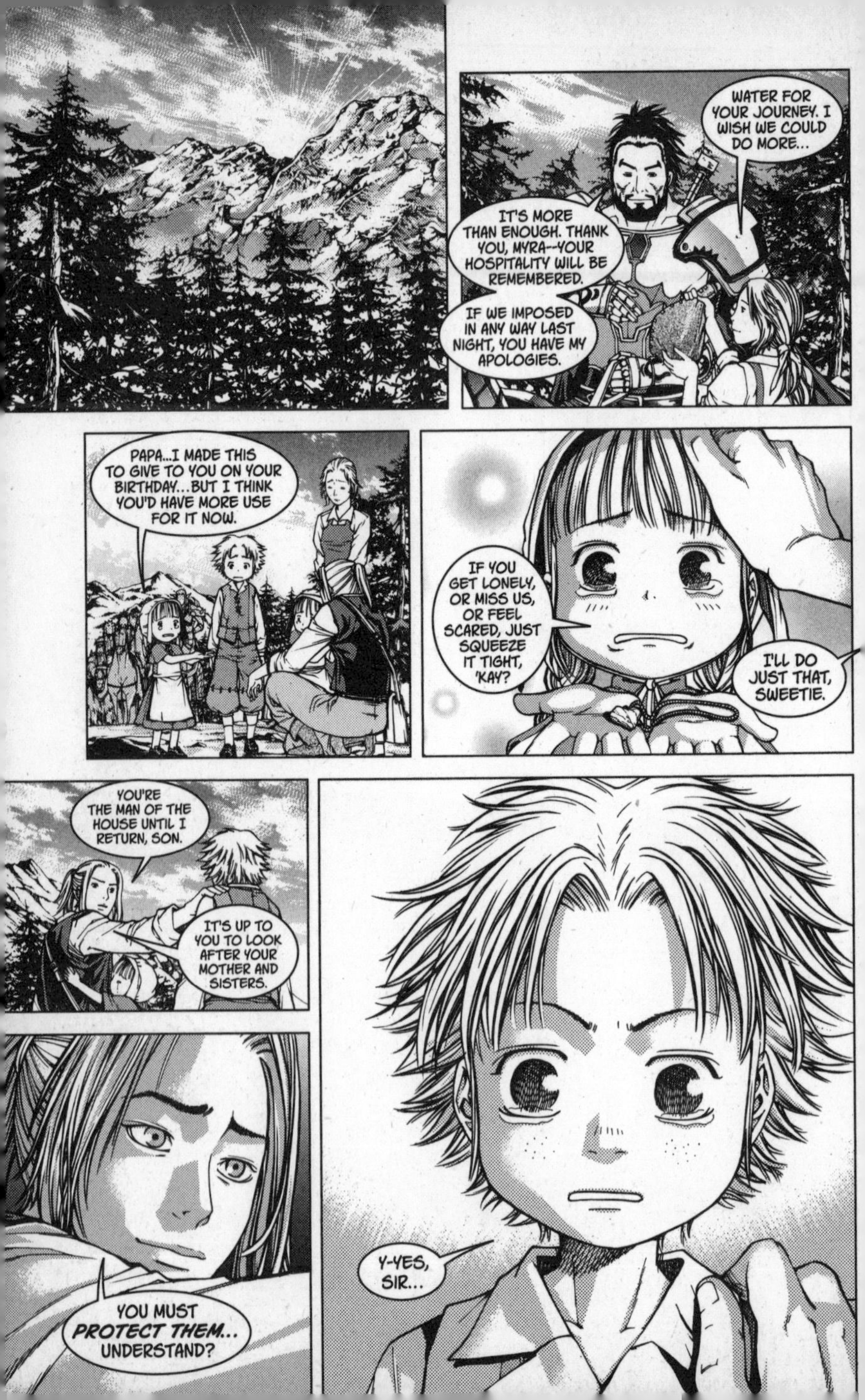
WATER FOR YOUR JOURNEY. I WISH WE COULD DO MORE...
IT'S MORE THAN ENOUGH. THANK YOU, MYRA--YOUR HOSPITALITY WILL BE REMEMBERED.
IF WE IMPOSED IN ANY WAY LAST NIGHT, YOU HAVE MY APOLOGIES.
PAPA...I MADE THIS TO GIVE TO YOU ON YOUR BIRTHDAY...BUT I THINK YOU'D HAVE MORE USE FOR IT NOW.
IF YOU GET LONELY, OR MISS US, OR FEEL SCARED, JUST SQUEEZE IT TIGHT, 'KAY?
I'LL DO JUST THAT, SWEETIE.
YOU'RE THE MAN OF THE HOUSE UNTIL I RETURN, SON.
IT'S UP TO YOU TO LOOK AFTER YOUR MOTHER AND SISTERS.
YOU MUST *PROTECT THEM...* UNDERSTAND?
Y-YES, SIR...

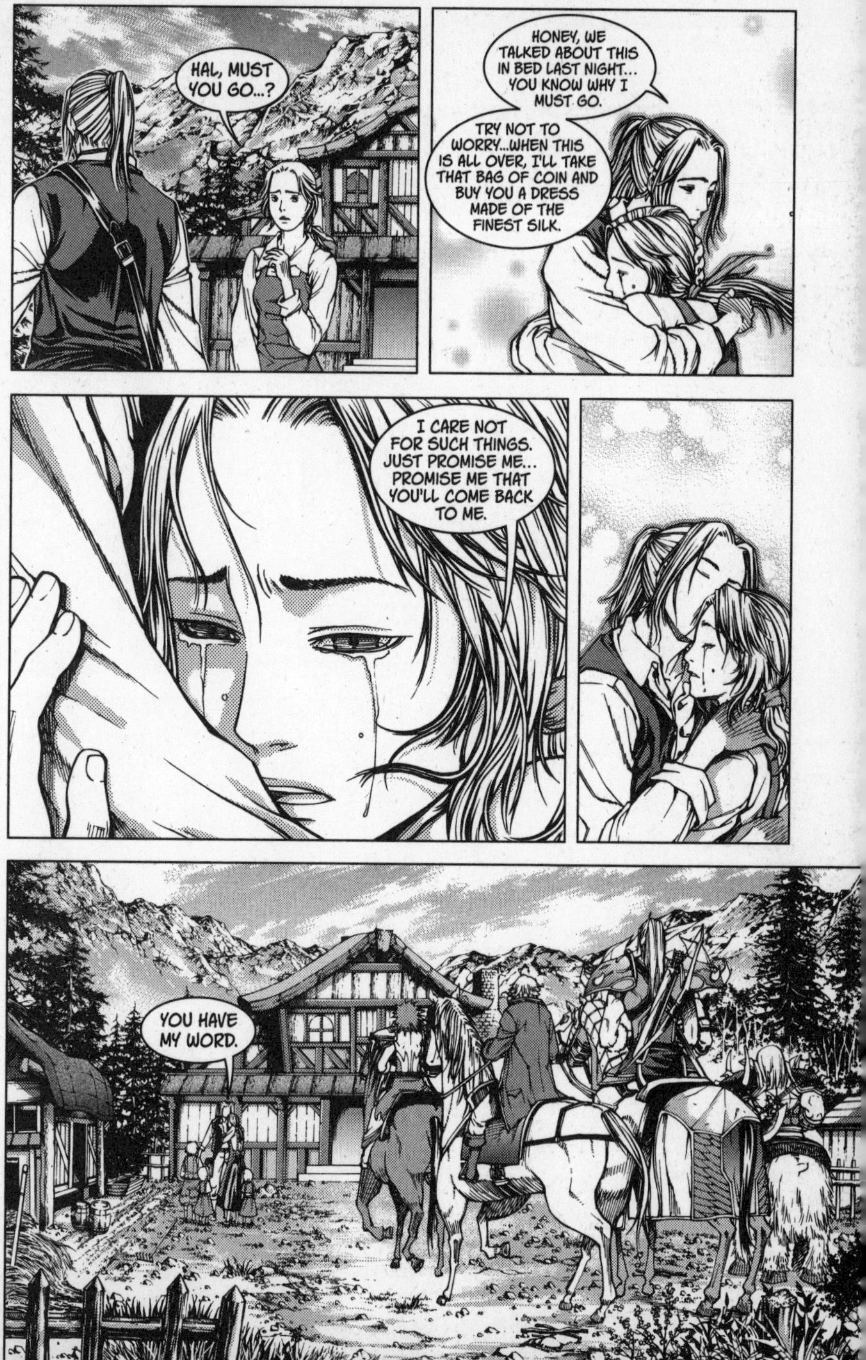
HAL, MUST YOU GO...?
HONEY, WE TALKED ABOUT THIS IN BED LAST NIGHT... YOU KNOW WHY I MUST GO.
TRY NOT TO WORRY...WHEN THIS IS ALL OVER, I'LL TAKE THAT BAG OF COIN AND BUY YOU A DRESS MADE OF THE FINEST SILK.
I CARE NOT FOR SUCH THINGS. JUST PROMISE ME... PROMISE ME THAT YOU'LL COME BACK TO ME.
YOU HAVE MY WORD.

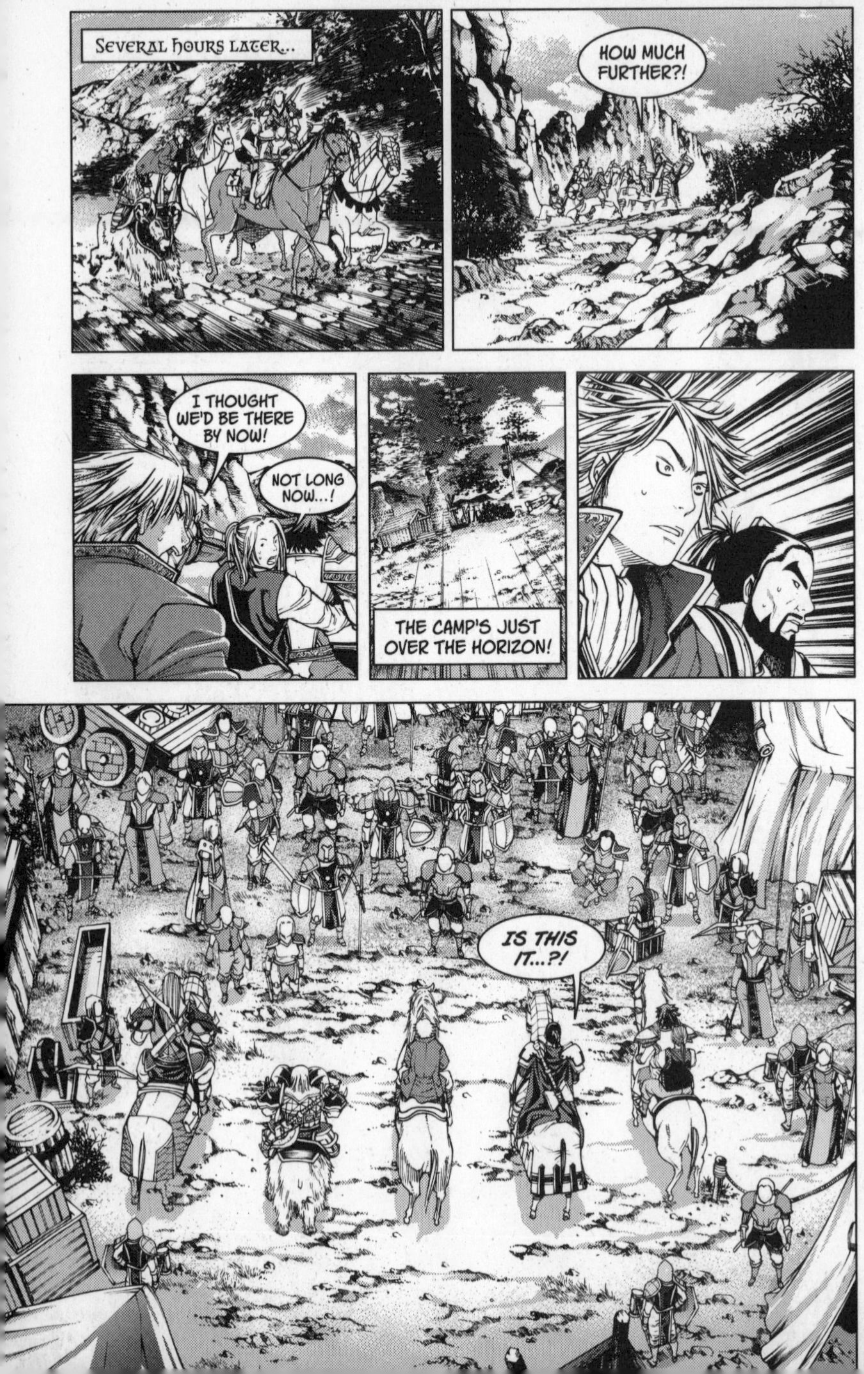
Several hours later...
HOW MUCH FURTHER?!
I THOUGHT WE'D BE THERE BY NOW!
NOT LONG NOW...!
THE CAMP'S JUST OVER THE HORIZON!
IS THIS IT...?!

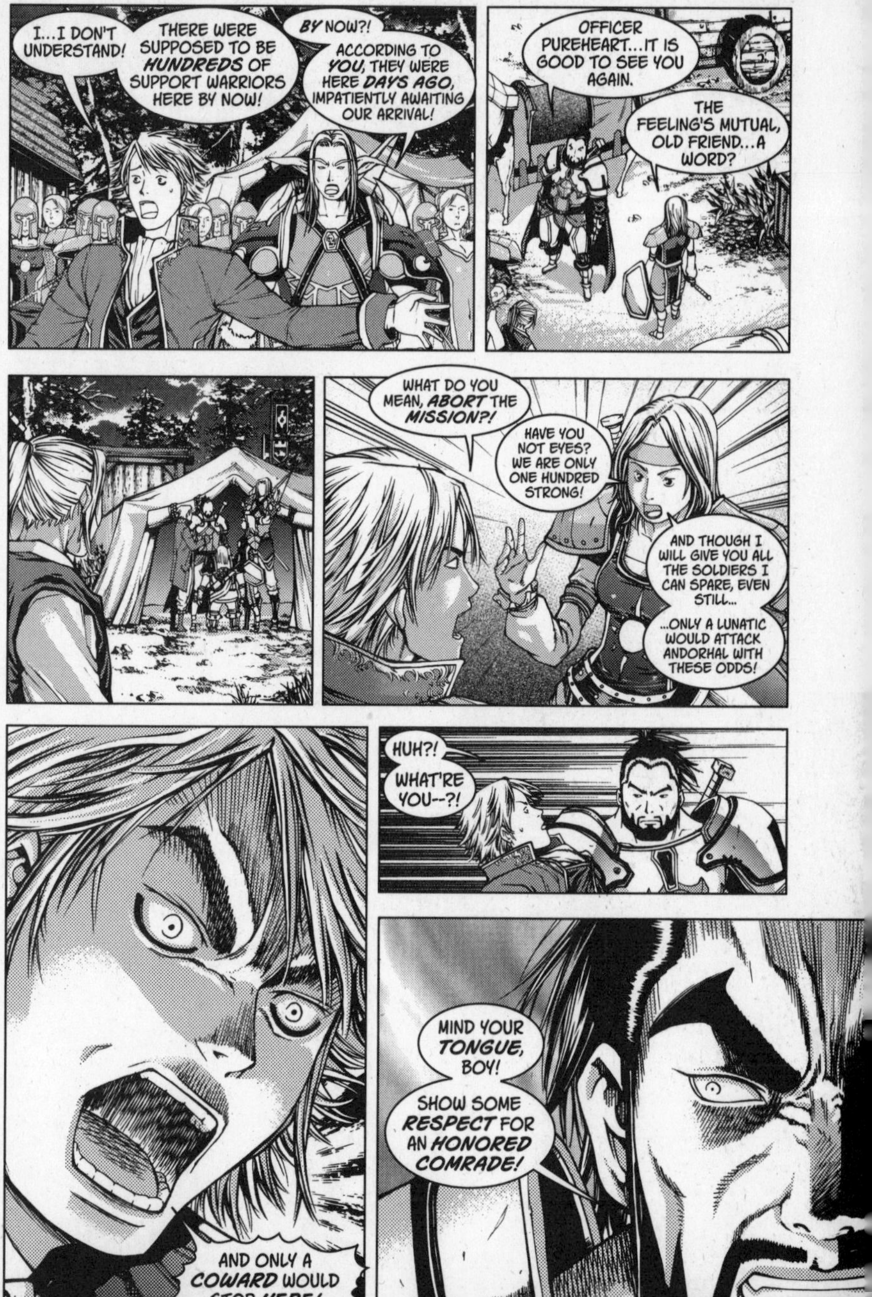

I...I DON'T UNDERSTAND!
THERE WERE SUPPOSED TO BE HUNDREDS OF SUPPORT WARRIORS HERE BY NOW!
BY NOW?!
ACCORDING TO YOU, THEY WERE HERE DAYS AGO, IMPATIENTLY AWAITING OUR ARRIVAL!
OFFICER PUREHEART...IT IS GOOD TO SEE YOU AGAIN.
THE FEELING'S MUTUAL, OLD FRIEND...A WORD?
WHAT DO YOU MEAN, ABORT THE MISSION?!
HAVE YOU NOT EYES? WE ARE ONLY ONE HUNDRED STRONG!
AND THOUGH I WILL GIVE YOU ALL THE SOLDIERS I CAN SPARE, EVEN STILL...
...ONLY A LUNATIC WOULD ATTACK ANDORHAL WITH THESE ODDS!
AND ONLY A COWARD WOULD STOP HERE!
HUH?!
WHAT'RE YOU--?!
MIND YOUR TONGUE, BOY!
SHOW SOME RESPECT FOR AN HONORED COMRADE!

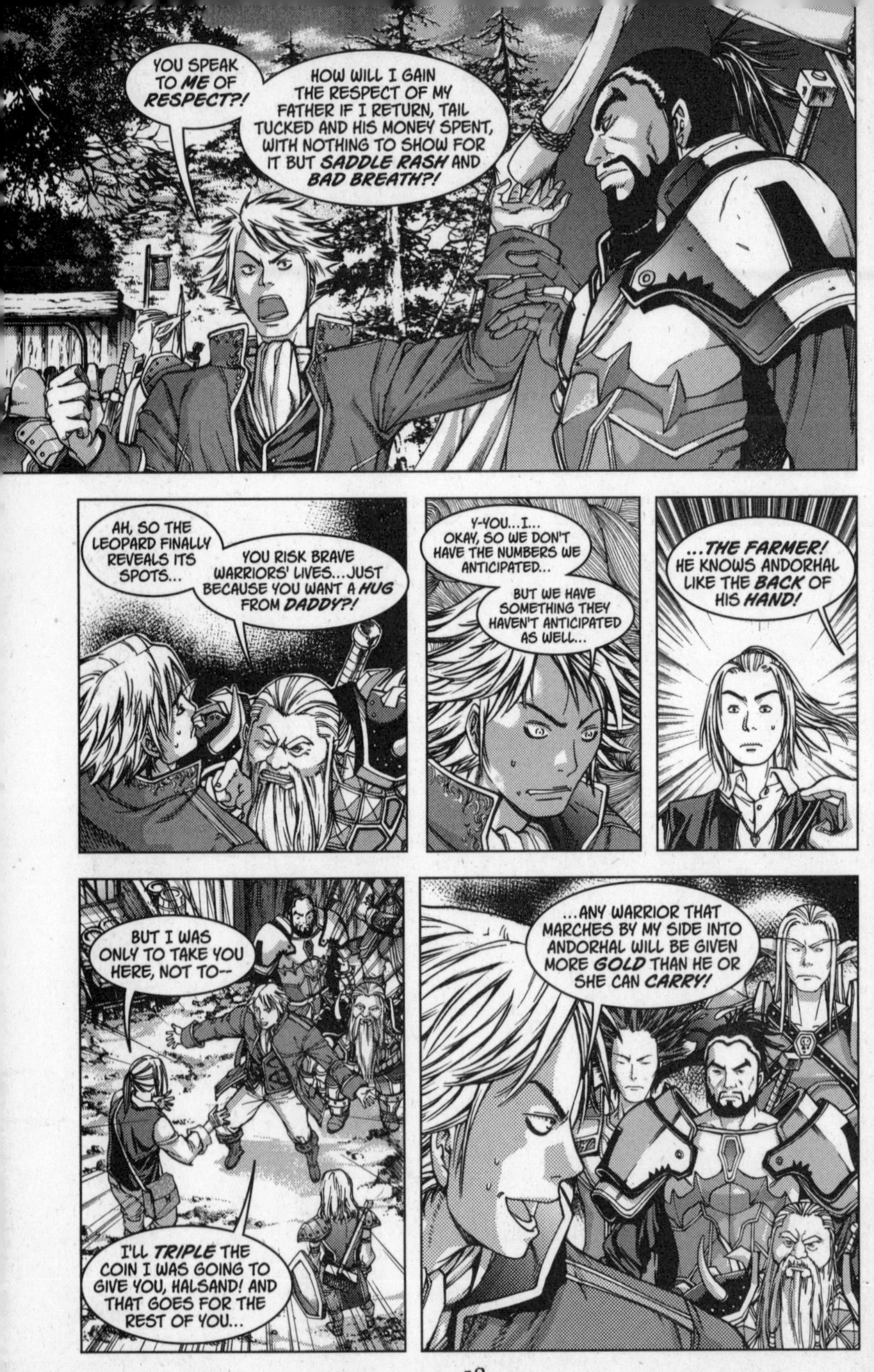
YOU SPEAK TO ME OF RESPECT?!
HOW WILL I GAIN THE RESPECT OF MY FATHER IF I RETURN, TAIL TUCKED AND HIS MONEY SPENT, WITH NOTHING TO SHOW FOR IT BUT SADDLE RASH AND BAD BREATH?!
AH, SO THE LEOPARD FINALLY REVEALS ITS SPOTS...
YOU RISK BRAVE WARRIORS' LIVES...JUST BECAUSE YOU WANT A HUG FROM DADDY?!
Y-YOU...I... OKAY, SO WE DON'T HAVE THE NUMBERS WE ANTICIPATED...
BUT WE HAVE SOMETHING THEY HAVEN'T ANTICIPATED AS WELL...
...THE FARMER! HE KNOWS ANDORHAL LIKE THE BACK OF HIS HAND!
BUT I WAS ONLY TO TAKE YOU HERE, NOT TO--
I'LL TRIPLE THE COIN I WAS GOING TO GIVE YOU, HALSAND! AND THAT GOES FOR THE REST OF YOU...
...ANY WARRIOR THAT MARCHES BY MY SIDE INTO ANDORHAL WILL BE GIVEN MORE GOLD THAN HE OR SHE CAN CARRY!

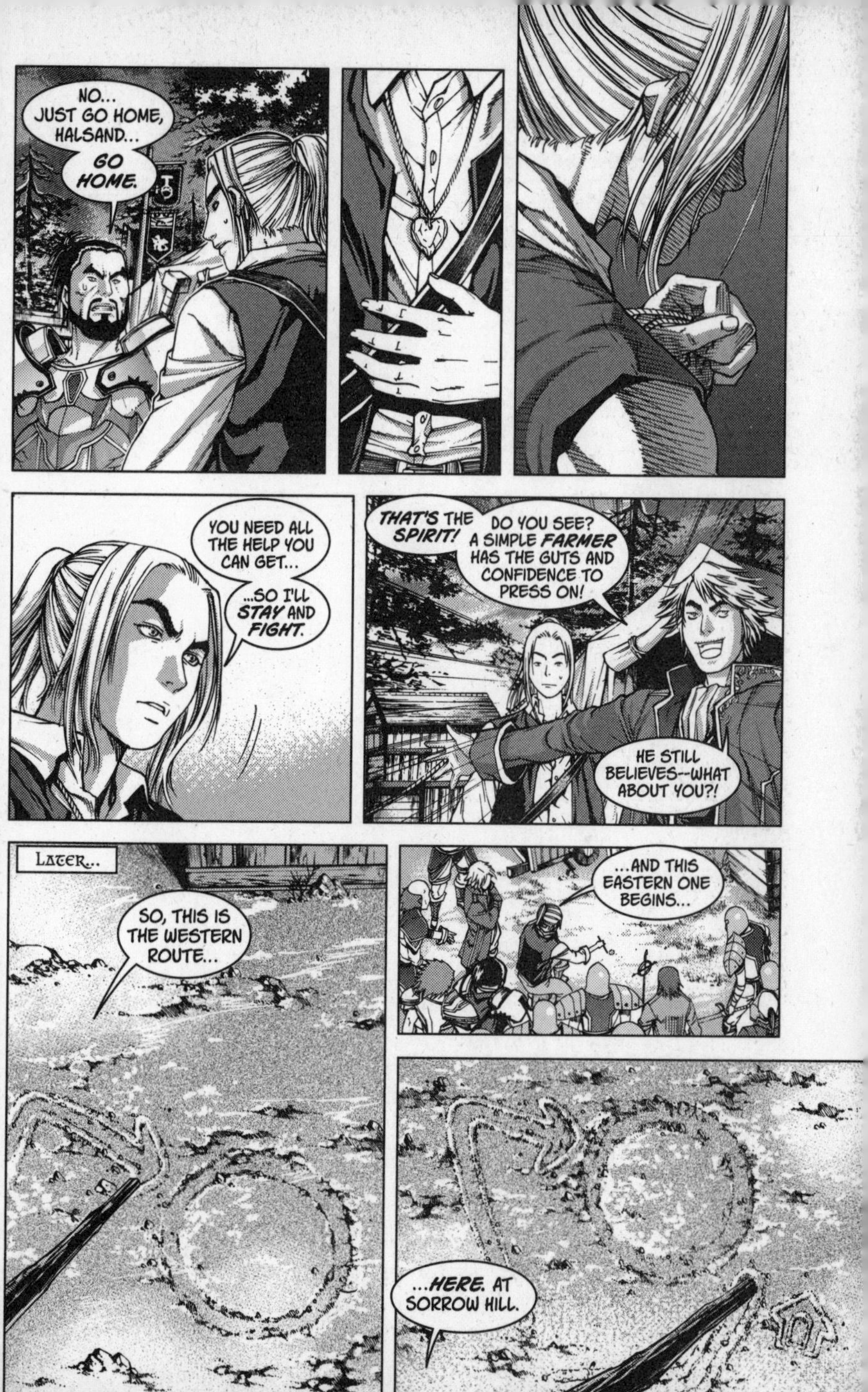
NO... JUST GO HOME, HALSAND...
GO HOME.
YOU NEED ALL THE HELP YOU CAN GET...
...SO I'LL STAY AND FIGHT.
THAT'S THE SPIRIT!
DO YOU SEE? A SIMPLE FARMER HAS THE GUTS AND CONFIDENCE TO PRESS ON!
HE STILL BELIEVES--WHAT ABOUT YOU?!
LATER...
SO, THIS IS THE WESTERN ROUTE...
...AND THIS EASTERN ONE BEGINS...
...HERE. AT SORROW HILL.

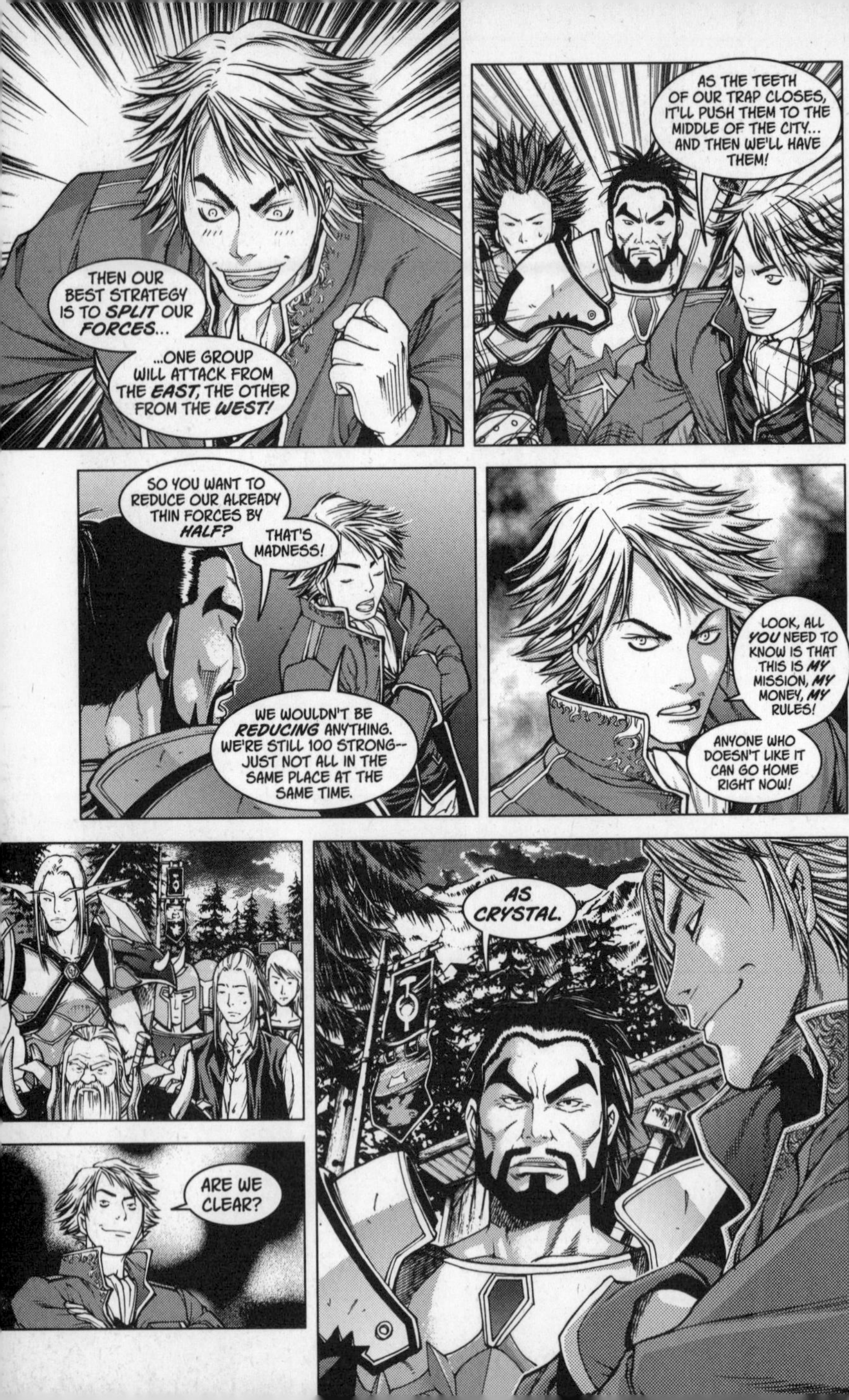
THEN OUR BEST STRATEGY IS TO *SPLIT* OUR *FORCES*...
...ONE GROUP WILL ATTACK FROM THE *EAST*, THE OTHER FROM THE *WEST!*
AS THE TEETH OF OUR TRAP CLOSES, IT'LL PUSH THEM TO THE MIDDLE OF THE CITY... AND THEN WE'LL HAVE THEM!
SO YOU WANT TO REDUCE OUR ALREADY THIN FORCES BY *HALF?*
THAT'S MADNESS!
WE WOULDN'T BE *REDUCING* ANYTHING. WE'RE STILL 100 STRONG--JUST NOT ALL IN THE SAME PLACE AT THE SAME TIME.
LOOK, ALL *YOU* NEED TO KNOW IS THAT THIS IS *MY* MISSION, *MY* MONEY, *MY* RULES!
ANYONE WHO DOESN'T LIKE IT CAN GO HOME RIGHT NOW!
ARE WE CLEAR?
AS CRYSTAL.

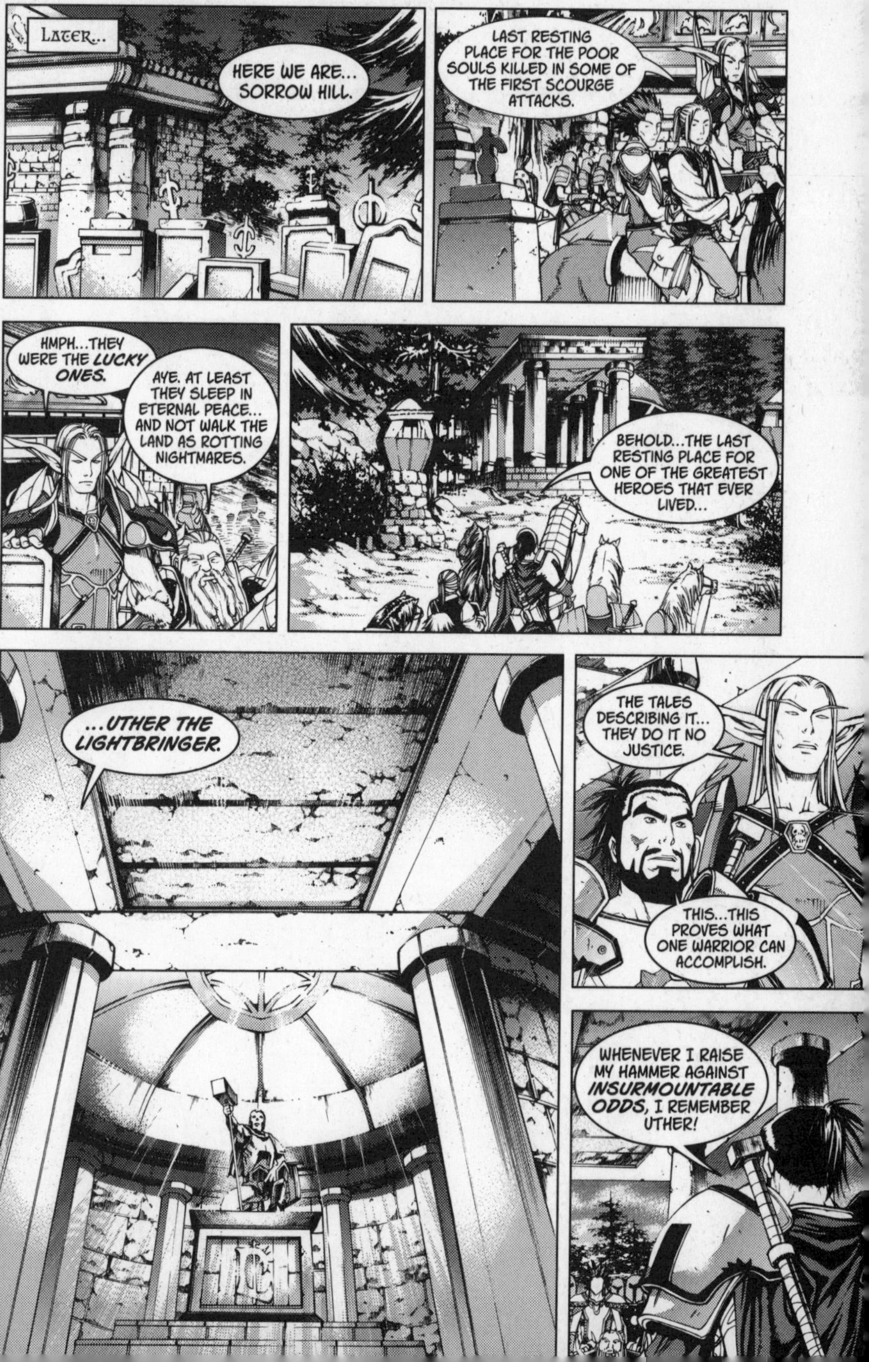
LATER...
HERE WE ARE... SORROW HILL.
LAST RESTING PLACE FOR THE POOR SOULS KILLED IN SOME OF THE FIRST SCOURGE ATTACKS.
HMPH...THEY WERE THE LUCKY ONES.
AYE. AT LEAST THEY SLEEP IN ETERNAL PEACE... AND NOT WALK THE LAND AS ROTTING NIGHTMARES.
BEHOLD...THE LAST RESTING PLACE FOR ONE OF THE GREATEST HEROES THAT EVER LIVED...
...UTHER THE LIGHTBRINGER.
THE TALES DESCRIBING IT... THEY DO IT NO JUSTICE.
THIS...THIS PROVES WHAT ONE WARRIOR CAN ACCOMPLISH.
WHENEVER I RAISE MY HAMMER AGAINST INSURMOUNTABLE ODDS, I REMEMBER UTHER!

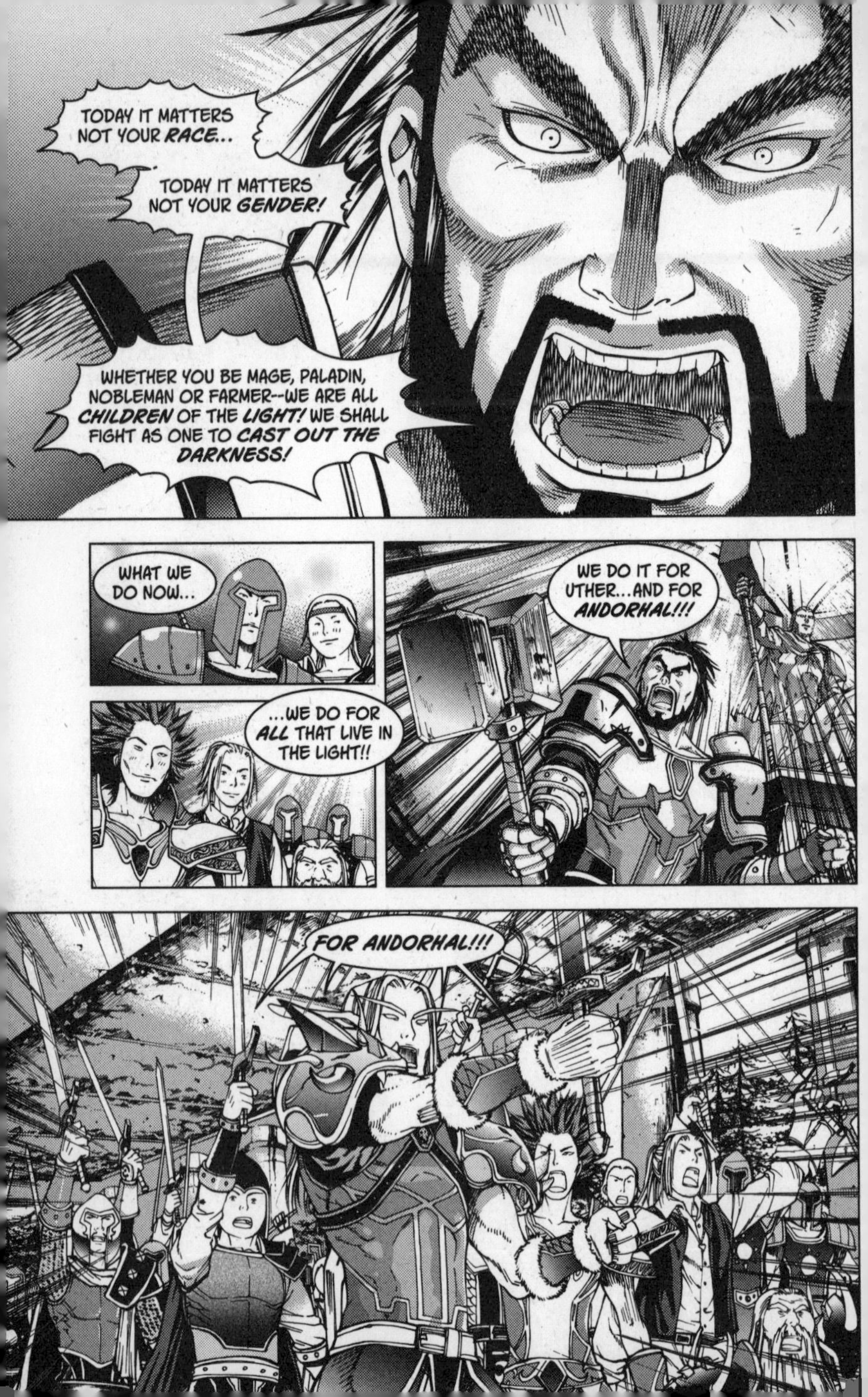
TODAY IT MATTERS NOT YOUR RACE...
TODAY IT MATTERS NOT YOUR GENDER!
WHETHER YOU BE MAGE, PALADIN, NOBLEMAN OR FARMER--WE ARE ALL CHILDREN OF THE LIGHT! WE SHALL FIGHT AS ONE TO CAST OUT THE DARKNESS!
WHAT WE DO NOW...
...WE DO FOR ALL THAT LIVE IN THE LIGHT!!
WE DO IT FOR UTHER...AND FOR ANDORHAL!!!
FOR ANDORHAL!!!

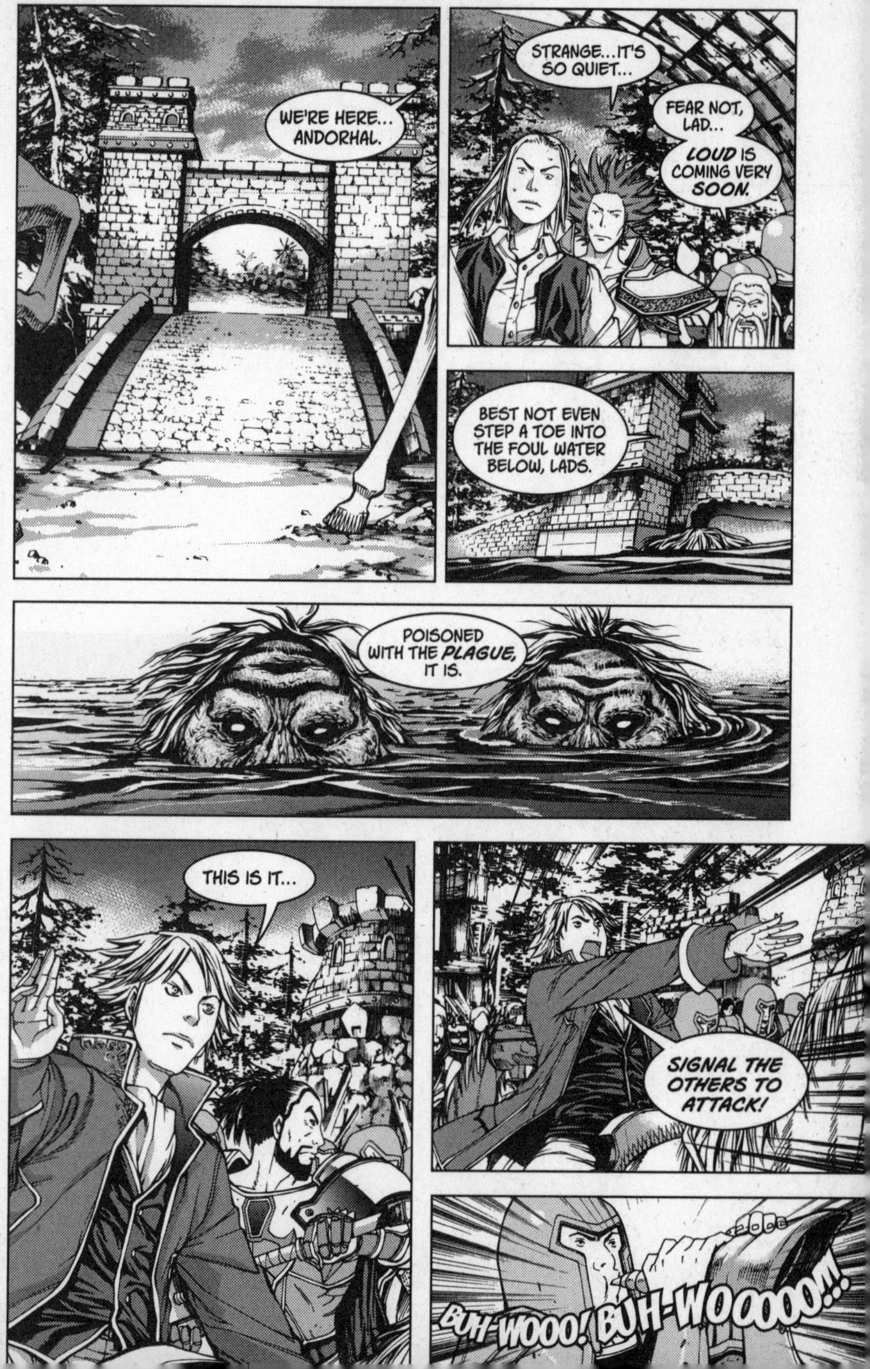
WE'RE HERE... ANDORHAL.
STRANGE...IT'S SO QUIET...
FEAR NOT, LAD... LOUD IS COMING VERY SOON.
BEST NOT EVEN STEP A TOE INTO THE FOUL WATER BELOW, LADS.
POISONED WITH THE PLAGUE, IT IS.
THIS IS IT...
SIGNAL THE OTHERS TO ATTACK!
BUH-WOOO! BUH-WOOOOO!!

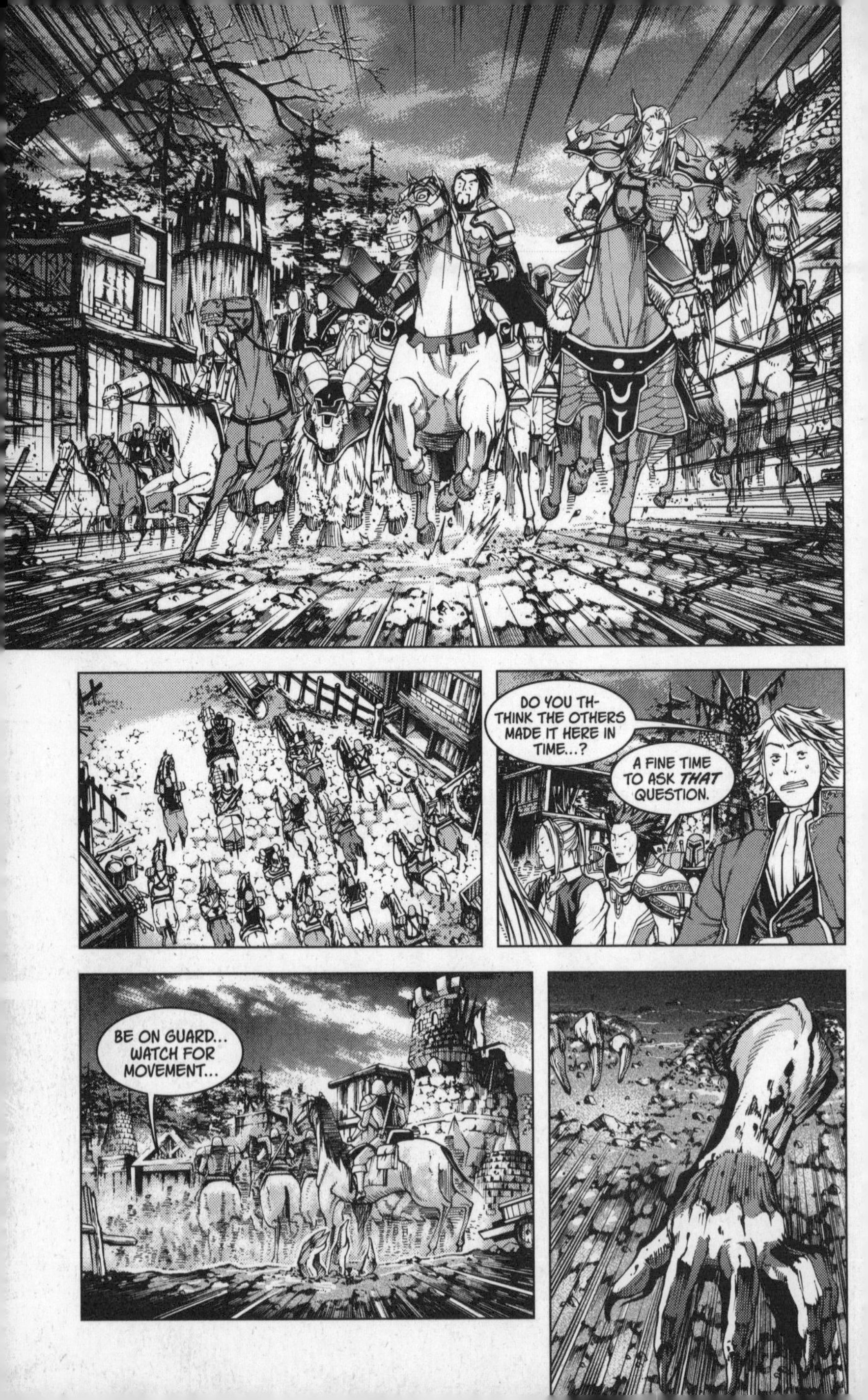
DO YOU TH-THINK THE OTHERS MADE IT HERE IN TIME...?
A FINE TIME TO ASK *THAT* QUESTION.
BE ON GUARD... WATCH FOR MOVEMENT...

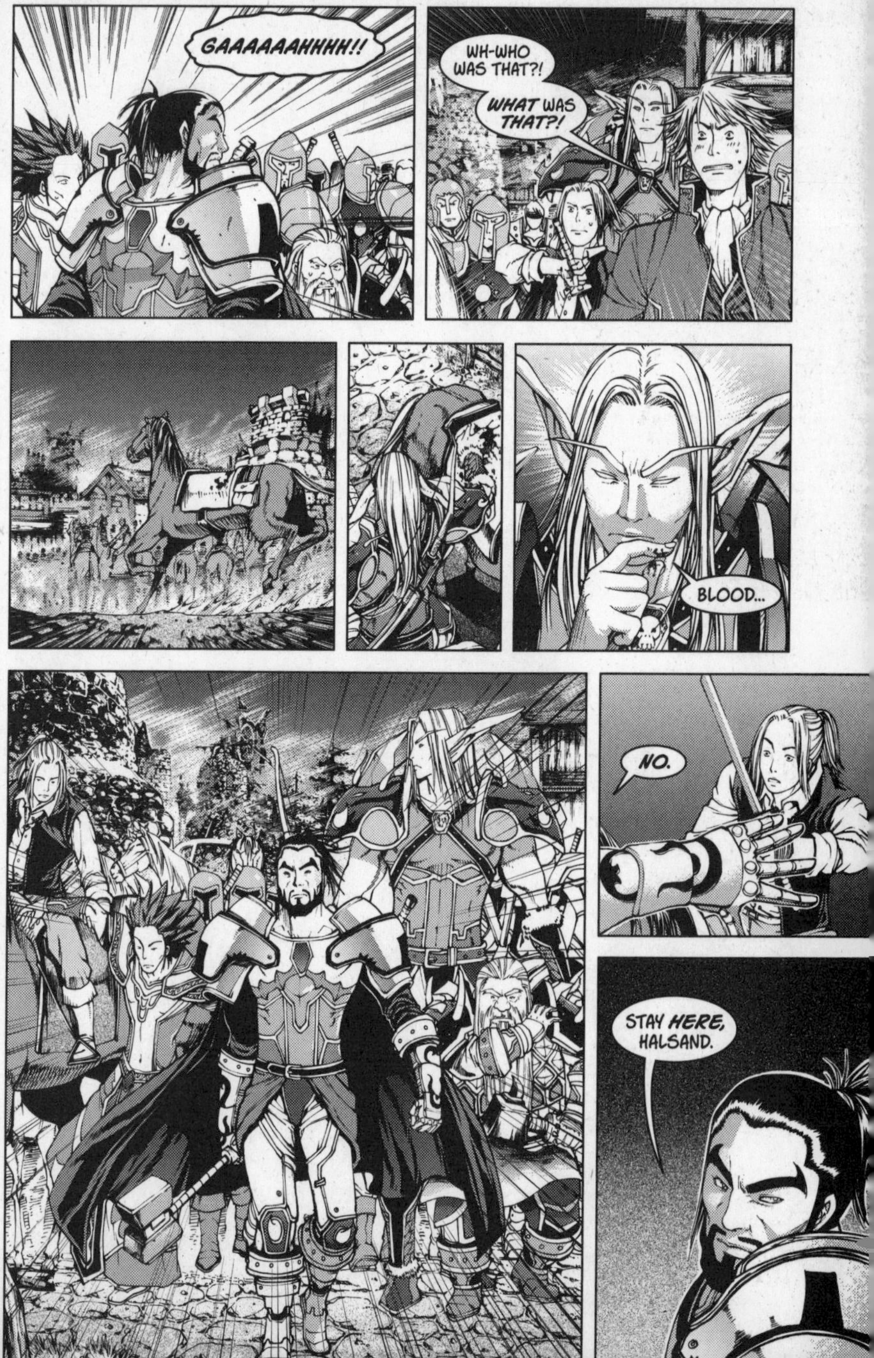
GAAAAAAHHHH!!
WH-WHO WAS THAT?!
WHAT WAS THAT?!
BLOOD...
NO.
STAY HERE, HALSAND.

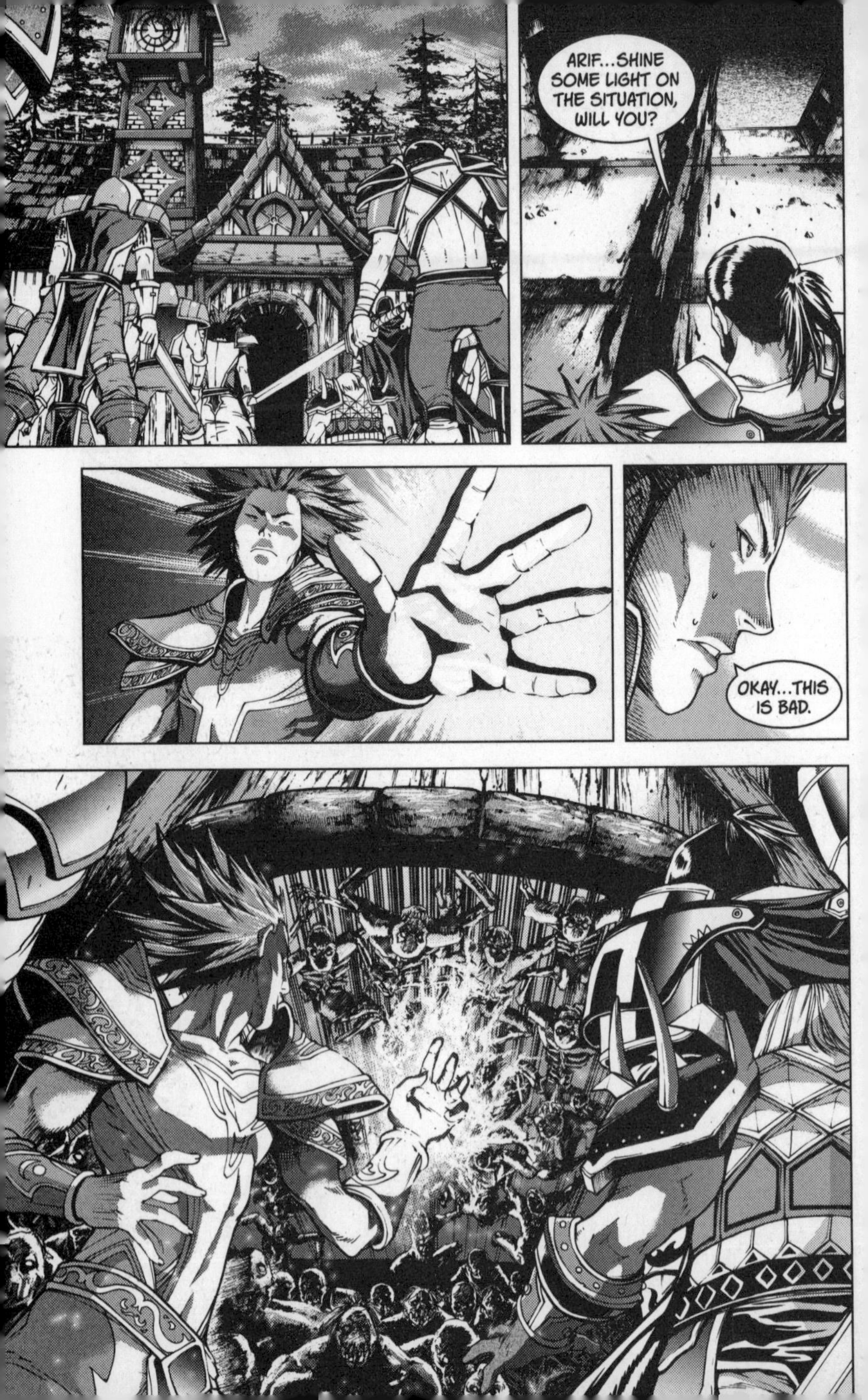
ARIF...SHINE SOME LIGHT ON THE SITUATION, WILL YOU?
OKAY...THIS IS BAD.

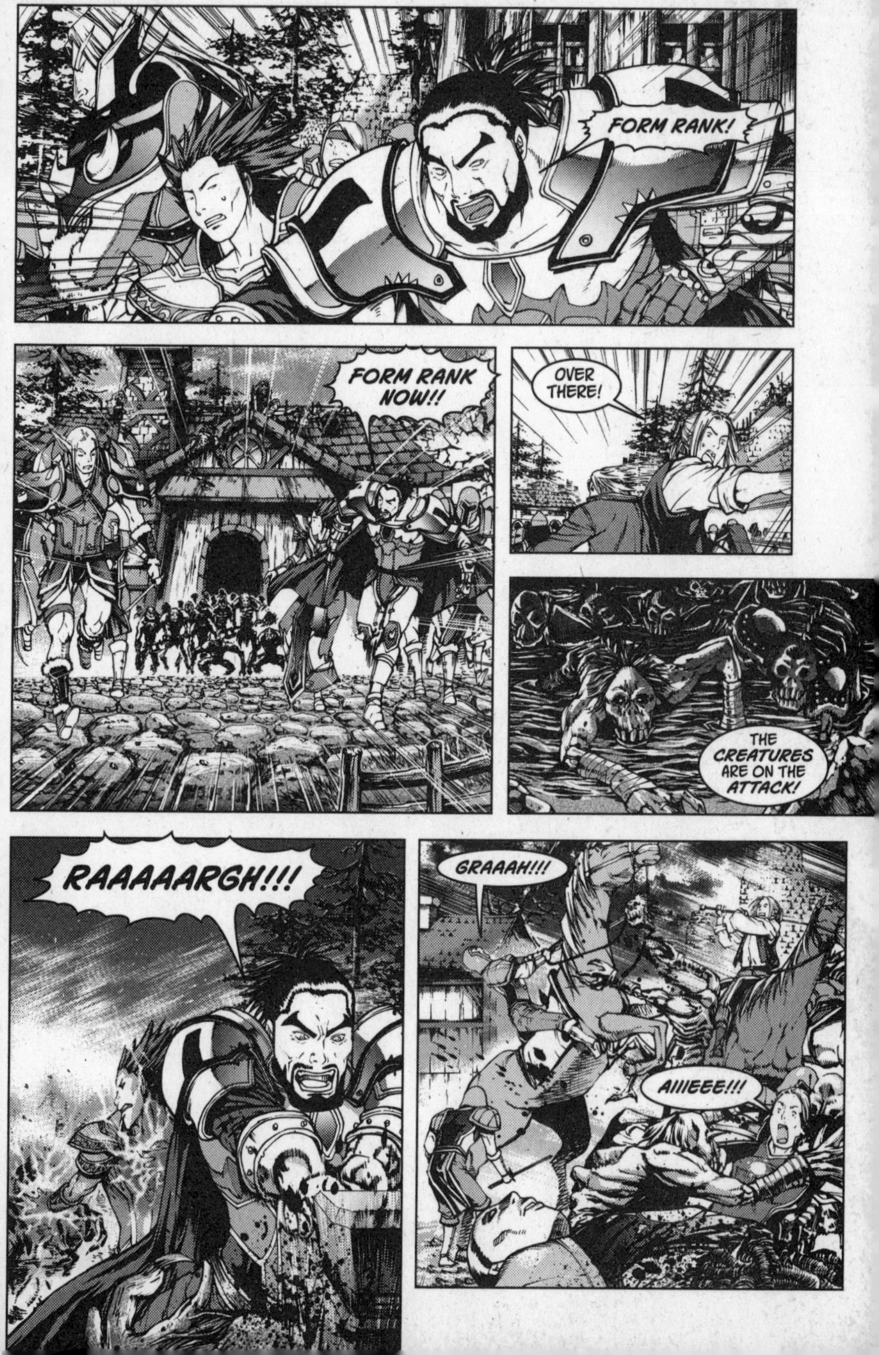
FORM RANK!
FORM RANK NOW!!
OVER THERE!
THE CREATURES ARE ON THE ATTACK!
RAAAAARGH!!!
GRAAAH!!!
AIIIEEE!!!

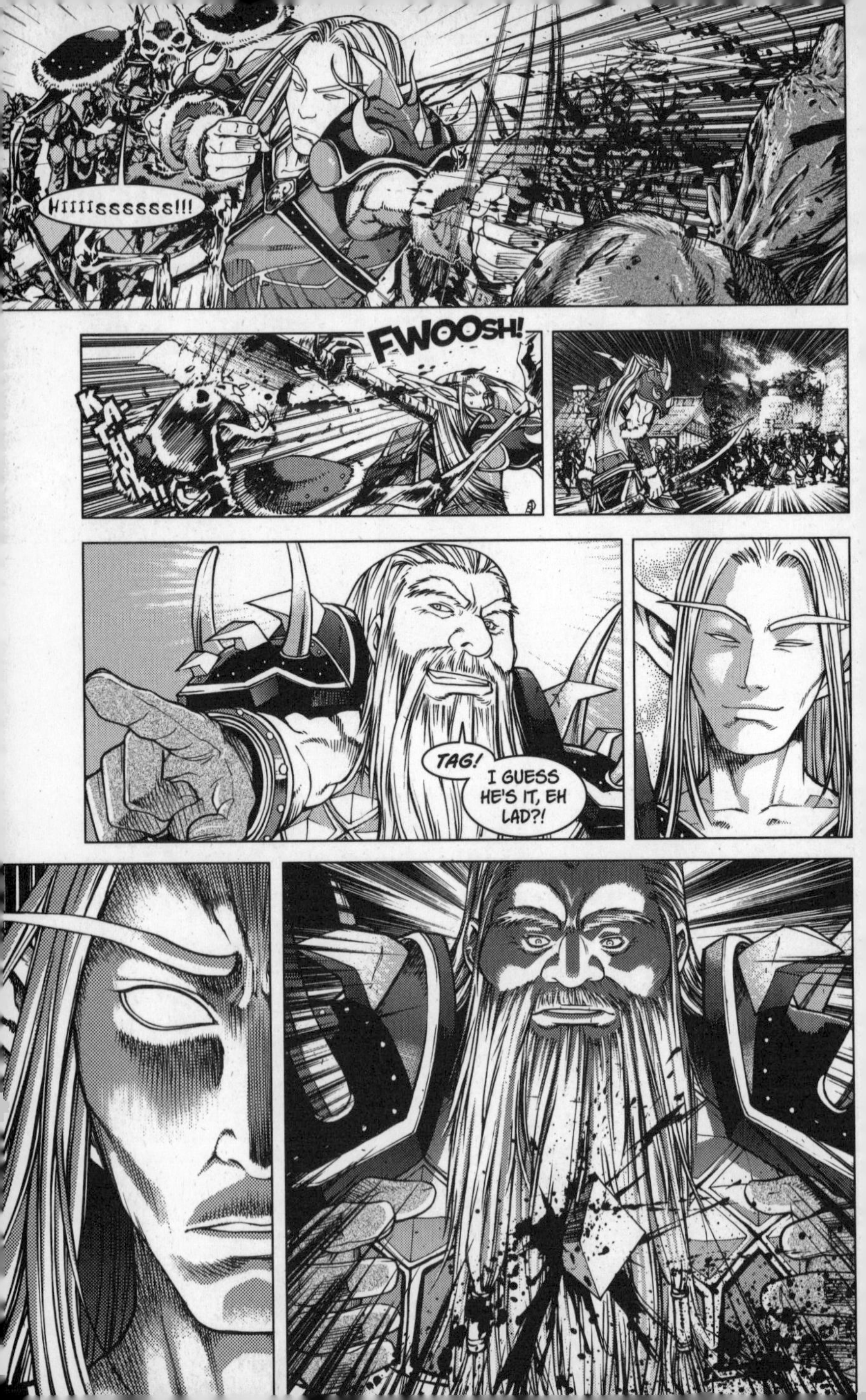
Hiiiissssss!!!
FWOOSH!
KA-THUNK!!
TAG!
I GUESS HE'S IT, EH LAD?!

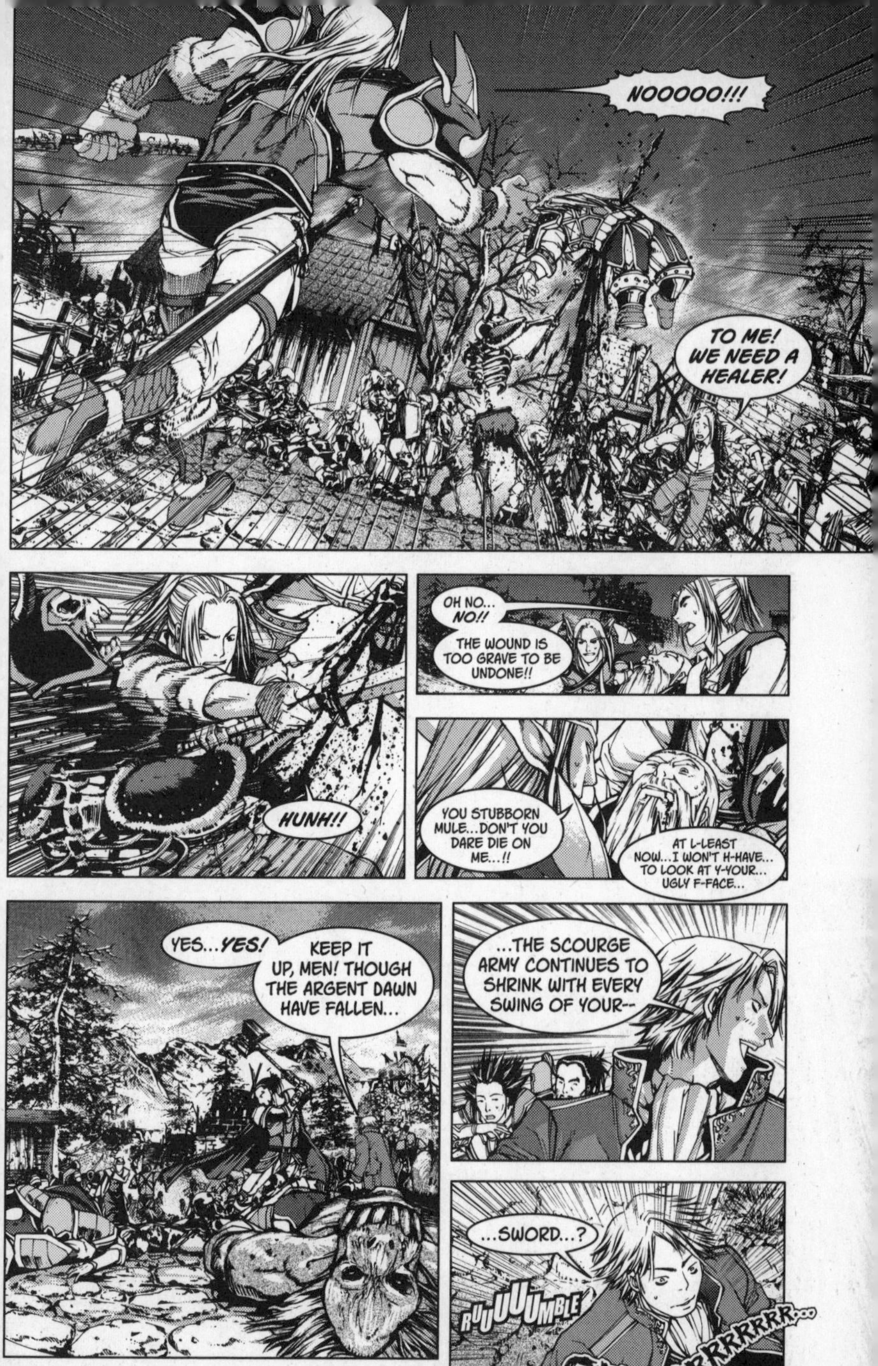
NOOOOO!!!
TO ME! WE NEED A HEALER!
HUNH!!
OH NO... NO!!
THE WOUND IS TOO GRAVE TO BE UNDONE!!
YOU STUBBORN MULE...DON'T YOU DARE DIE ON ME...!!
AT L-LEAST NOW...I WON'T H-HAVE... TO LOOK AT Y-YOUR... UGLY F-FACE...
YES...YES!
KEEP IT UP, MEN! THOUGH THE ARGENT DAWN HAVE FALLEN...
...THE SCOURGE ARMY CONTINUES TO SHRINK WITH EVERY SWING OF YOUR--
...SWORD...?
RUUUUUMBLE
GRRRRRRRRRRRR...

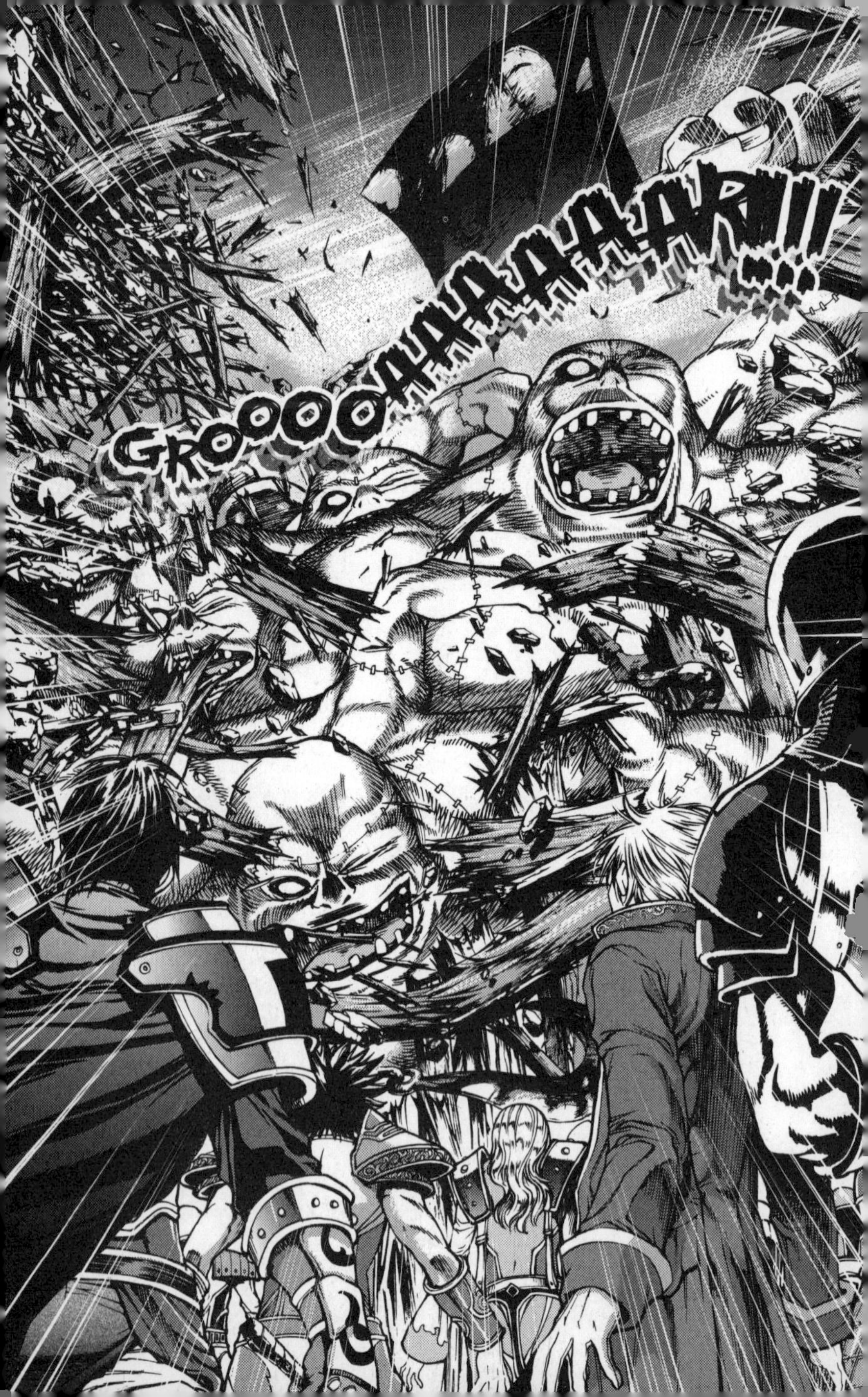
GROOOOOAAAAAAAR!!!

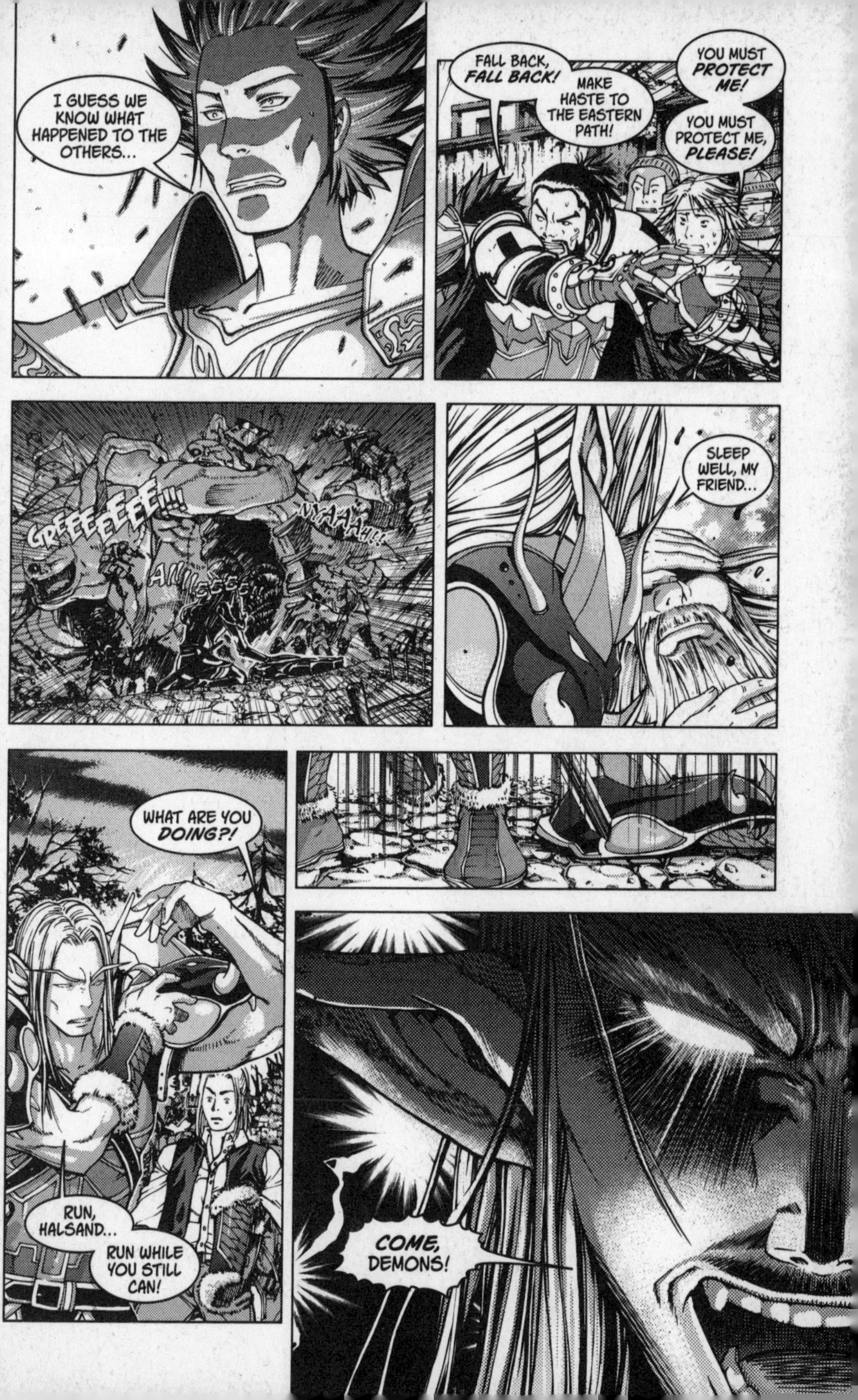
I GUESS WE KNOW WHAT HAPPENED TO THE OTHERS...
FALL BACK, *FALL BACK!*
MAKE HASTE TO THE EASTERN PATH!
YOU MUST *PROTECT ME!*
YOU MUST PROTECT ME, *PLEASE!*
GREEEEEEE!!!!
AIIIEEEEE!!
NYAAAAH!!!
SLEEP WELL, MY FRIEND...
WHAT ARE YOU *DOING?!*
RUN, HALSAND...
RUN WHILE YOU STILL CAN!
COME, DEMONS!

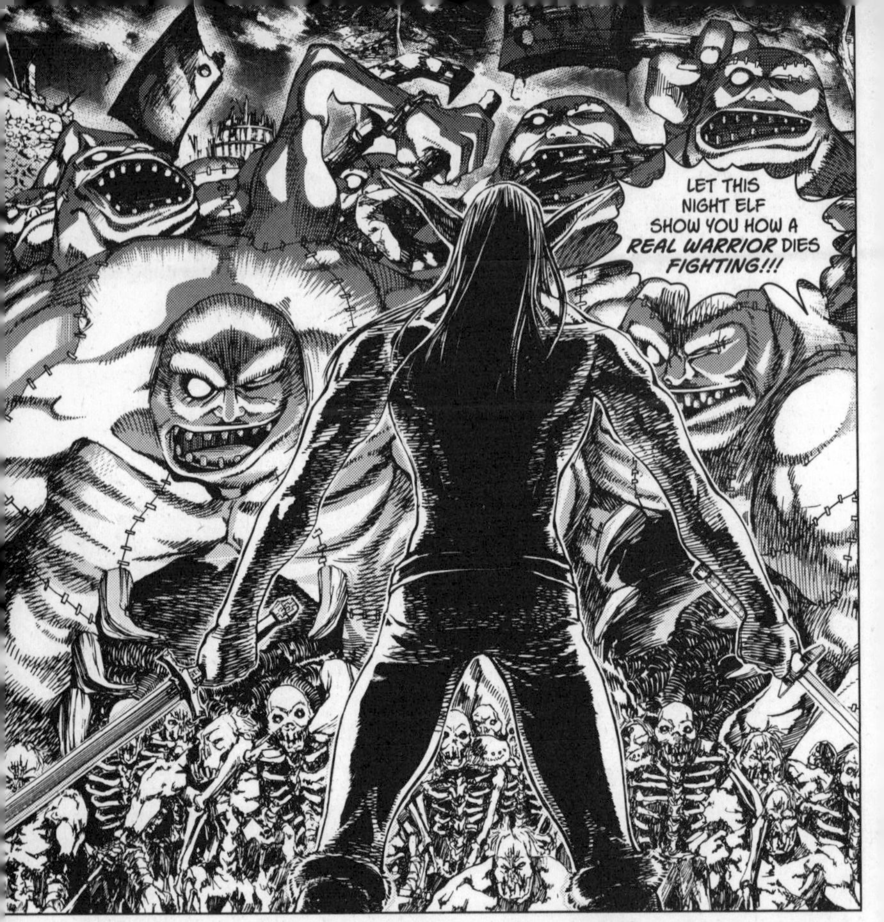
LET THIS NIGHT ELF SHOW YOU HOW A REAL WARRIOR DIES FIGHTING!!!
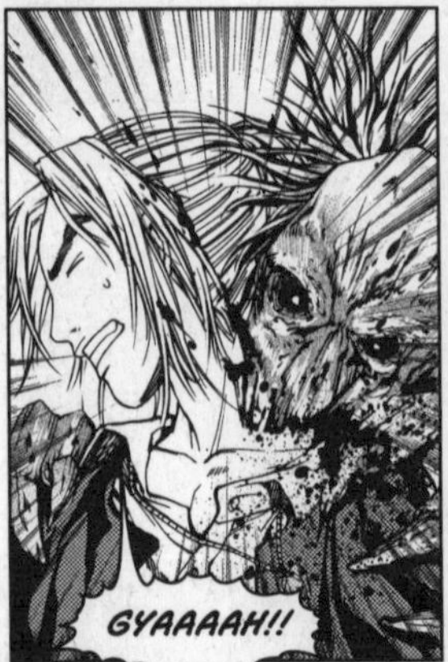
GYAAAAH!!
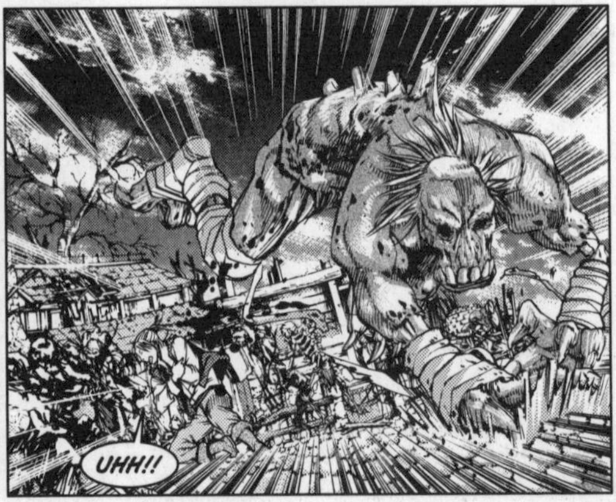
UHH!!

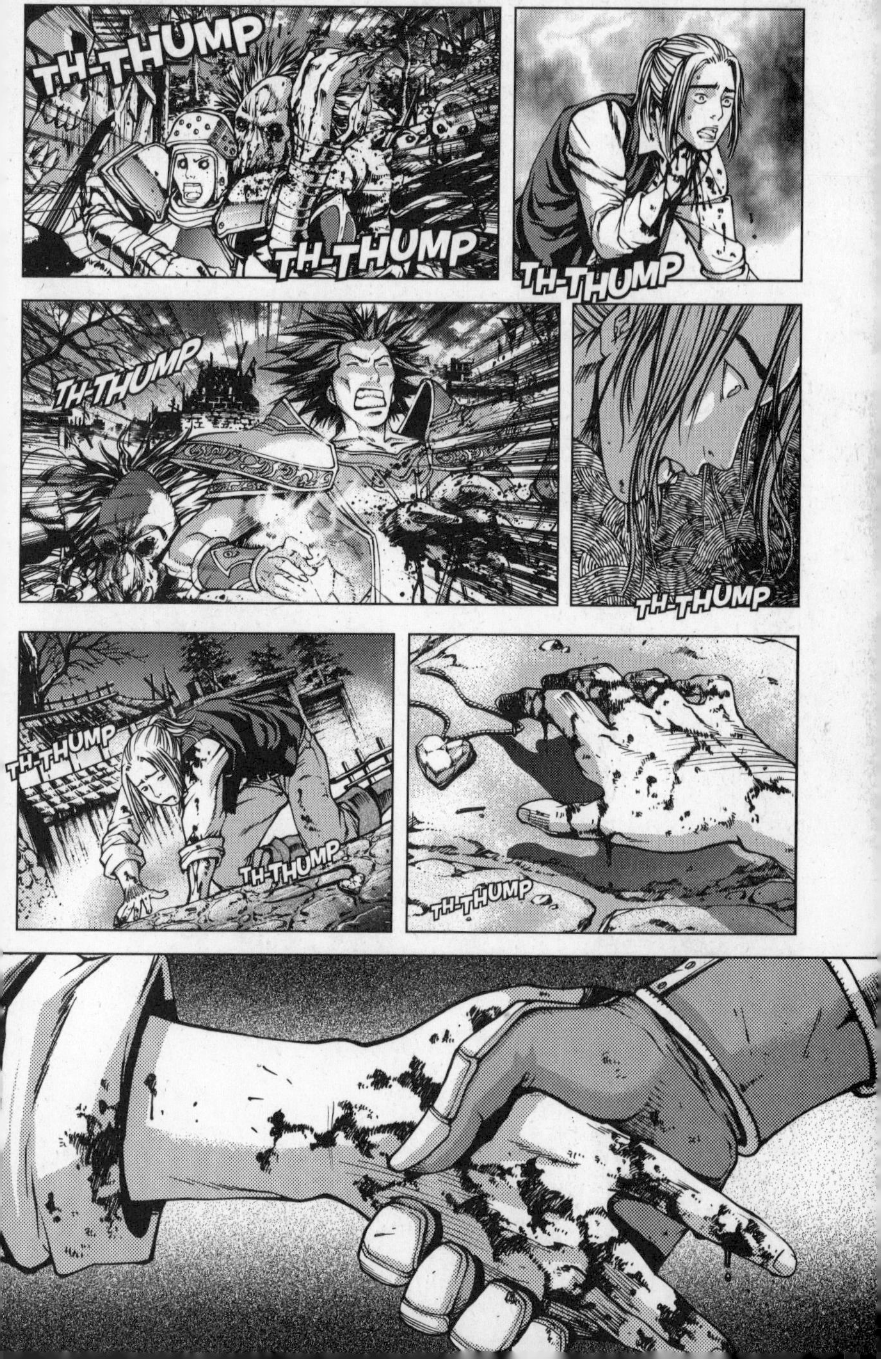
TH-THUMP
TH-THUMP
TH-THUMP
TH-THUMP
TH-THUMP
TH-THUMP
TH-THUMP
TH-THUMP

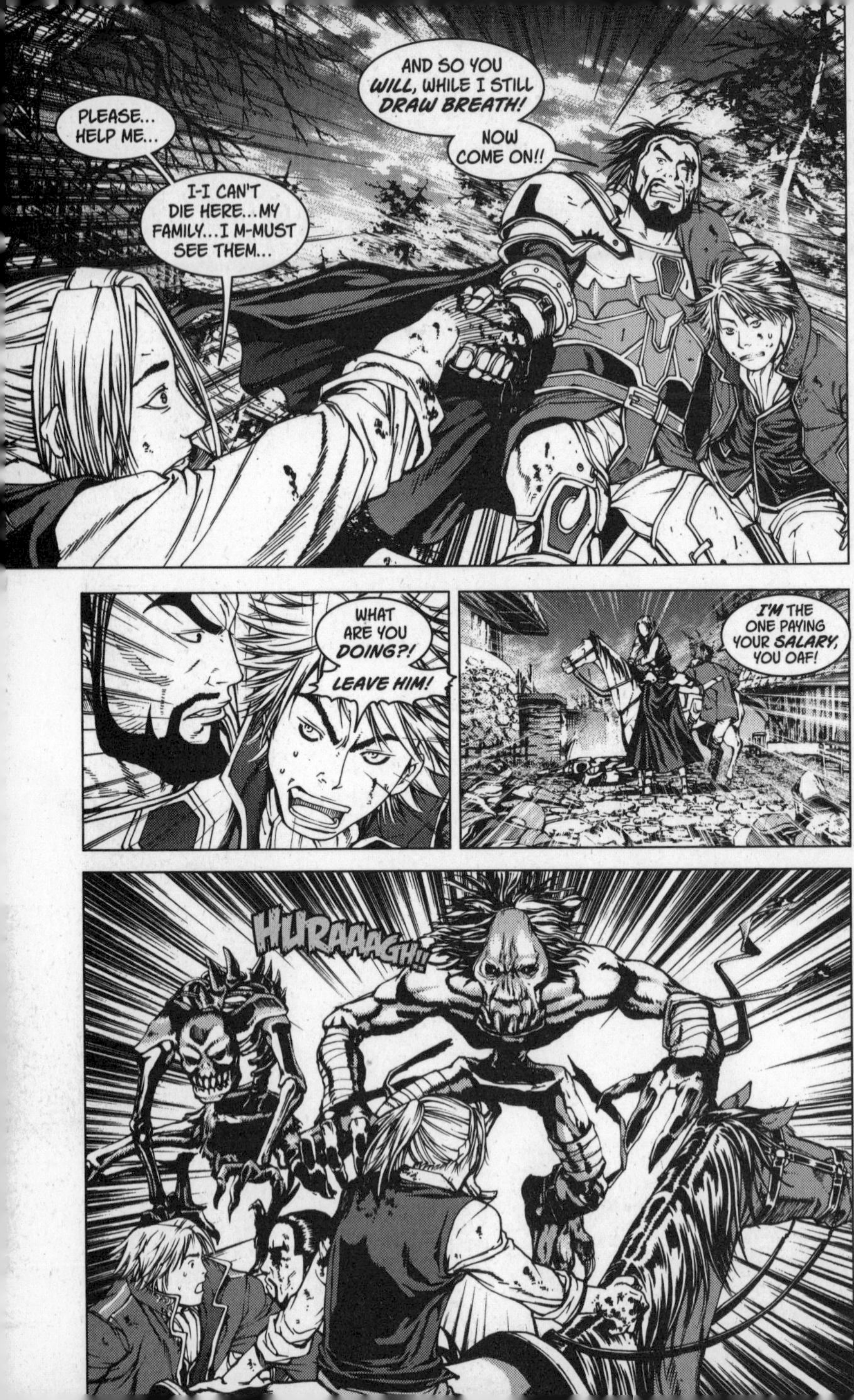
PLEASE... HELP ME...
I-I CAN'T DIE HERE...MY FAMILY...I M-MUST SEE THEM...
AND SO YOU *WILL*, WHILE I STILL *DRAW BREATH!*
NOW COME ON!!
WHAT ARE YOU *DOING?!*
LEAVE HIM!
I'M THE ONE PAYING YOUR *SALARY*, YOU OAF!
HURAAAGH!!

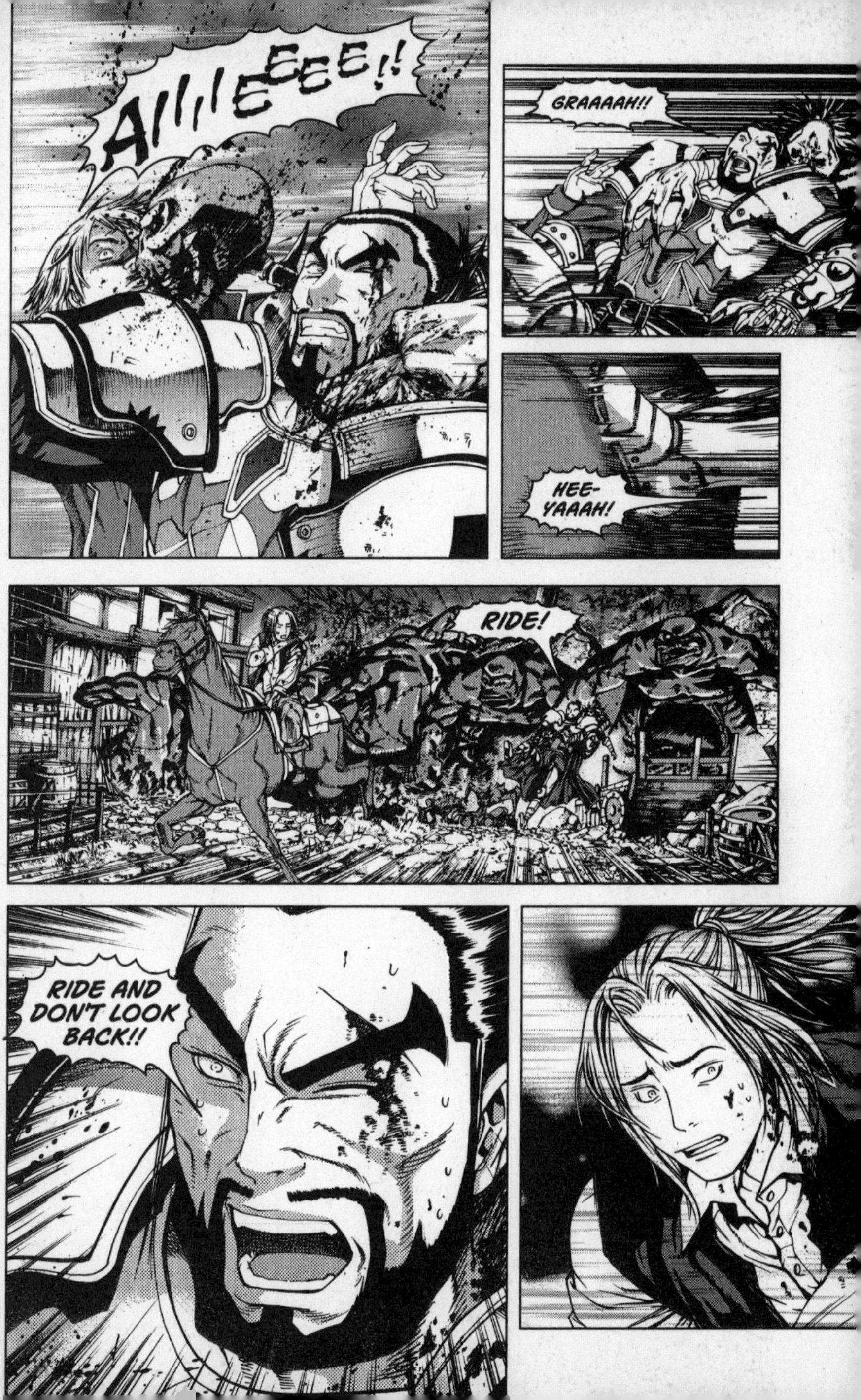
AIIIIEEEEE!!
GRAAAAH!!
HEE-YAAAH!
RIDE!
RIDE AND DON'T LOOK BACK!!

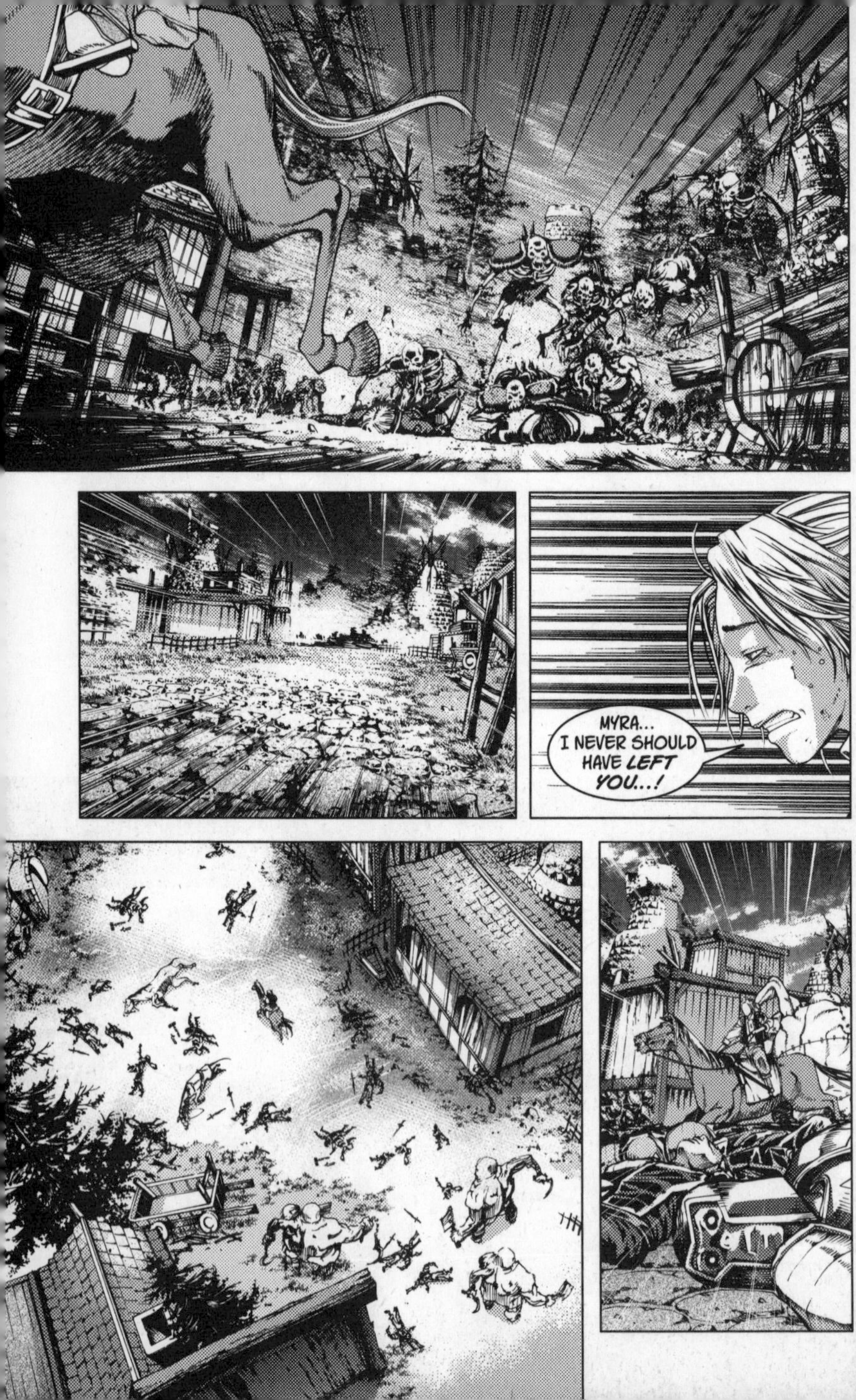
MYRA... I NEVER SHOULD HAVE LEFT YOU...!

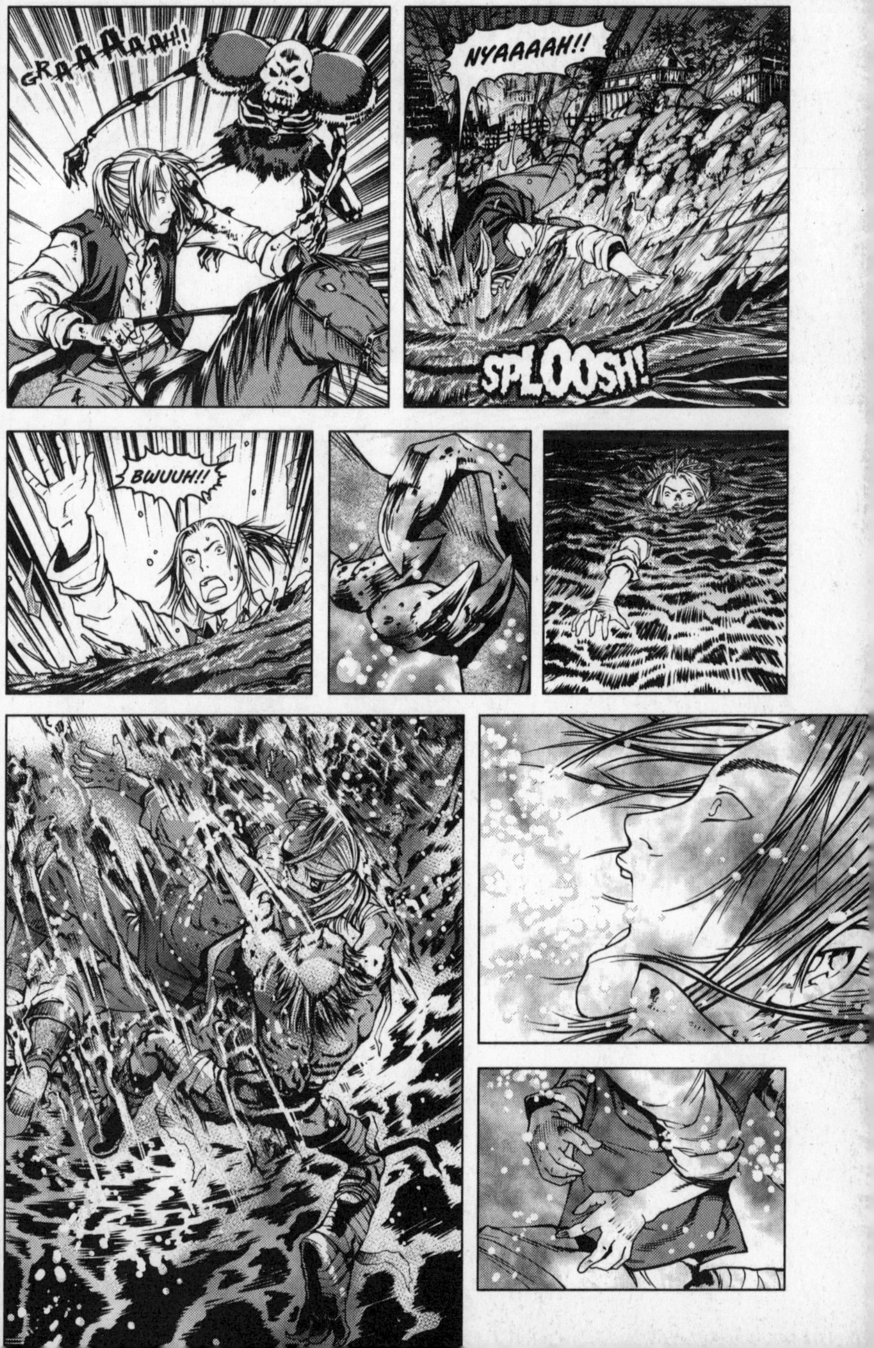
GRAAAAAAH!!
NYAAAAH!!
SPLOOSH!
BWUUH!!

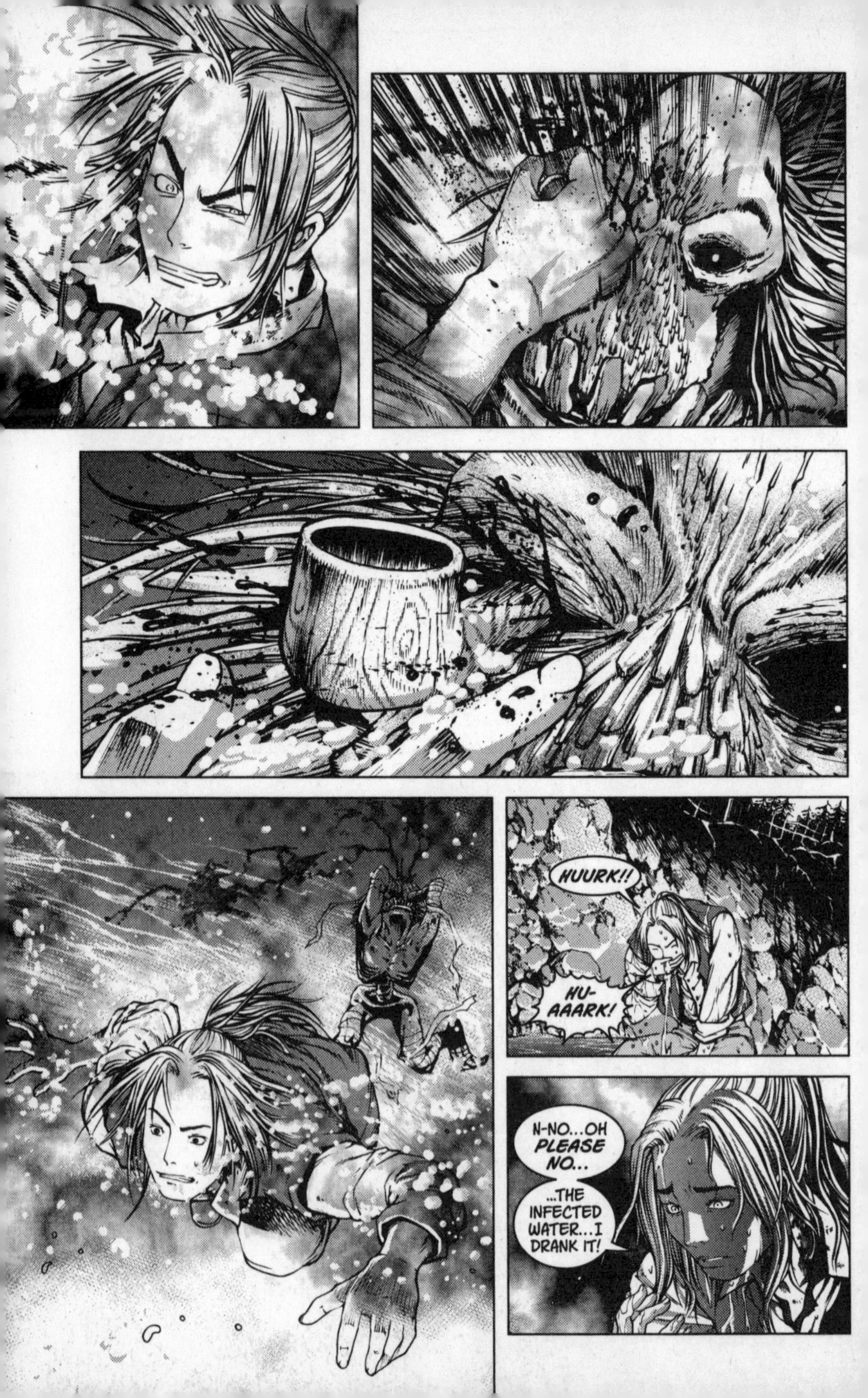
HUURK!!
HU-AAARK!
N-NO...OH PLEASE NO...
...THE INFECTED WATER...I DRANK IT!

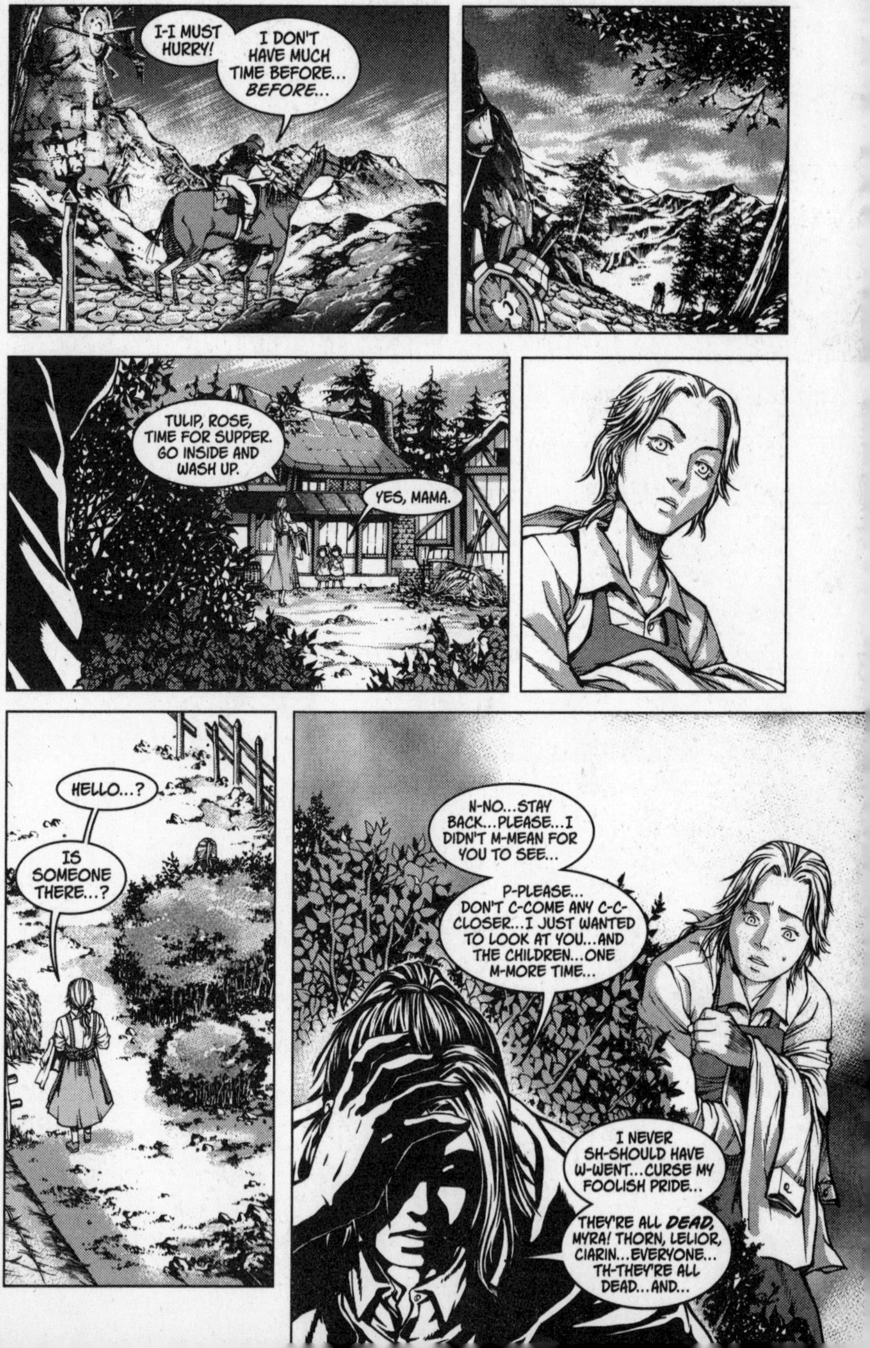
I-I MUST HURRY!
I DON'T HAVE MUCH TIME BEFORE... *BEFORE...*
TULIP, ROSE, TIME FOR SUPPER. GO INSIDE AND WASH UP.
YES, MAMA.
HELLO...?
IS SOMEONE THERE...?
N-NO...STAY BACK...PLEASE...I DIDN'T M-MEAN FOR YOU TO SEE...
P-PLEASE... DON'T C-COME ANY C-C-CLOSER...I JUST WANTED TO LOOK AT YOU...AND THE CHILDREN...ONE M-MORE TIME...
I NEVER SH-SHOULD HAVE W-WENT...CURSE MY FOOLISH PRIDE...
THEY'RE ALL ***DEAD***, MYRA! THORN, LELIOR, CIARIN...EVERYONE... TH-THEY'RE ALL DEAD...AND...

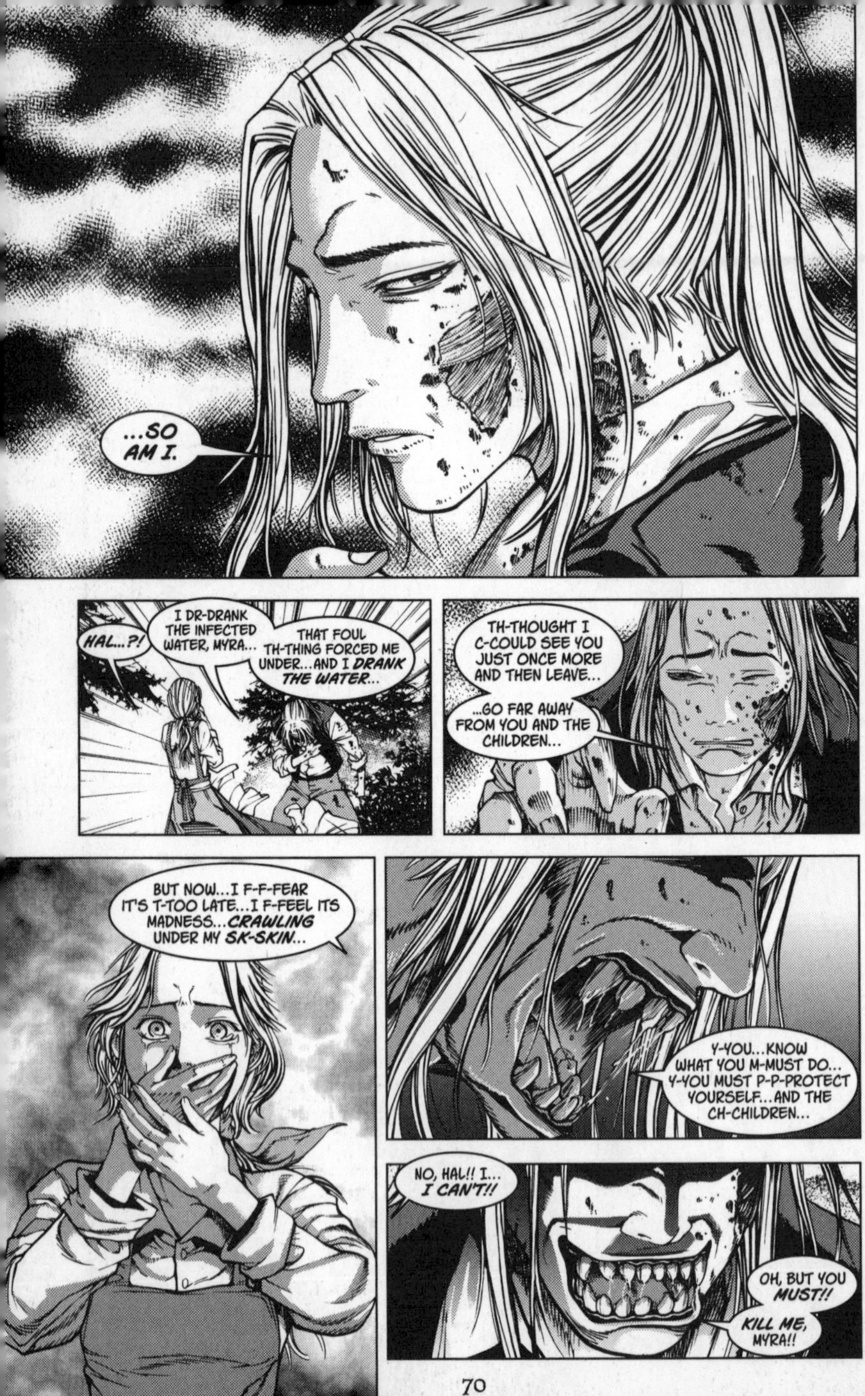
...SO AM I.
HAL...?!
I DR-DRANK THE INFECTED WATER, MYRA...
THAT FOUL TH-THING FORCED ME UNDER...AND I DRANK THE WATER...
TH-THOUGHT I C-COULD SEE YOU JUST ONCE MORE AND THEN LEAVE...
...GO FAR AWAY FROM YOU AND THE CHILDREN...
BUT NOW...I F-F-FEAR IT'S T-TOO LATE...I F-FEEL ITS MADNESS...CRAWLING UNDER MY SK-SKIN...
Y-YOU...KNOW WHAT YOU M-MUST DO... Y-YOU MUST P-P-PROTECT YOURSELF...AND THE CH-CHILDREN...
NO, HAL!! I... I CAN'T!!
OH, BUT YOU MUST!!
KILL ME, MYRA!!

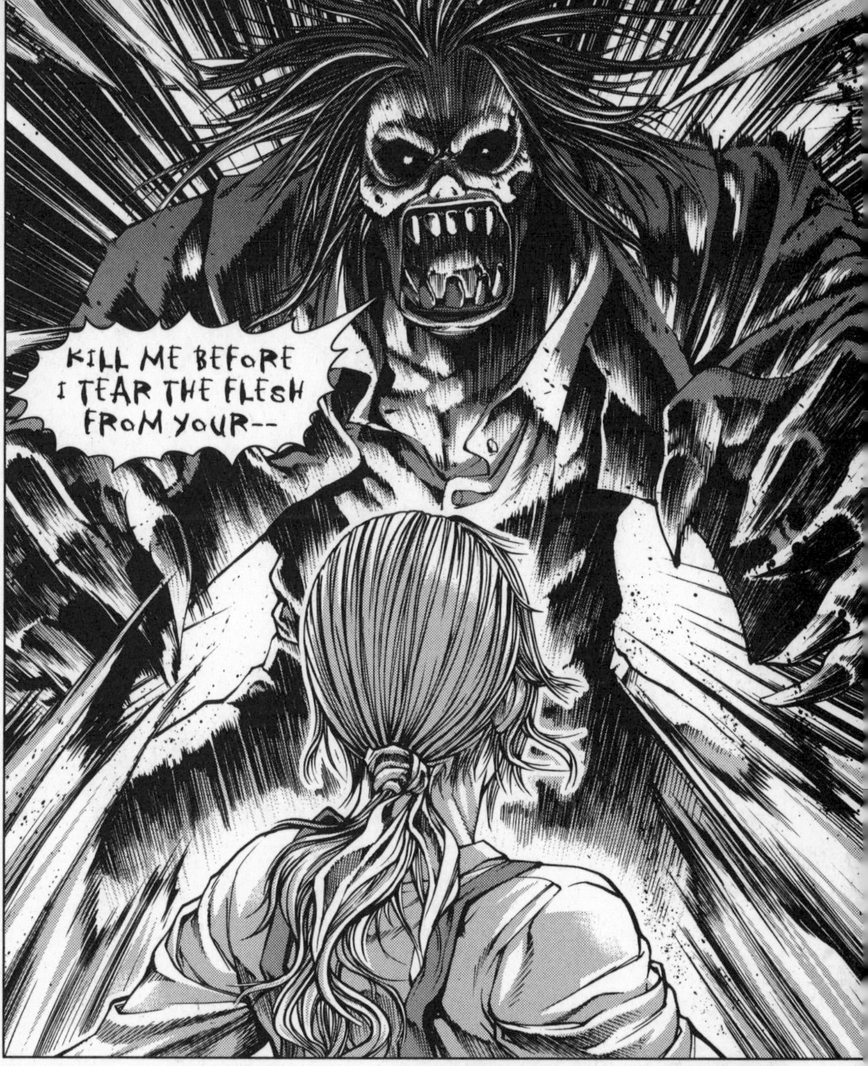
KILL ME BEFORE I TEAR THE FLESH FROM YOUR--
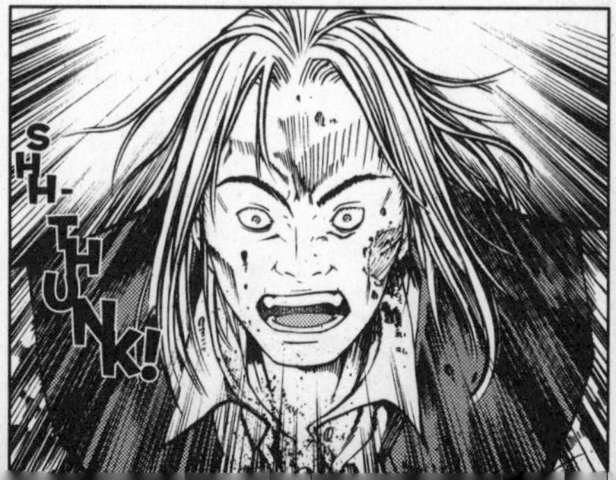
SHH-THUNK!
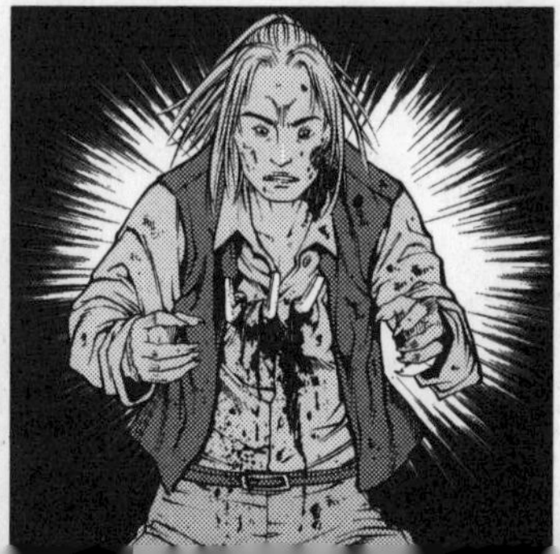

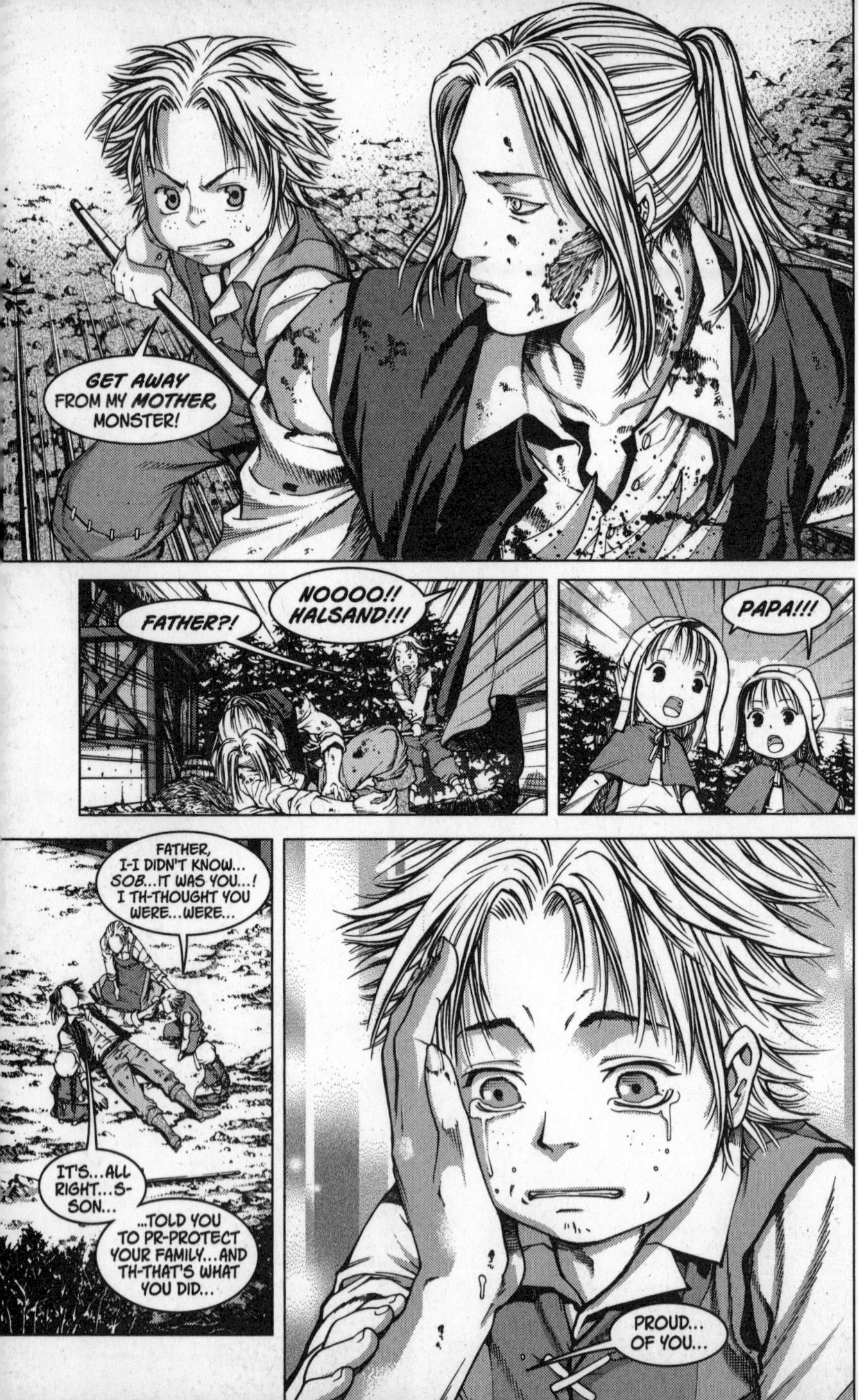
GET AWAY FROM MY MOTHER, MONSTER!
FATHER?!
NOOOO!! HALSAND!!!
PAPA!!!
FATHER, I-I DIDN'T KNOW... SOB...IT WAS YOU...! I TH-THOUGHT YOU WERE...WERE...
IT'S...ALL RIGHT...S-SON...
...TOLD YOU TO PR-PROTECT YOUR FAMILY...AND TH-THAT'S WHAT YOU DID...
PROUD... OF YOU...

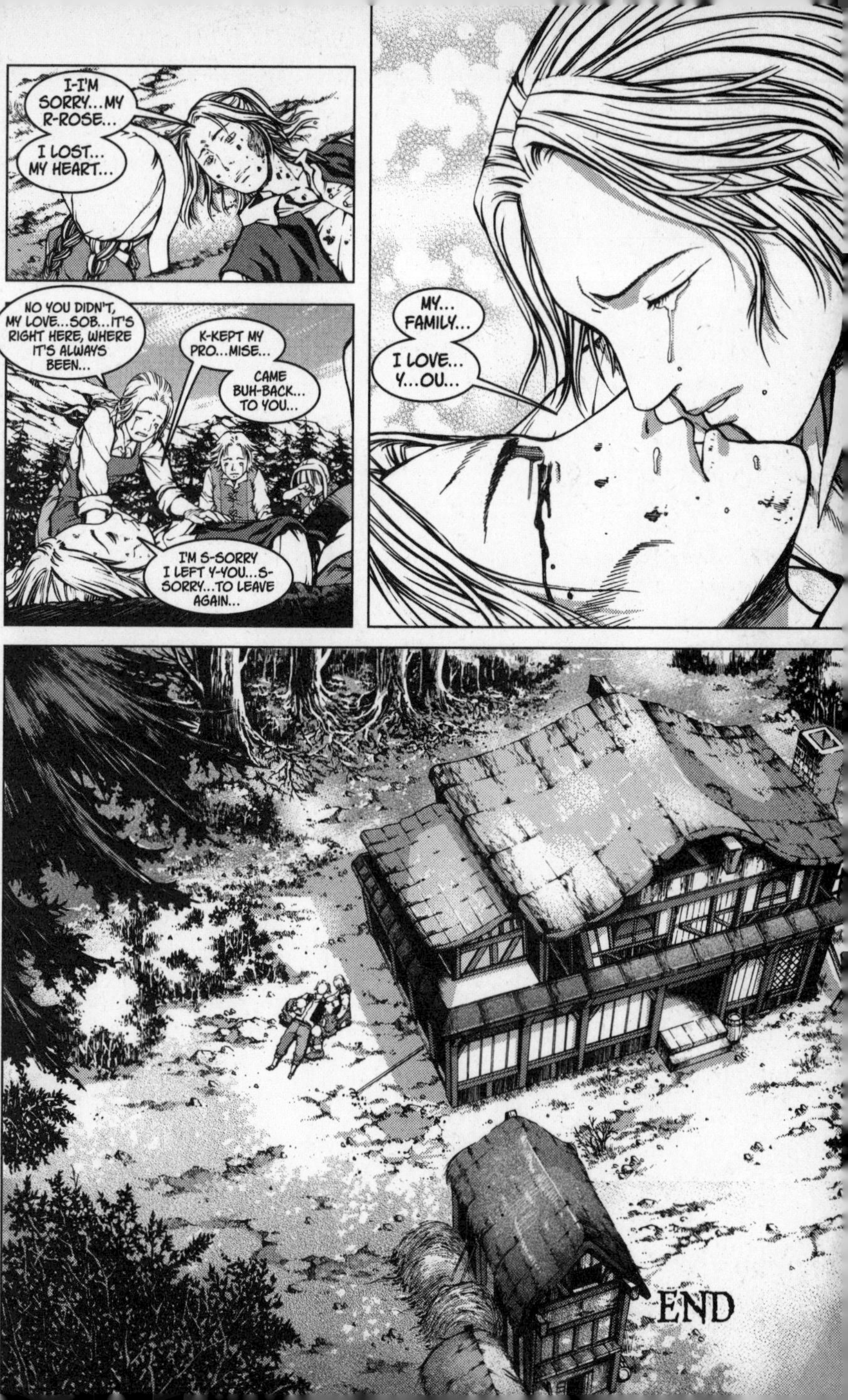
I-I'M SORRY...MY R-ROSE...
I LOST... MY HEART...
NO YOU DIDN'T, MY LOVE...SOB...IT'S RIGHT HERE, WHERE IT'S ALWAYS BEEN...
K-KEPT MY PRO...MISE...
CAME BUH-BACK... TO YOU...
I'M S-SORRY I LEFT Y-YOU...S-SORRY...TO LEAVE AGAIN...
MY... FAMILY...
I LOVE... Y...OU...
END

WarCraft

LEGENDS
VOLUME ONE

HOW TO WIN FRIENDS

WRITTEN BY DAN JOLLEY

PENCILS BY CARLOS OLIVARES
INKS & TONES BY CARLOS OLIVARES, MARC RUEDA
& JANINA GORRISSEIN

EDITOR: TROY LEWTER
ASSOCIATE EDITOR: SHANNON WATTERS
LETTERER: LUCAS RIVERA

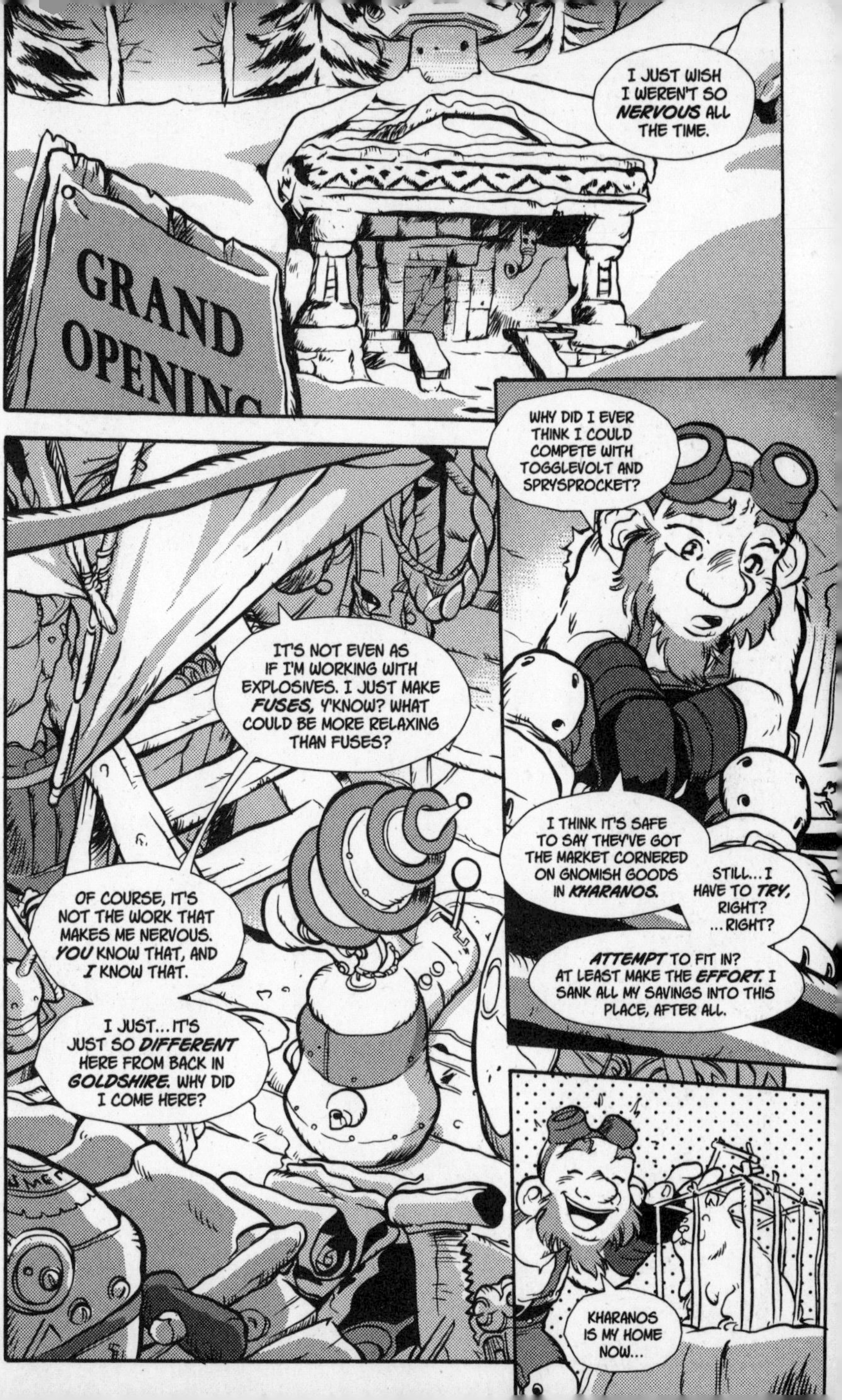
GRAND OPENIN
I JUST WISH I WEREN'T SO *NERVOUS* ALL THE TIME.
IT'S NOT EVEN AS IF I'M WORKING WITH EXPLOSIVES. I JUST MAKE *FUSES,* Y'KNOW? WHAT COULD BE MORE RELAXING THAN FUSES?
OF COURSE, IT'S NOT THE WORK THAT MAKES ME NERVOUS. *YOU* KNOW THAT, AND *I* KNOW THAT.
I JUST... IT'S JUST SO *DIFFERENT* HERE FROM BACK IN *GOLDSHIRE*. WHY DID I COME HERE?
WHY DID I EVER THINK I COULD COMPETE WITH TOGGLEVOLT AND SPRYSPROCKET?
I THINK IT'S SAFE TO SAY THEY'VE GOT THE MARKET CORNERED ON GNOMISH GOODS IN *KHARANOS*.
STILL... I HAVE TO *TRY,* RIGHT? ...RIGHT?
ATTEMPT TO FIT IN? AT LEAST MAKE THE *EFFORT.* I SANK ALL MY SAVINGS INTO THIS PLACE, AFTER ALL.
KHARANOS IS MY HOME NOW...

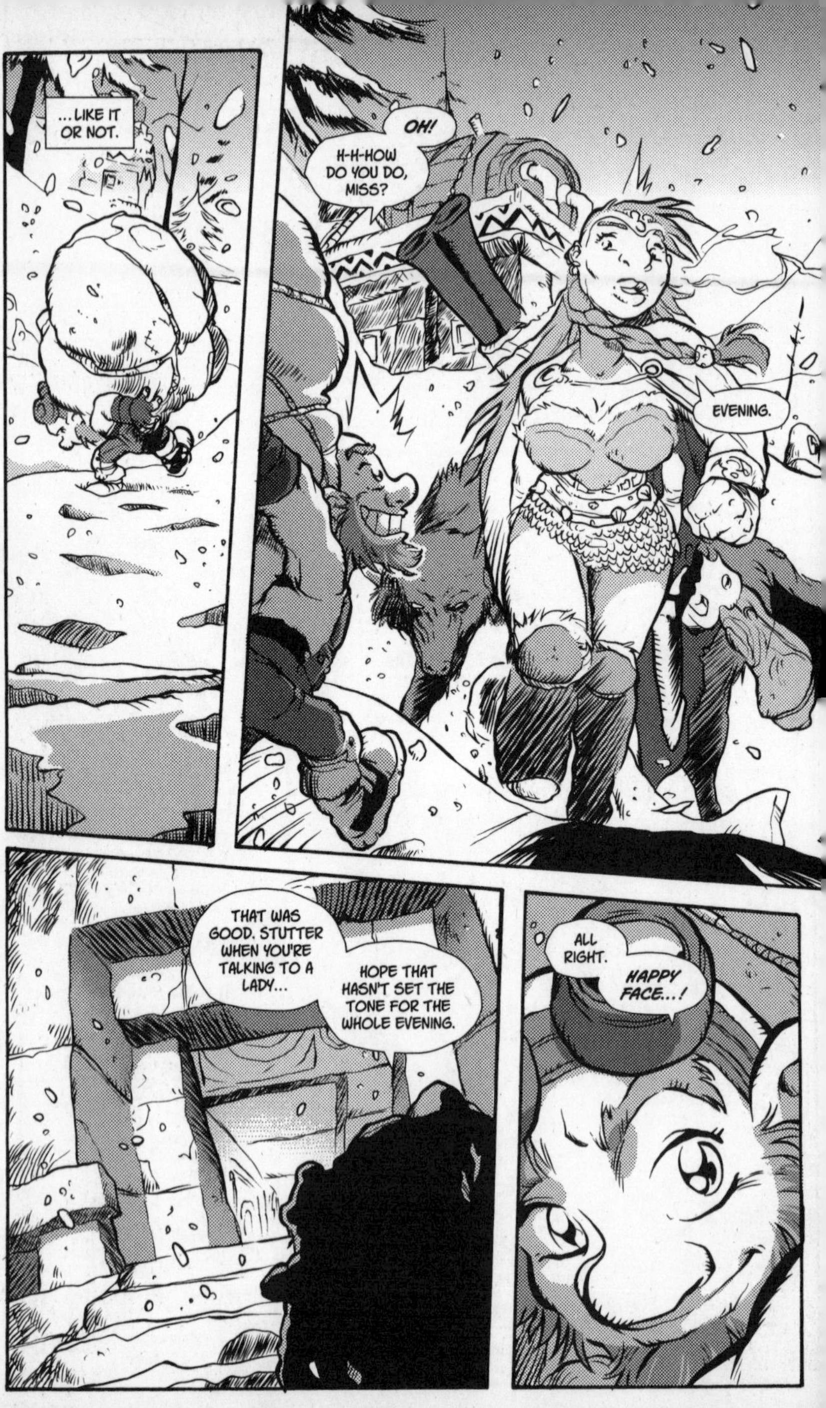
...LIKE IT OR NOT.
OH!
H-H-HOW DO YOU DO, MISS?
EVENING.
THAT WAS GOOD. STUTTER WHEN YOU'RE TALKING TO A LADY...
HOPE THAT HASN'T SET THE TONE FOR THE WHOLE EVENING.
ALL RIGHT.
HAPPY FACE...!

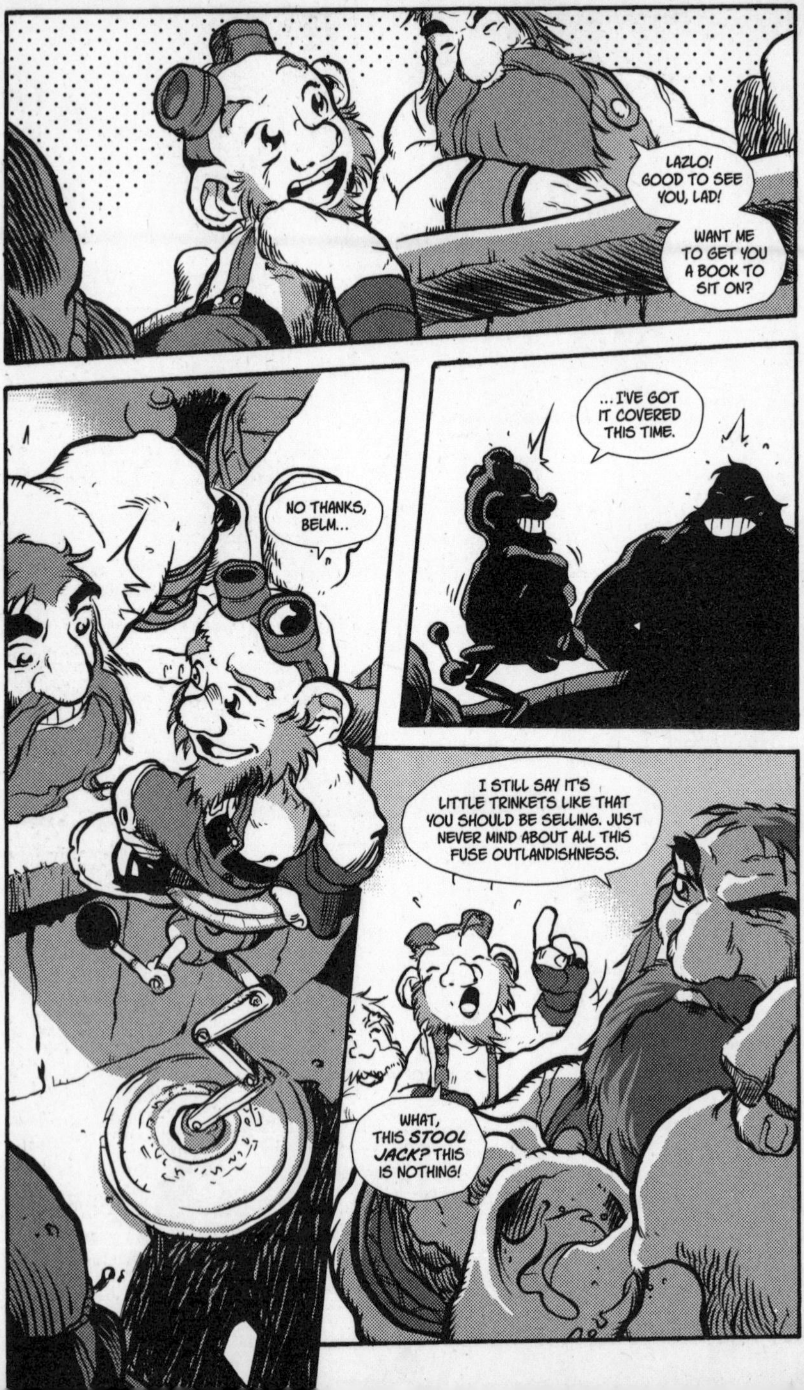
LAZLO! GOOD TO SEE YOU, LAD!
WANT ME TO GET YOU A BOOK TO SIT ON?
NO THANKS, BELM...
...I'VE GOT IT COVERED THIS TIME.
I STILL SAY IT'S LITTLE TRINKETS LIKE THAT YOU SHOULD BE SELLING. JUST NEVER MIND ABOUT ALL THIS FUSE OUTLANDISHNESS.
WHAT, THIS *STOOL JACK?* THIS IS NOTHING!

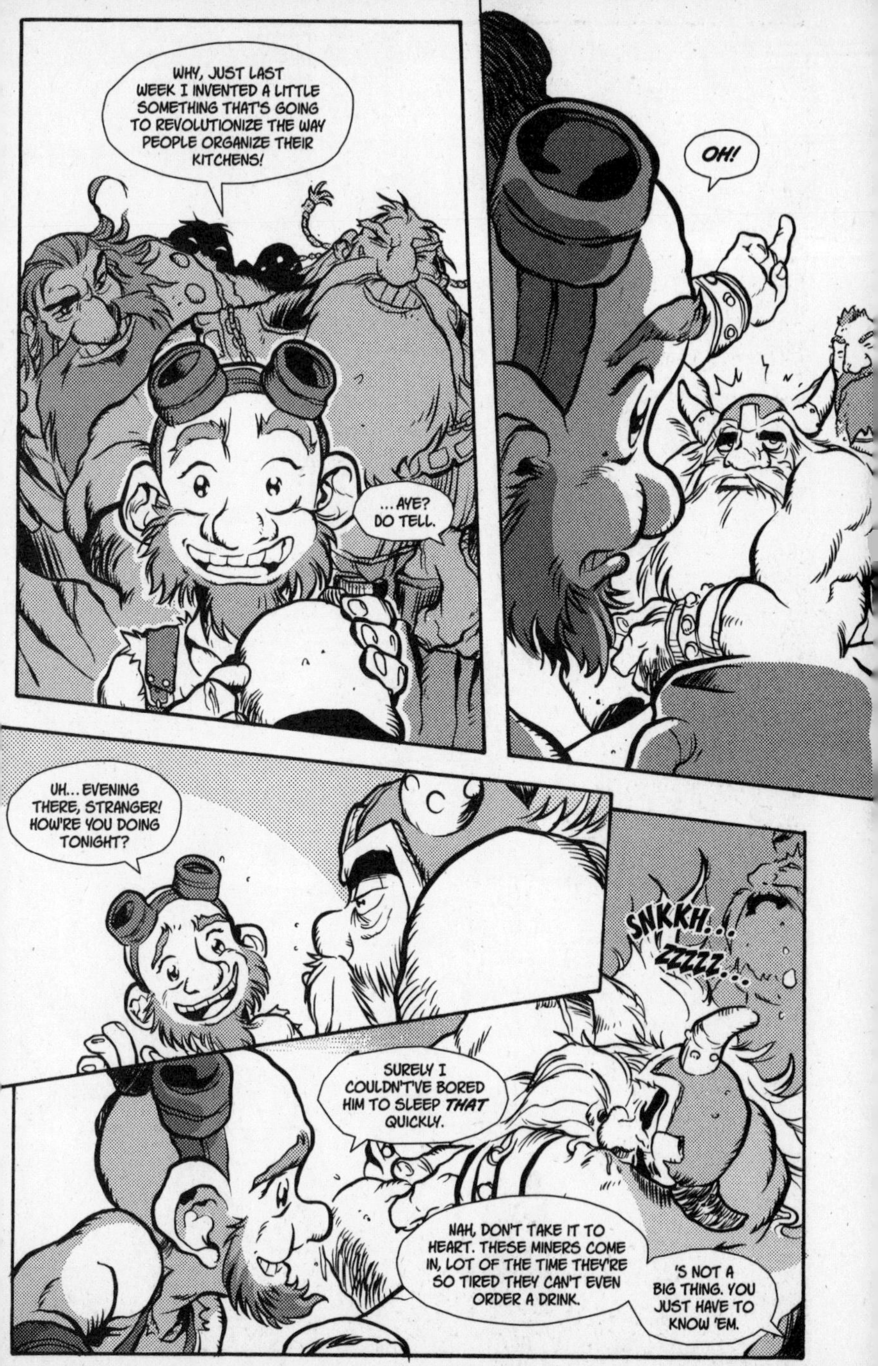
WHY, JUST LAST WEEK I INVENTED A LITTLE SOMETHING THAT'S GOING TO REVOLUTIONIZE THE WAY PEOPLE ORGANIZE THEIR KITCHENS!
...AYE? DO TELL.
OH!
UH... EVENING THERE, STRANGER! HOW'RE YOU DOING TONIGHT?
SNKKH...
ZZZZZ...
SURELY I COULDN'T'VE BORED HIM TO SLEEP *THAT* QUICKLY.
NAH, DON'T TAKE IT TO HEART. THESE MINERS COME IN, LOT OF THE TIME THEY'RE SO TIRED THEY CAN'T EVEN ORDER A DRINK.
'S NOT A BIG THING. YOU JUST HAVE TO KNOW 'EM.

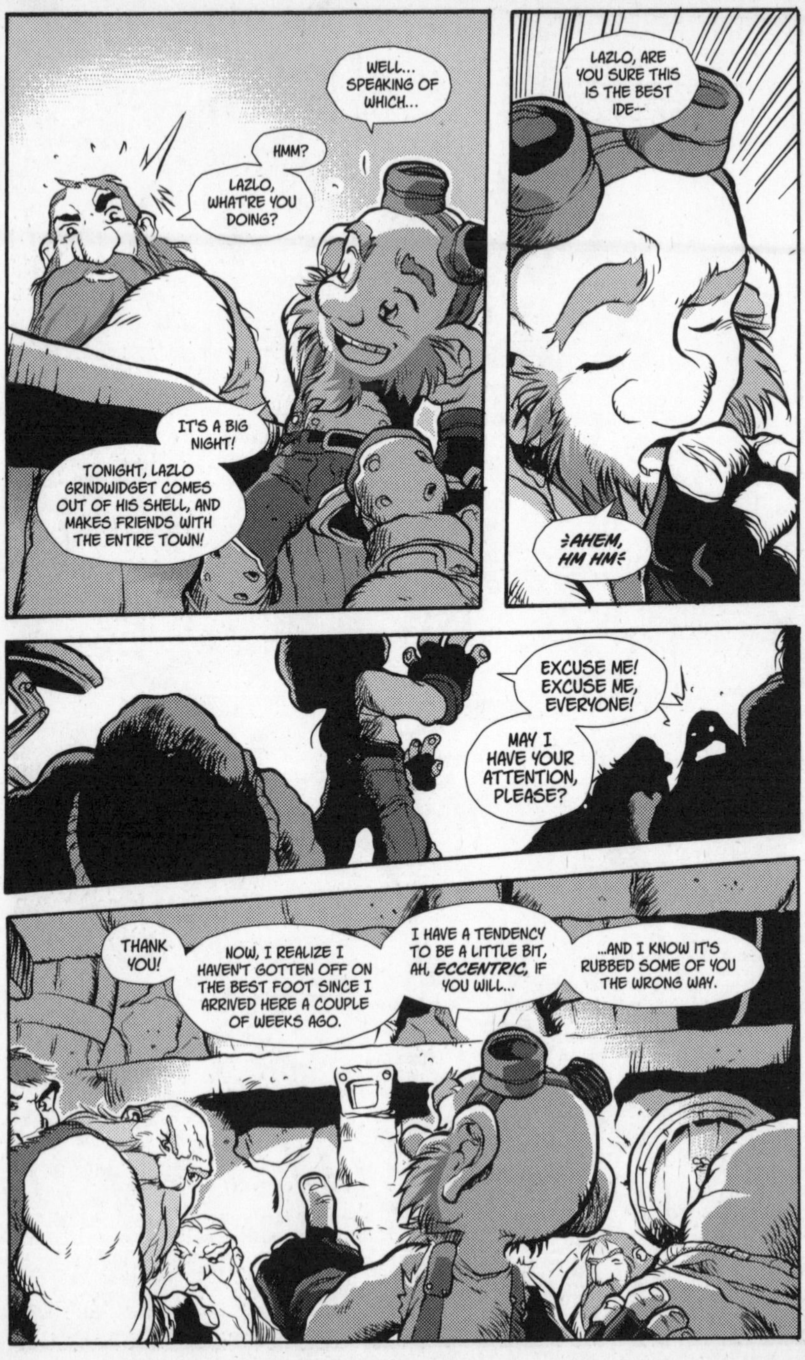
WELL... SPEAKING OF WHICH...
HMM?
LAZLO, WHAT'RE YOU DOING?
IT'S A BIG NIGHT!
TONIGHT, LAZLO GRINDWIDGET COMES OUT OF HIS SHELL, AND MAKES FRIENDS WITH THE ENTIRE TOWN!
LAZLO, ARE YOU SURE THIS IS THE BEST IDE--
AHEM, HM HM
EXCUSE ME! EXCUSE ME, EVERYONE!
MAY I HAVE YOUR ATTENTION, PLEASE?
THANK YOU!
NOW, I REALIZE I HAVEN'T GOTTEN OFF ON THE BEST FOOT SINCE I ARRIVED HERE A COUPLE OF WEEKS AGO.
I HAVE A TENDENCY TO BE A LITTLE BIT, AH, ECCENTRIC, IF YOU WILL...
...AND I KNOW IT'S RUBBED SOME OF YOU THE WRONG WAY.

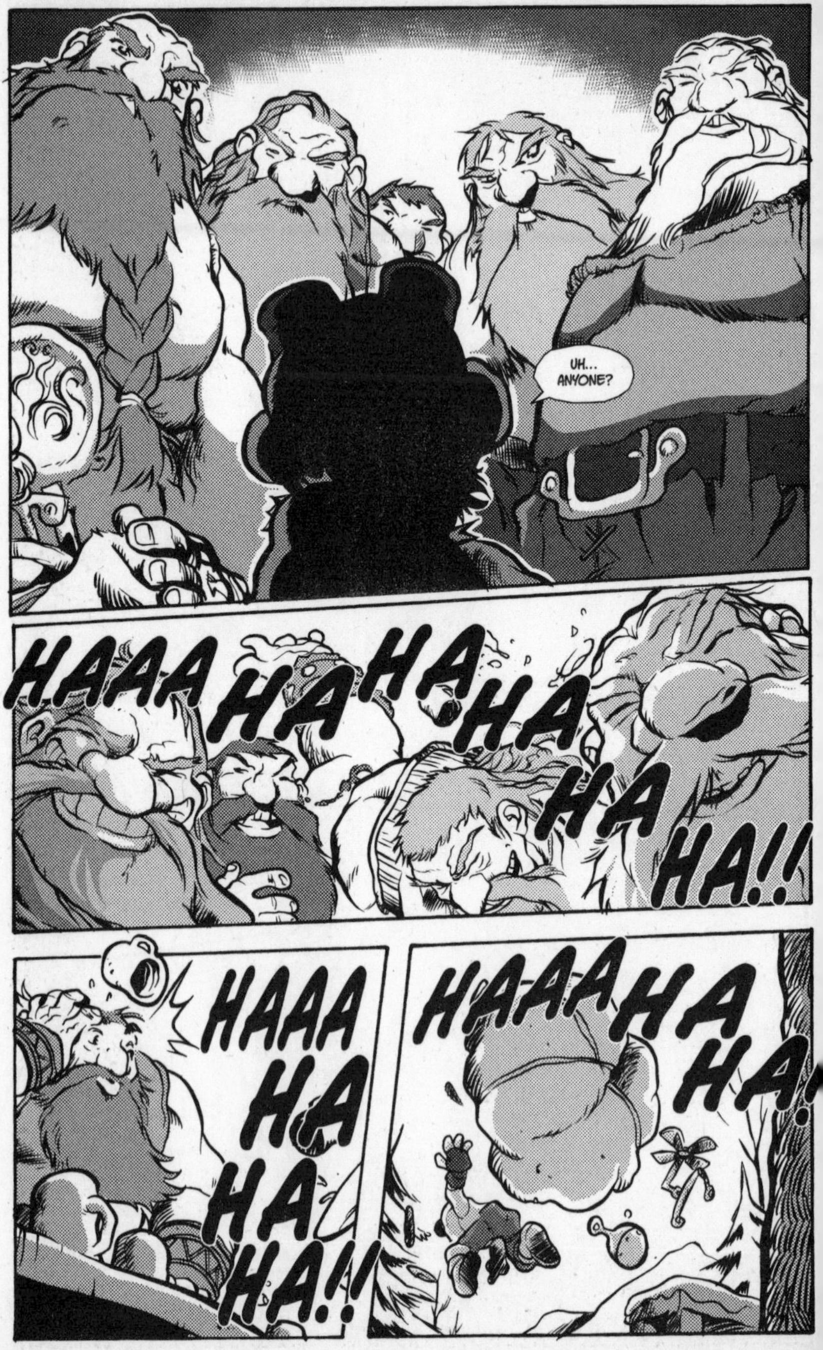
UH... ANYONE?
HAAAAHAHAHAHAHAHA!!
HAAAHAHAHA!!
HAAAAHAHAHA!

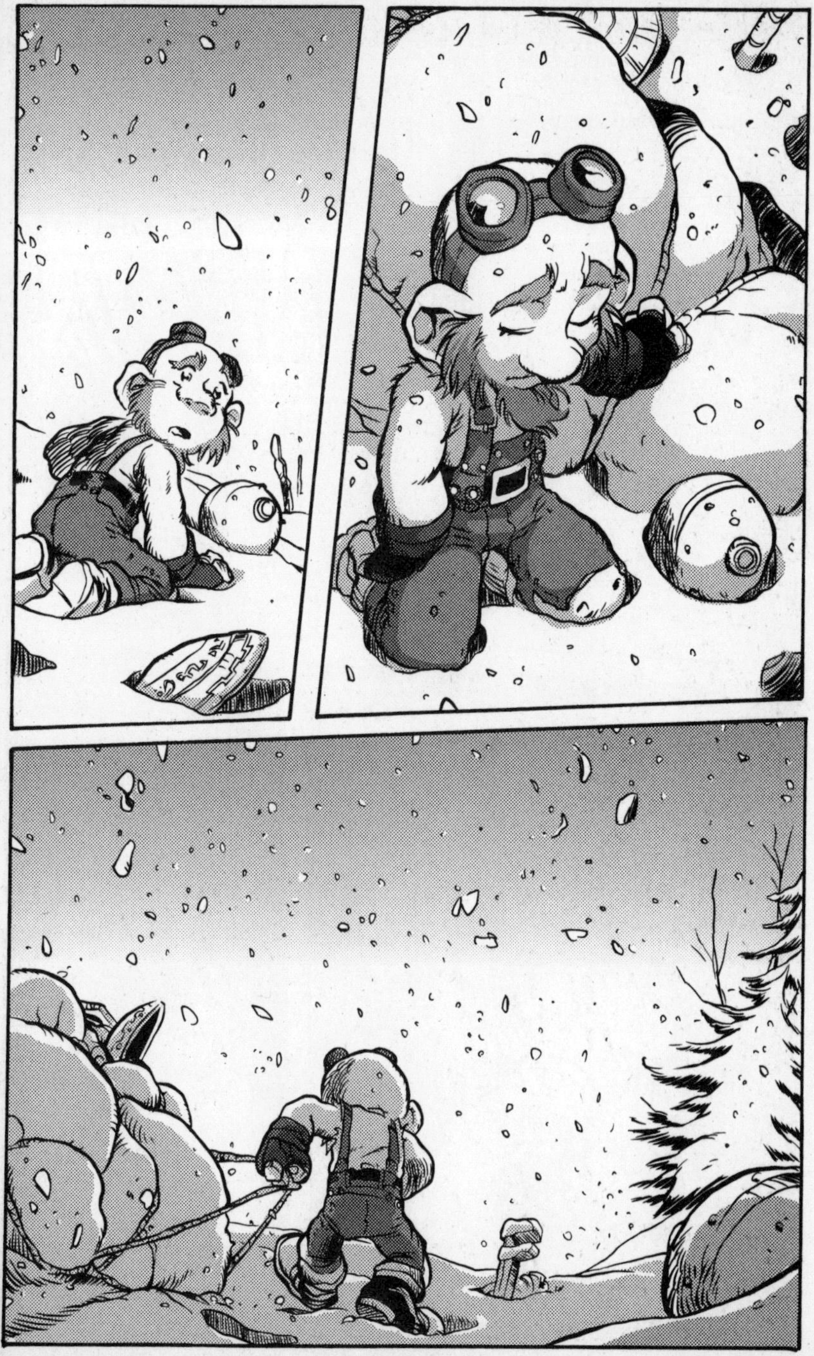

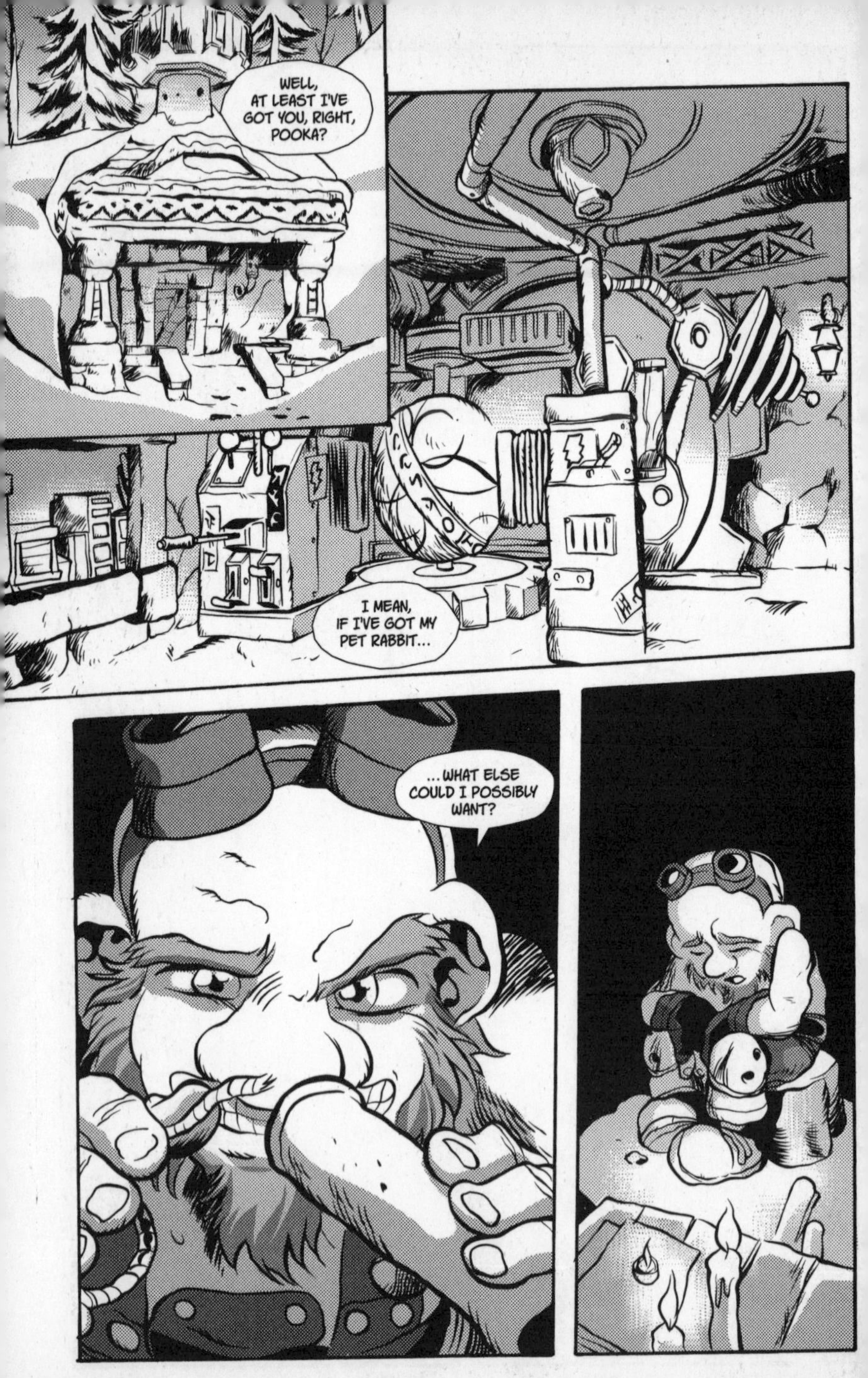
WELL, AT LEAST I'VE GOT YOU, RIGHT, POOKA?
I MEAN, IF I'VE GOT MY PET RABBIT...
...WHAT ELSE COULD I POSSIBLY WANT?

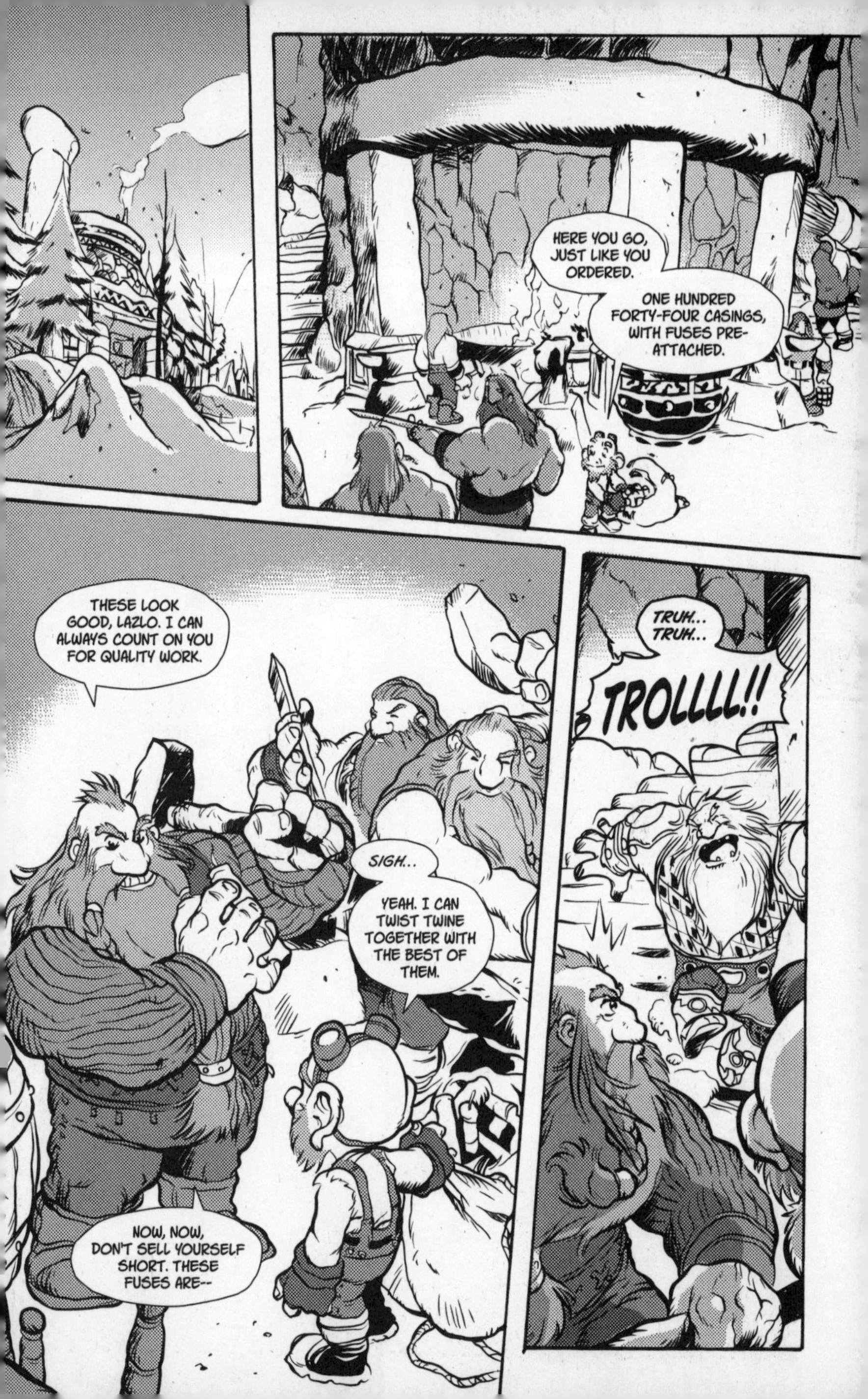
HERE YOU GO, JUST LIKE YOU ORDERED.
ONE HUNDRED FORTY-FOUR CASINGS, WITH FUSES PRE-ATTACHED.
THESE LOOK GOOD, LAZLO. I CAN ALWAYS COUNT ON YOU FOR QUALITY WORK.
SIGH...
YEAH. I CAN TWIST TWINE TOGETHER WITH THE BEST OF THEM.
NOW, NOW, DON'T SELL YOURSELF SHORT. THESE FUSES ARE--
TRUH... TRUH...
TROLLLL!!

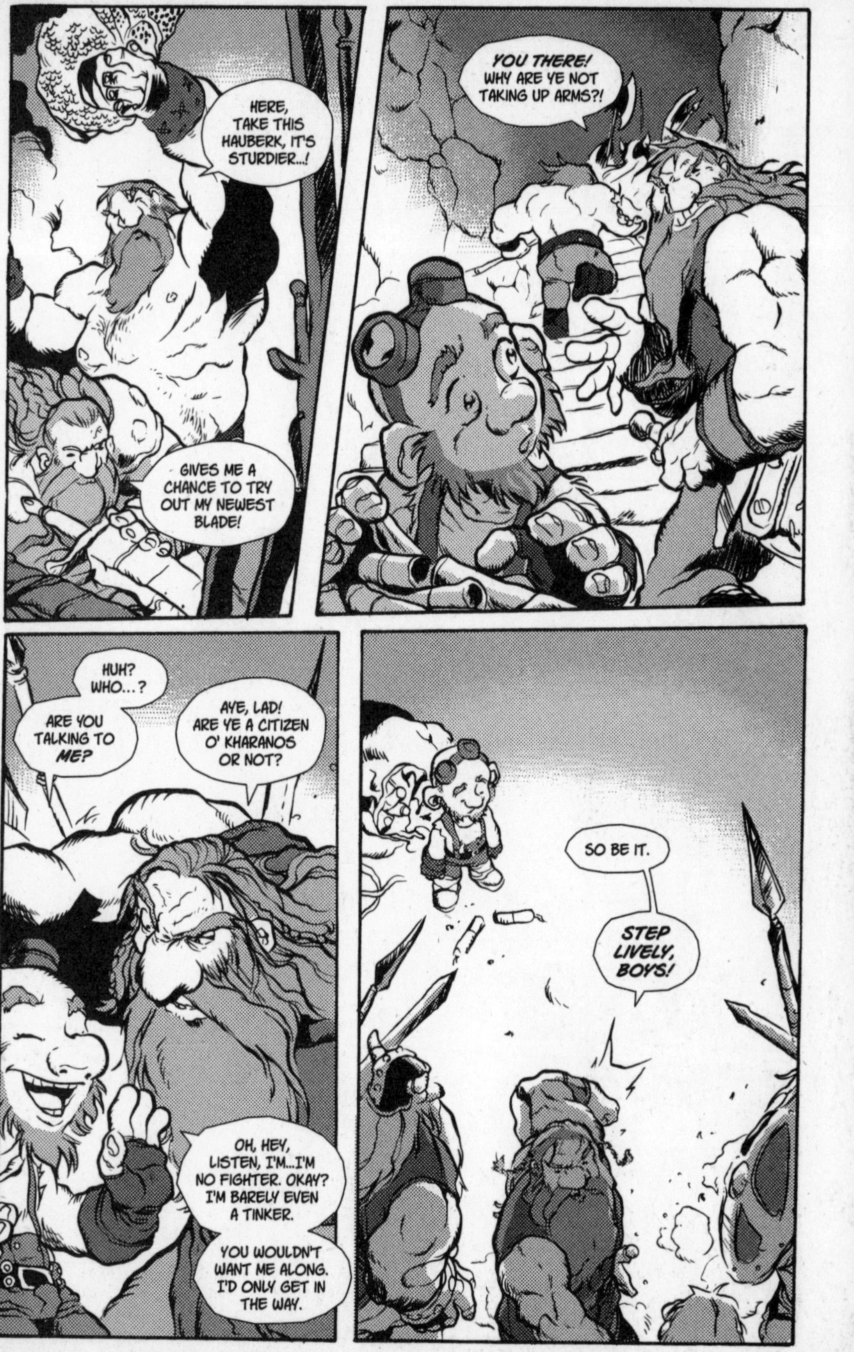
HERE, TAKE THIS HAUBERK, IT'S STURDIER...!
GIVES ME A CHANCE TO TRY OUT MY NEWEST BLADE!
YOU THERE! WHY ARE YE NOT TAKING UP ARMS?!
HUH? WHO...?
ARE YOU TALKING TO ME?
AYE, LAD! ARE YE A CITIZEN O' KHARANOS OR NOT?
OH, HEY, LISTEN, I'M...I'M NO FIGHTER. OKAY? I'M BARELY EVEN A TINKER.
YOU WOULDN'T WANT ME ALONG. I'D ONLY GET IN THE WAY.
SO BE IT.
STEP LIVELY, BOYS!

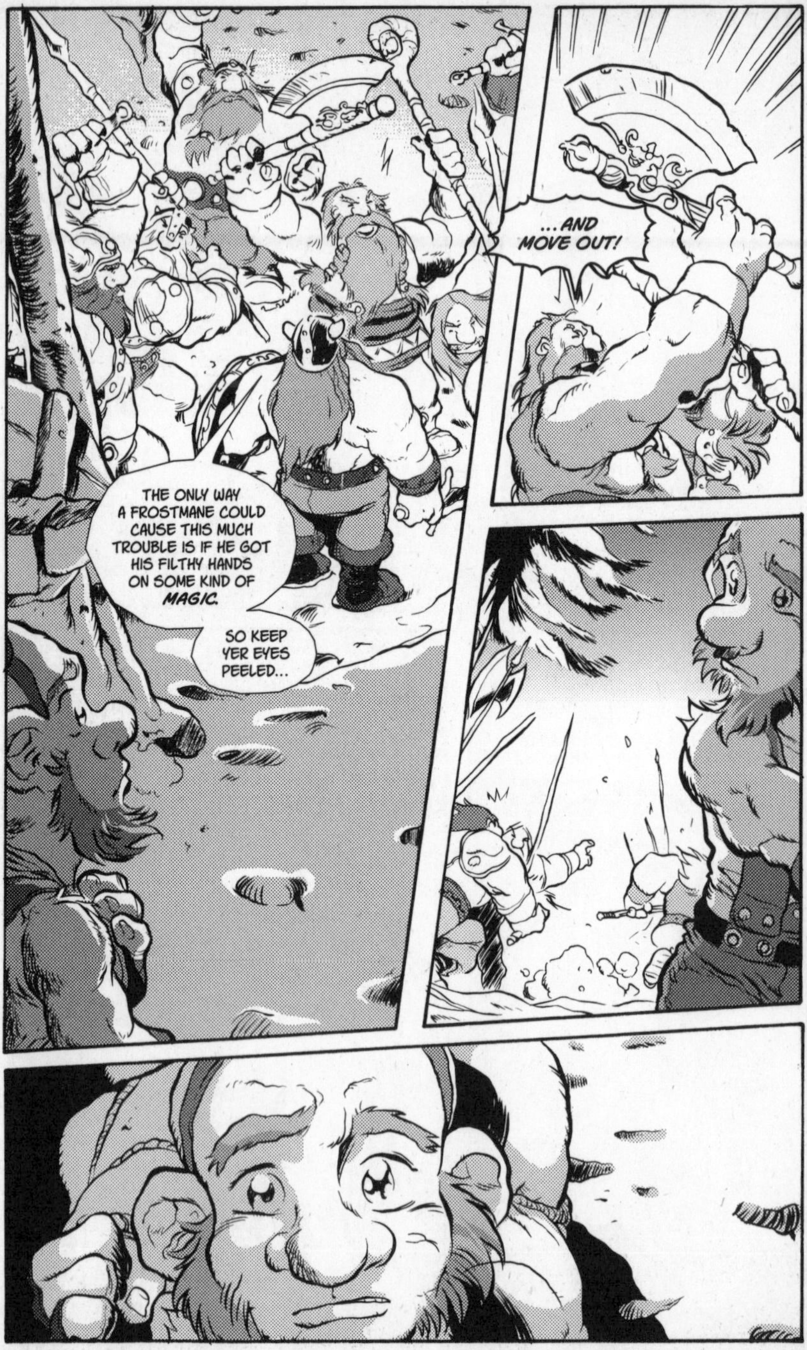
THE ONLY WAY A FROSTMANE COULD CAUSE THIS MUCH TROUBLE IS IF HE GOT HIS FILTHY HANDS ON SOME KIND OF *MAGIC.*
SO KEEP YER EYES PEELED...
...AND MOVE OUT!

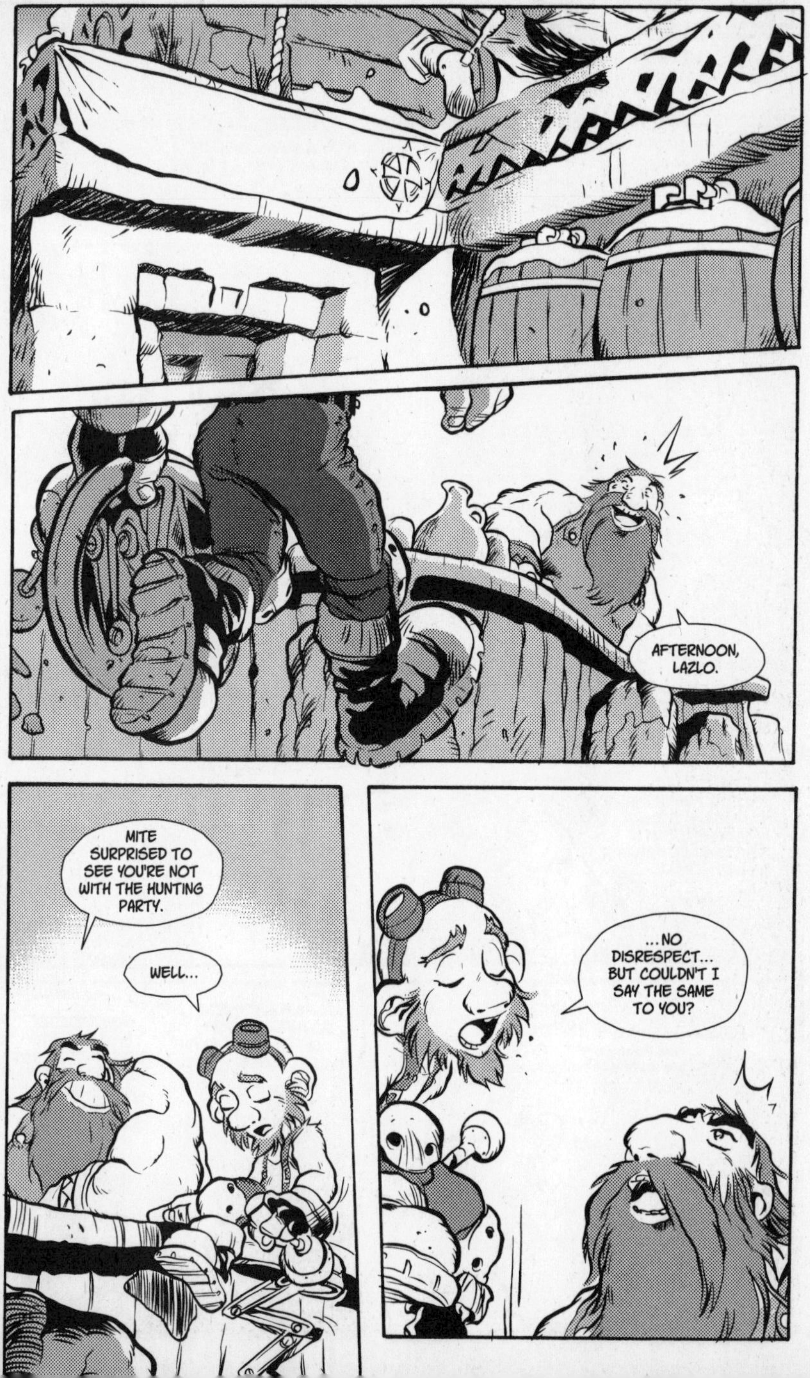
AFTERNOON, LAZLO.
MITE SURPRISED TO SEE YOU'RE NOT WITH THE HUNTING PARTY.
WELL...
...NO DISRESPECT... BUT COULDN'T I SAY THE SAME TO YOU?

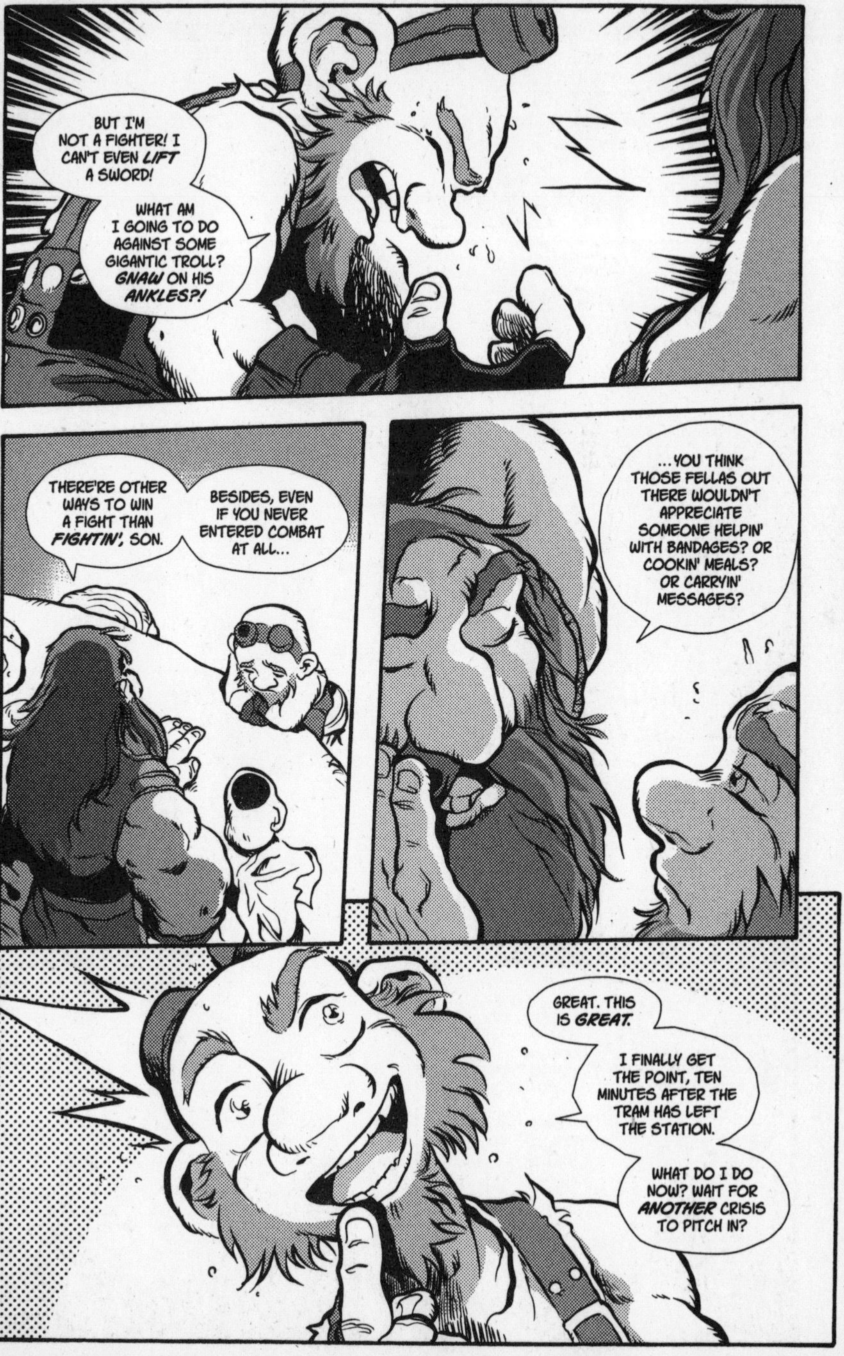
BUT I'M NOT A FIGHTER! I CAN'T EVEN *LIFT* A SWORD!
WHAT AM I GOING TO DO AGAINST SOME GIGANTIC TROLL? ***GNAW*** ON HIS ***ANKLES?!***
THERE'RE OTHER WAYS TO WIN A FIGHT THAN ***FIGHTIN',*** SON.
BESIDES, EVEN IF YOU NEVER ENTERED COMBAT AT ALL...
...YOU THINK THOSE FELLAS OUT THERE WOULDN'T APPRECIATE SOMEONE HELPIN' WITH BANDAGES? OR COOKIN' MEALS? OR CARRYIN' MESSAGES?
GREAT. THIS IS ***GREAT.***
I FINALLY GET THE POINT, TEN MINUTES AFTER THE TRAM HAS LEFT THE STATION.
WHAT DO I DO NOW? WAIT FOR ***ANOTHER*** CRISIS TO PITCH IN?

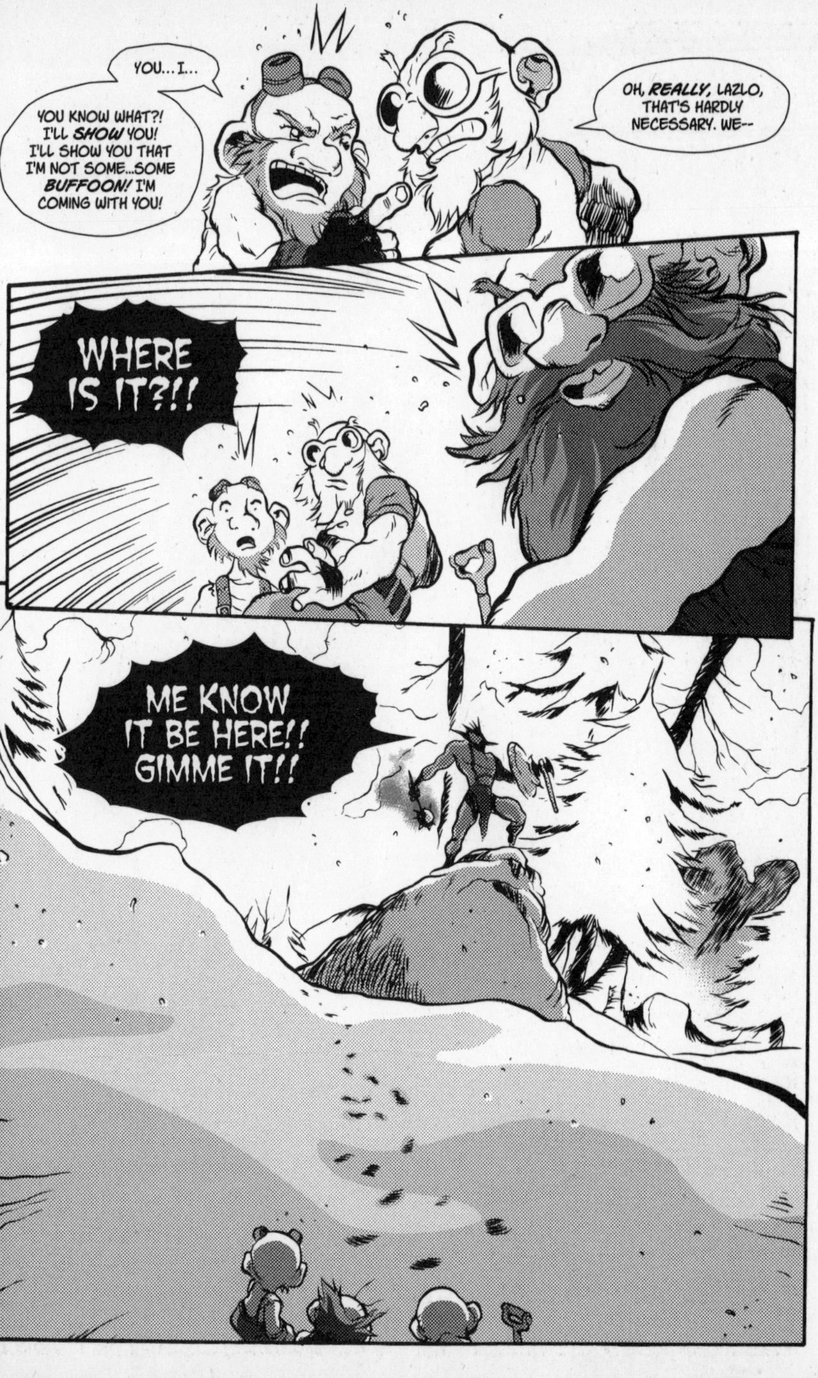
YOU... I...
YOU KNOW WHAT?! I'LL **SHOW** YOU! I'LL SHOW YOU THAT I'M NOT SOME...SOME **BUFFOON!** I'M COMING WITH YOU!
OH, **REALLY,** LAZLO, THAT'S HARDLY NECESSARY. WE--
WHERE IS IT?!!
ME KNOW IT BE HERE!! GIMME IT!!

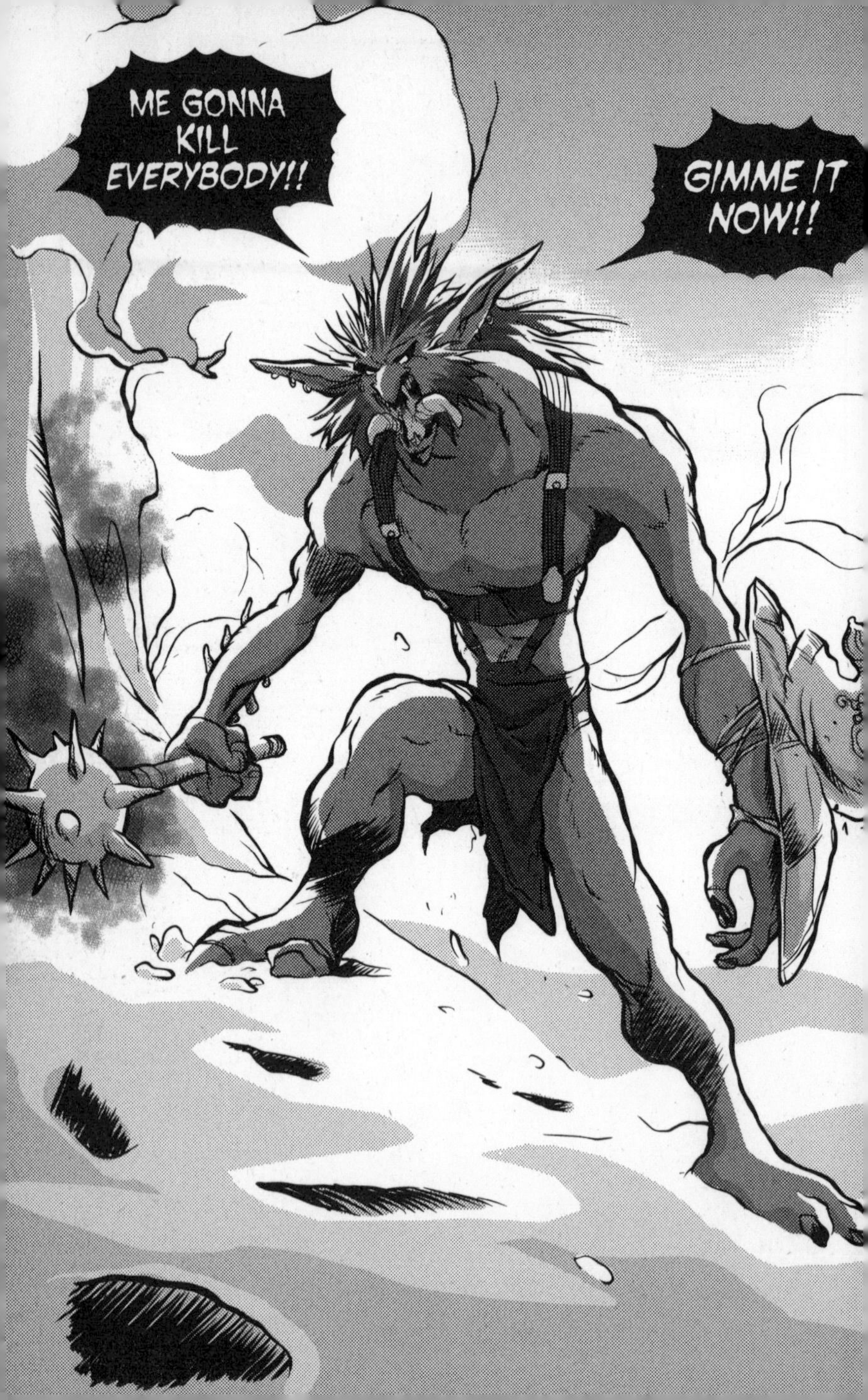
ME GONNA KILL EVERYBODY!!
GIMME IT NOW!!

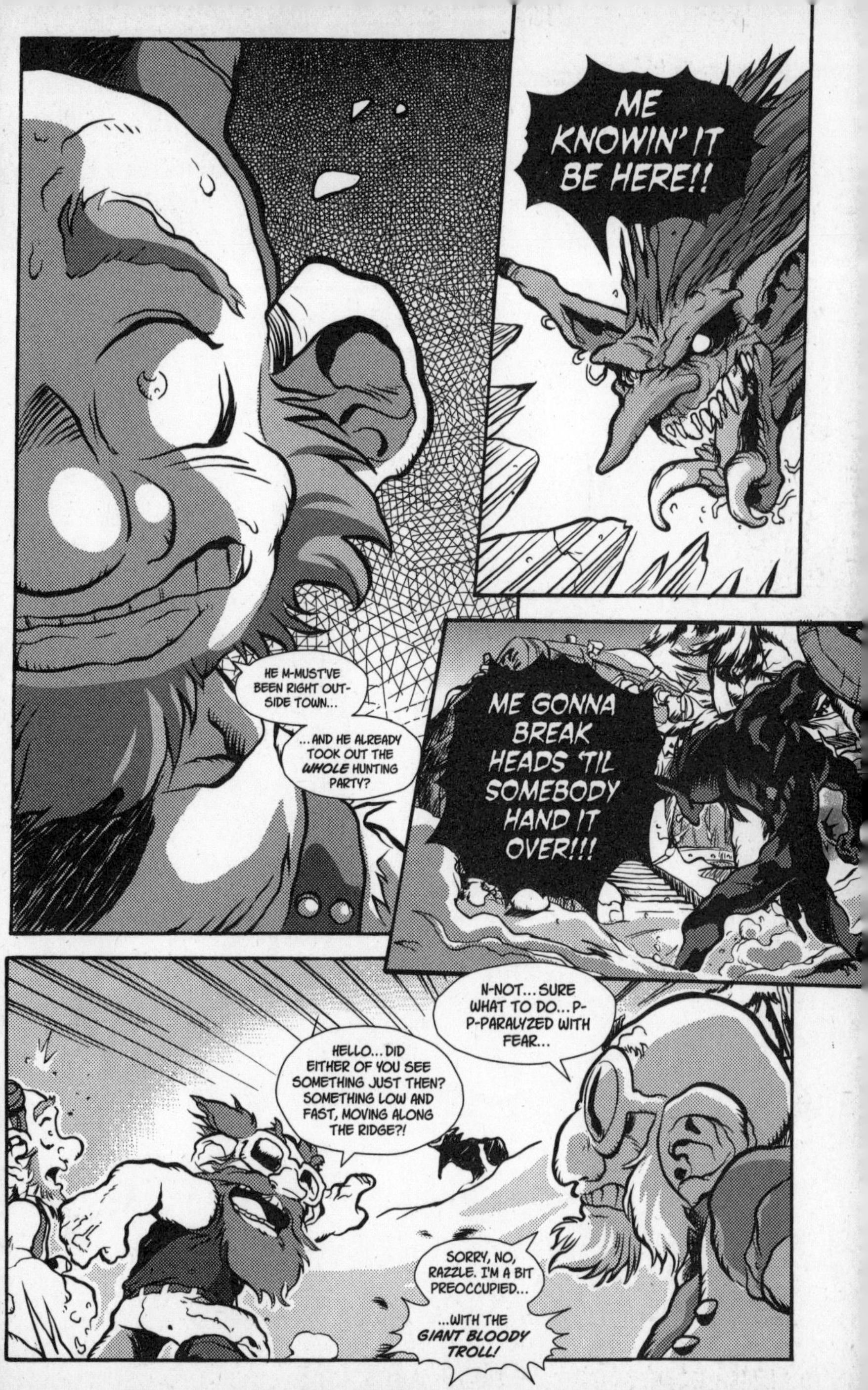

ME KNOWIN' IT BE HERE!!
HE M-MUST'VE BEEN RIGHT OUT-SIDE TOWN...
...AND HE ALREADY TOOK OUT THE *WHOLE* HUNTING PARTY?
ME GONNA BREAK HEADS 'TIL SOMEBODY HAND IT OVER!!!
HELLO... DID EITHER OF YOU SEE SOMETHING JUST THEN? SOMETHING LOW AND FAST, MOVING ALONG THE RIDGE?!
N-NOT... SURE WHAT TO DO... P-P-PARALYZED WITH FEAR...
SORRY, NO, RAZZLE. I'M A BIT PREOCCUPIED...
...WITH THE *GIANT BLOODY TROLL!*

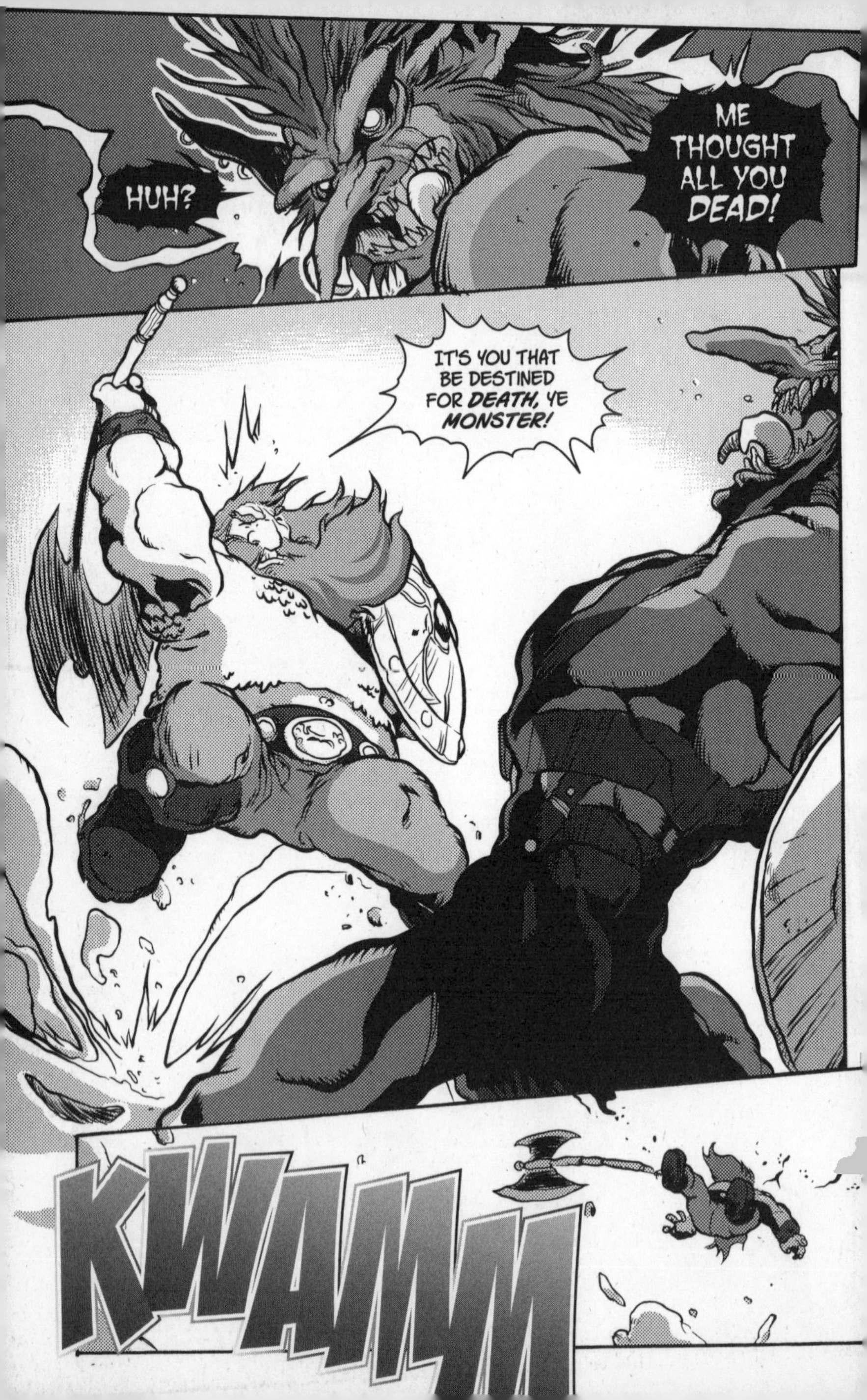
HUH?
ME THOUGHT ALL YOU DEAD!
IT'S YOU THAT BE DESTINED FOR DEATH, YE MONSTER!
KWAMM

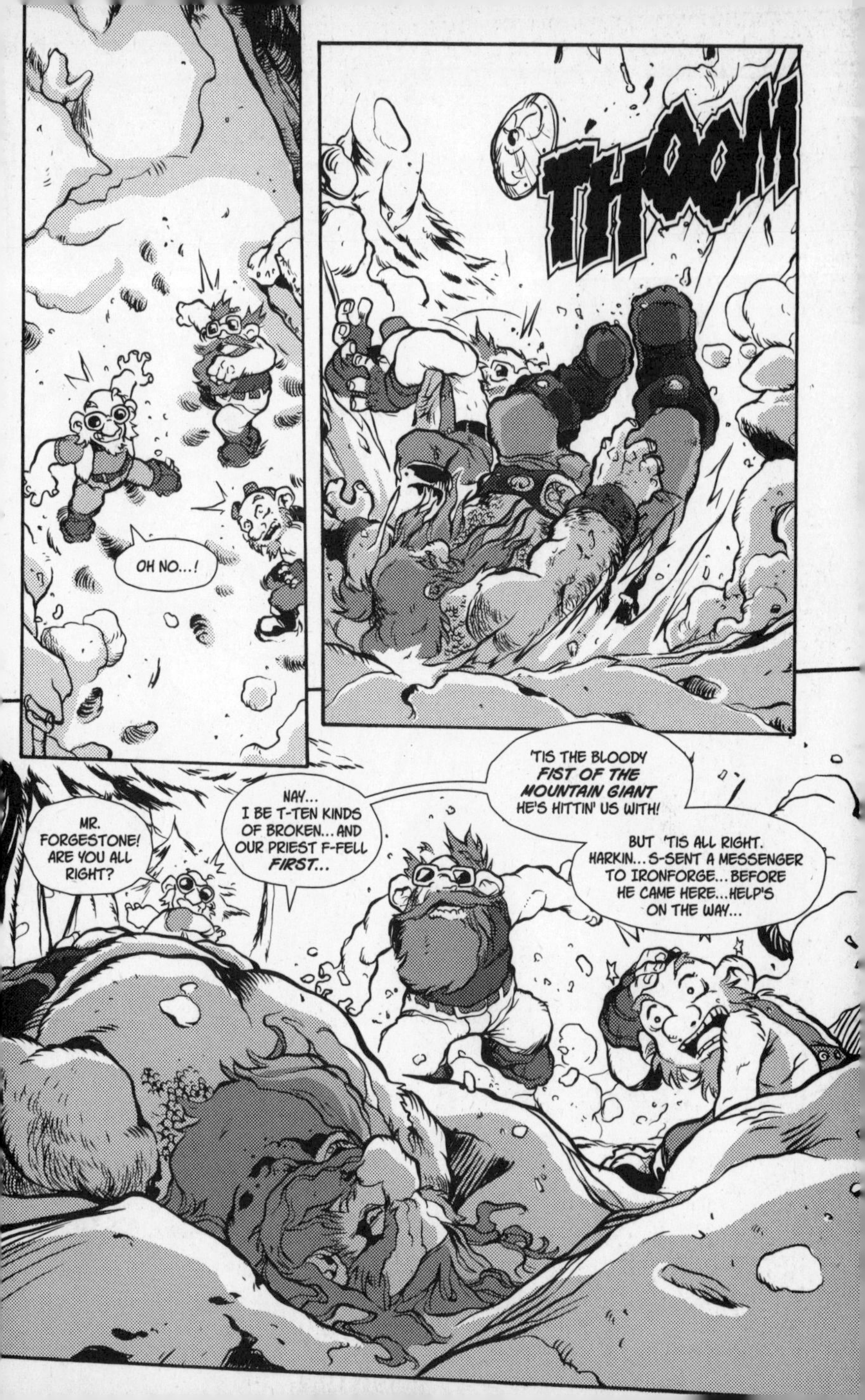
OH NO...!
THOOM
MR. FORGESTONE! ARE YOU ALL RIGHT?
NAY... I BE T-TEN KINDS OF BROKEN... AND OUR PRIEST F-FELL *FIRST*...
'TIS THE BLOODY ***FIST OF THE MOUNTAIN GIANT*** HE'S HITTIN' US WITH!
BUT 'TIS ALL RIGHT. HARKIN... S-SENT A MESSENGER TO IRONFORGE... BEFORE HE CAME HERE... HELP'S ON THE WAY...

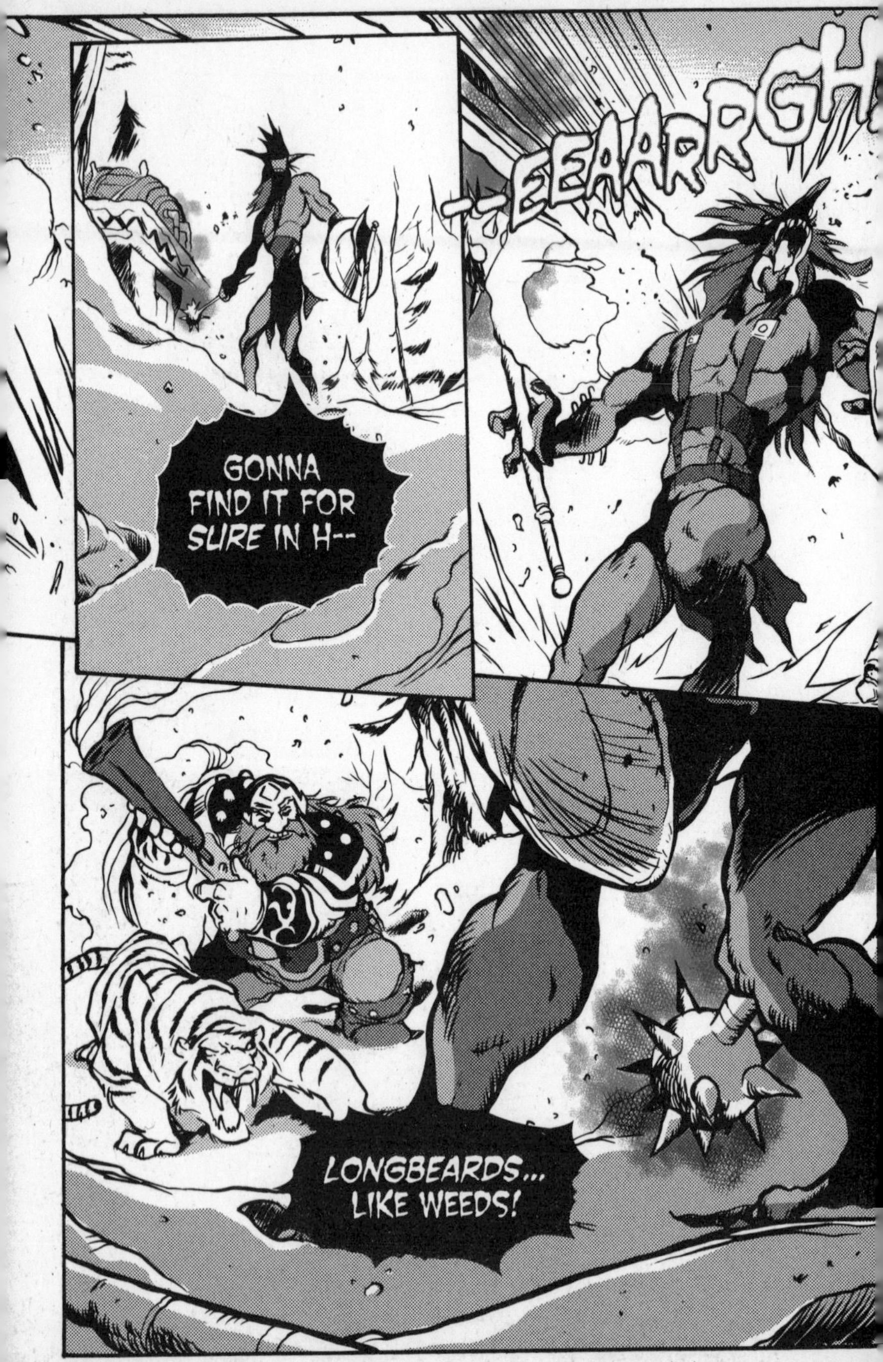
GONNA FIND IT FOR SURE IN H--
--EEAARRGH
LONGBEARDS... LIKE WEEDS!

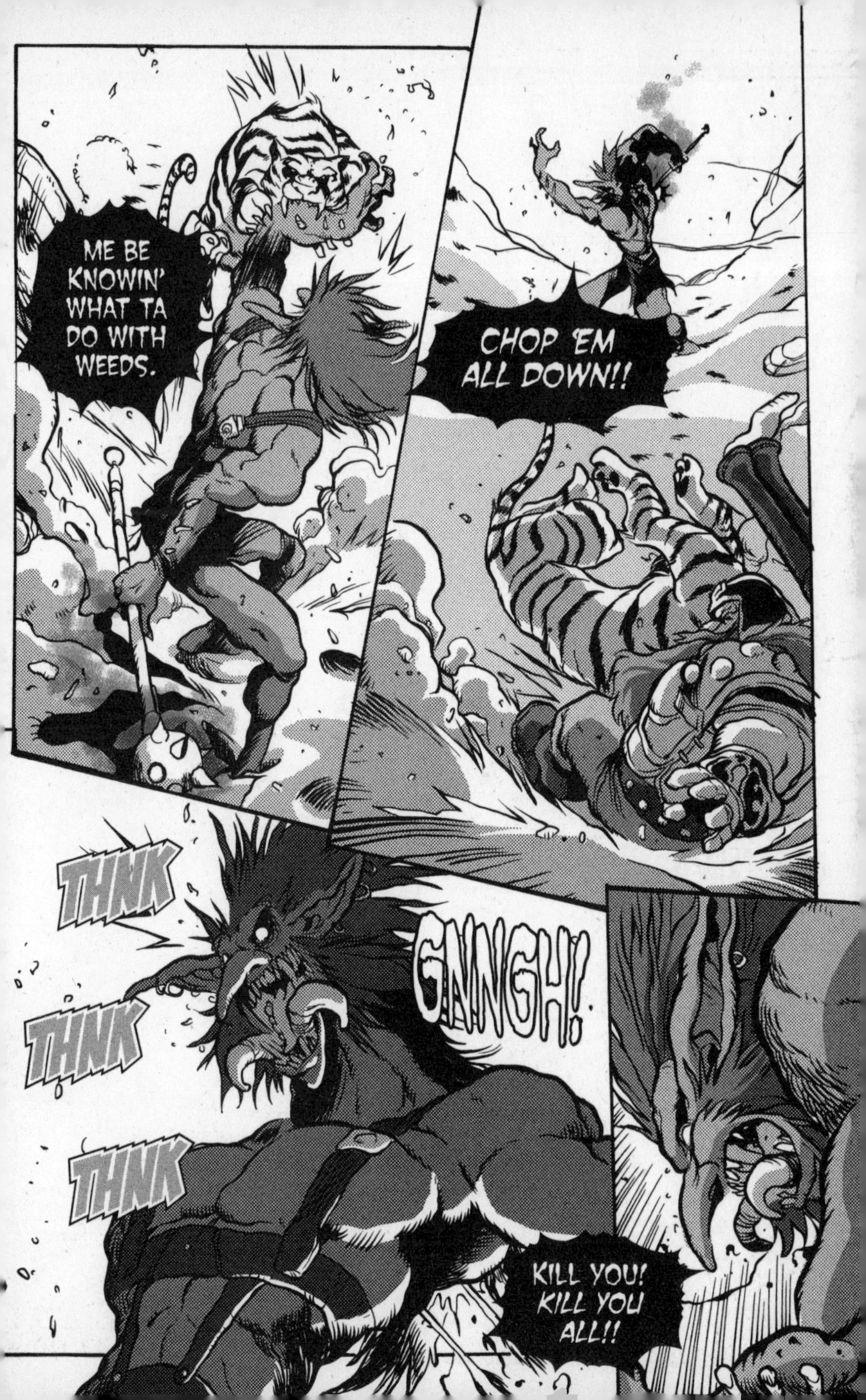
ME BE KNOWIN' WHAT TA DO WITH WEEDS.
CHOP 'EM ALL DOWN!!
THNK
THNK
THNK
GNNGH!
KILL YOU! KILL YOU ALL!!

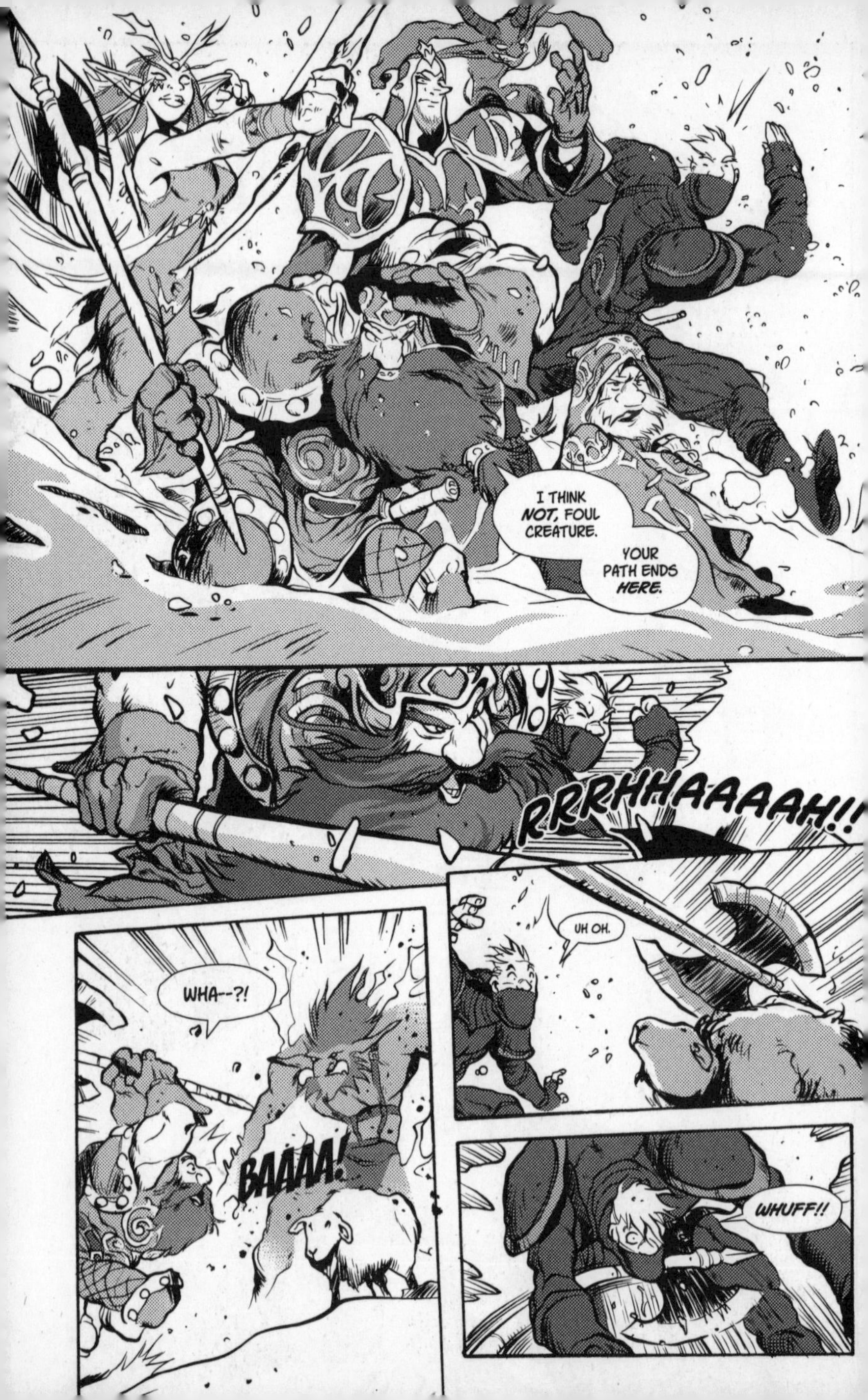
I THINK NOT, FOUL CREATURE.
YOUR PATH ENDS HERE.
RRRHHAAAAAH!!
WHA--?!
BAAAA!
UH OH.
WHUFF!!

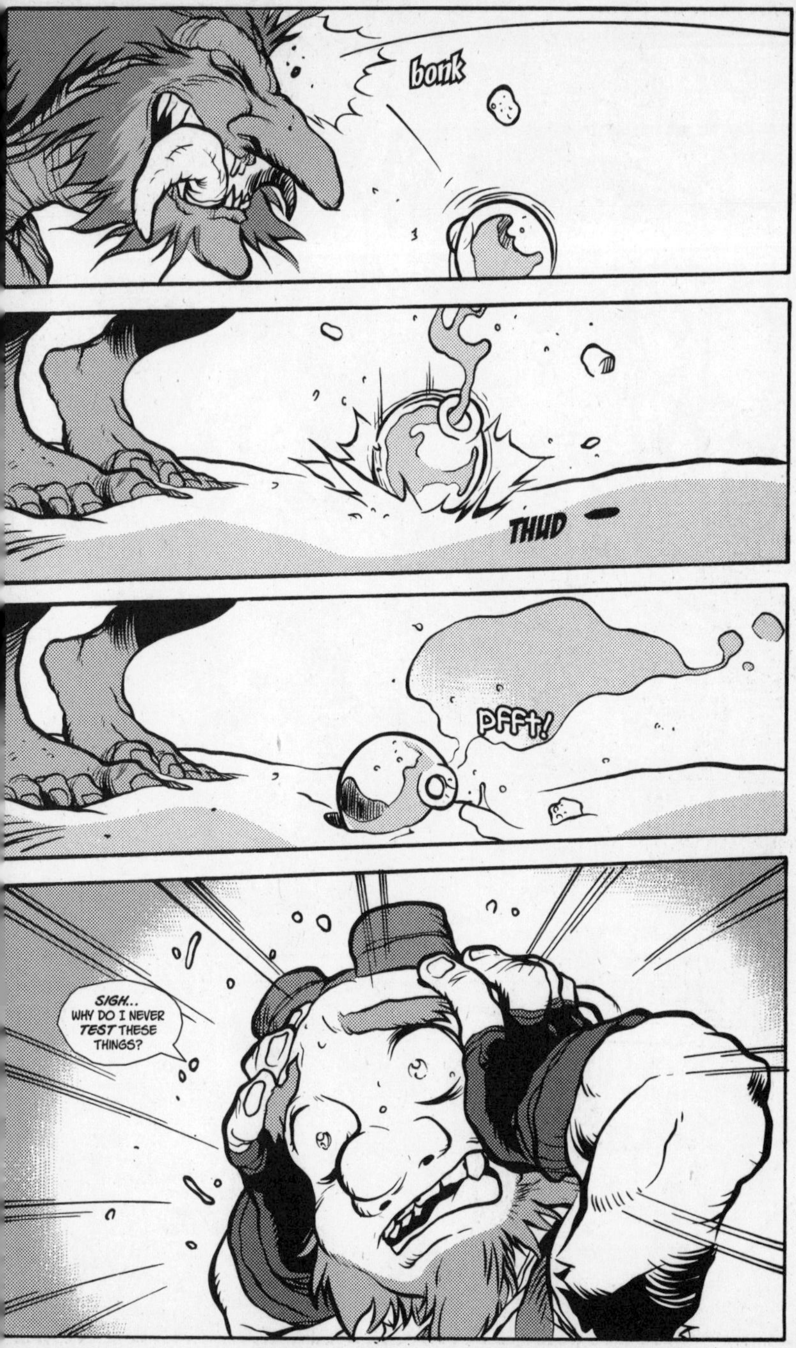
bonk
THUD
pfft!
SIGH... WHY DO I NEVER TEST THESE THINGS?

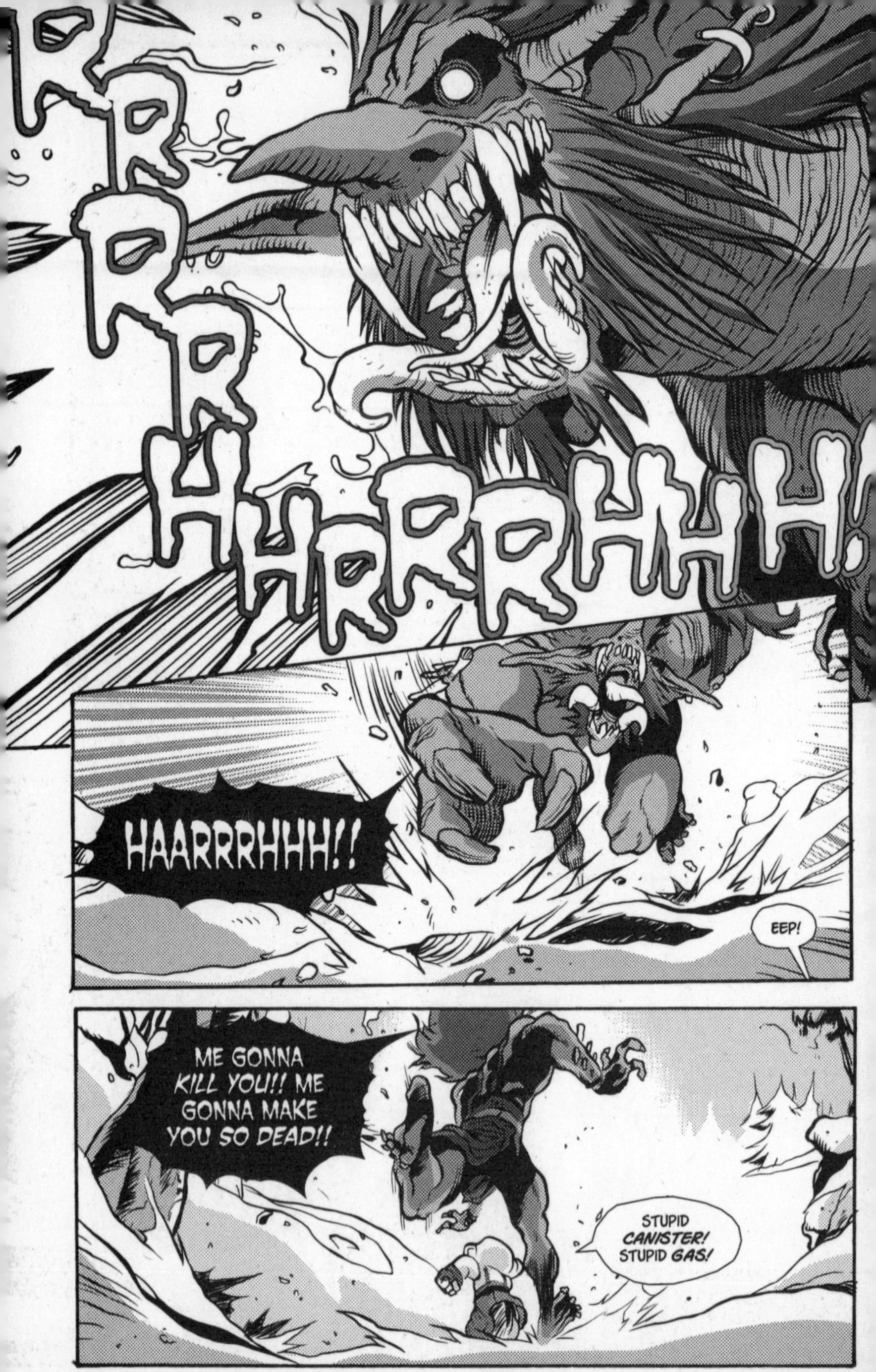
RRRHHRRRHHH!
HAARRRHHH!!
EEP!
ME GONNA KILL YOU!! ME GONNA MAKE YOU SO DEAD!!
STUPID CANISTER! STUPID GAS!

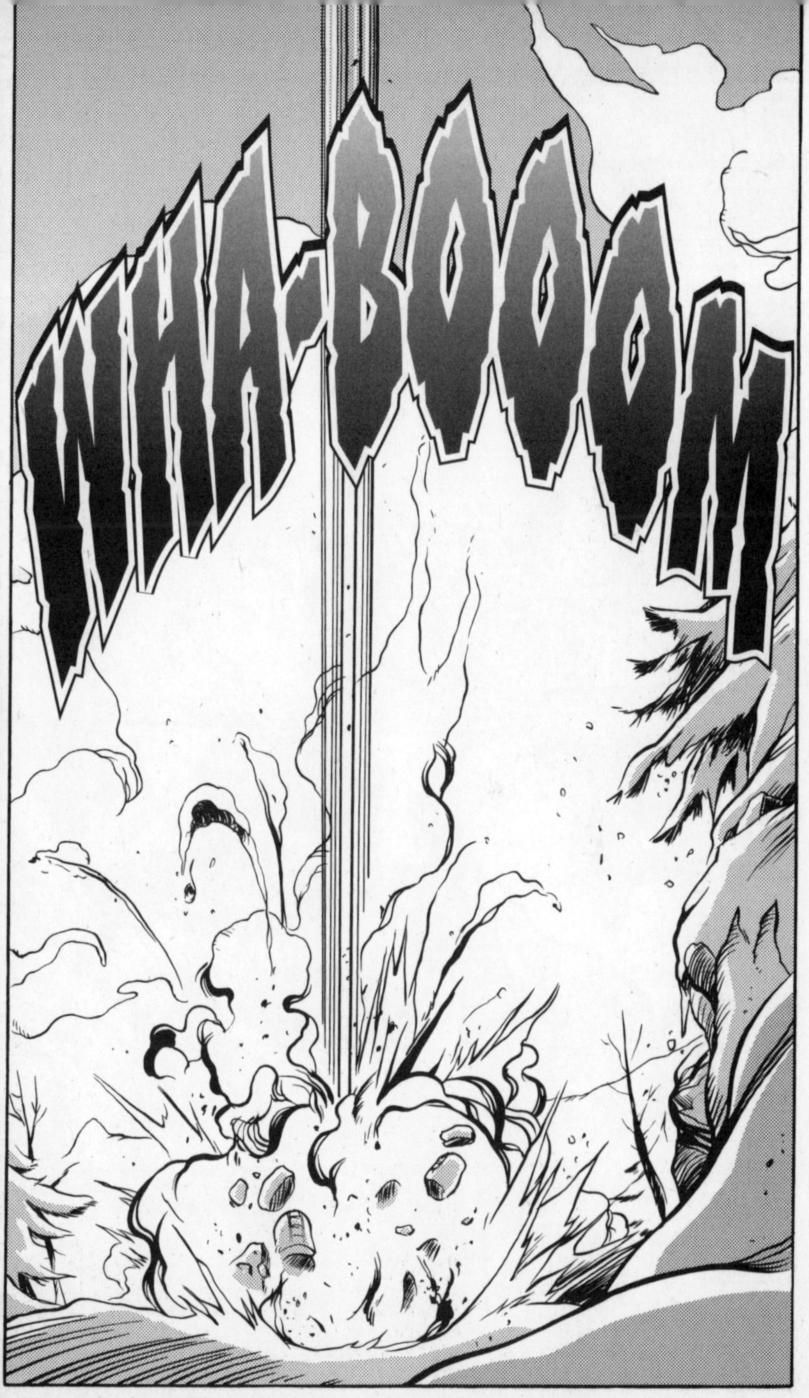
WHA-BOOOM

WARCRAFT

LEGENDS

VOLUME ONE

AN HONEST TRADE

WRITTEN BY TROY LEWTER

PENCILS BY NAM KIM & STUDIOIL
STUDIOIL STAFF: AJ FORD 3, BEN HARVEY & SHIWAH WONG
LAYOUTS BY J.M
INKS BY MATT DALTON, KÖSEN & ALISON ACTON
TONES BY CHOW HON LAM & MONICA KUBINA

EDITOR: TIM BEEDLE
ASSOCIATE EDITOR: SHANNON WATTERS
LETTERER: MICHAEL PAOLILLI

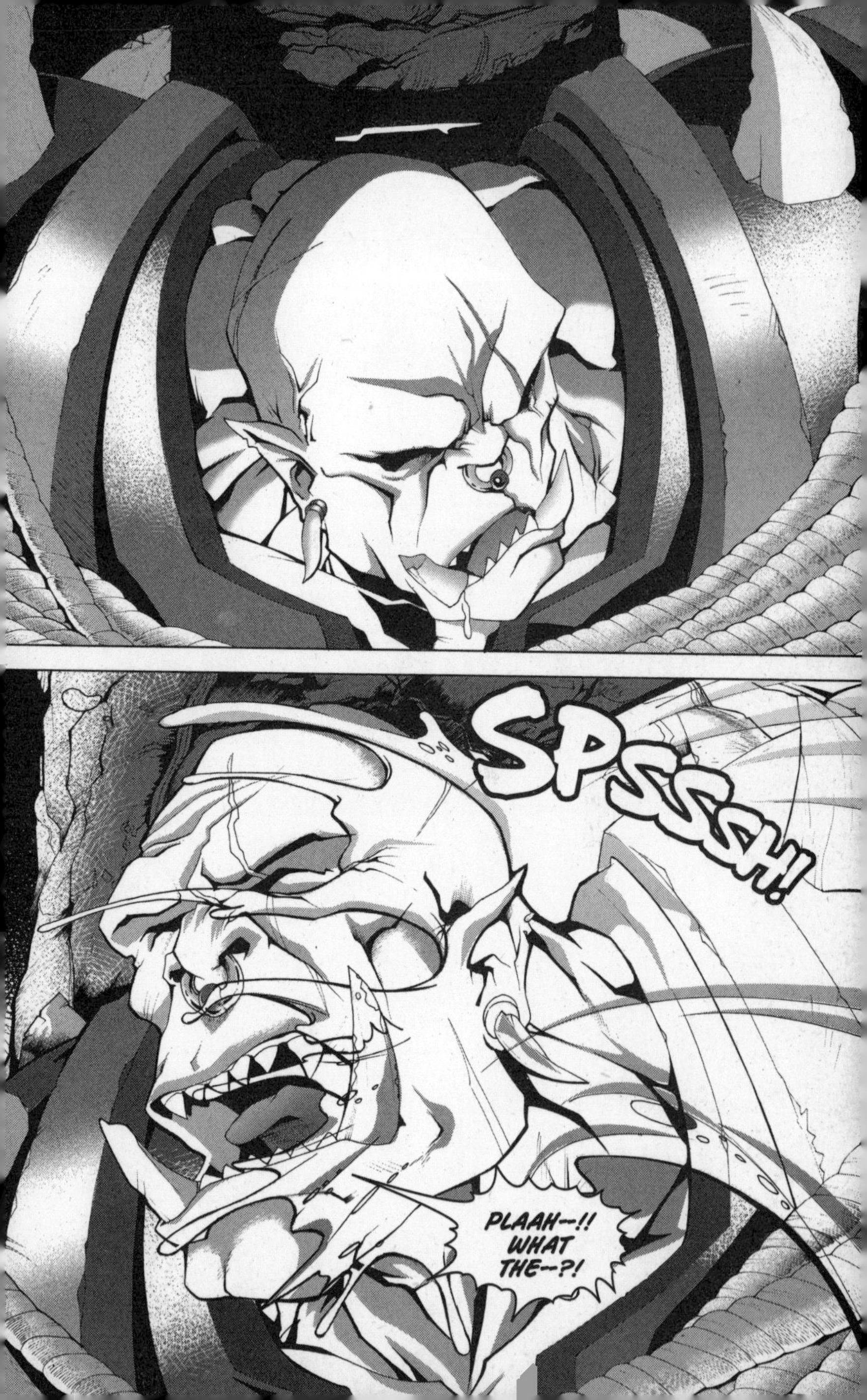
SPSSSH!
PLAAH--!! WHAT THE--?!

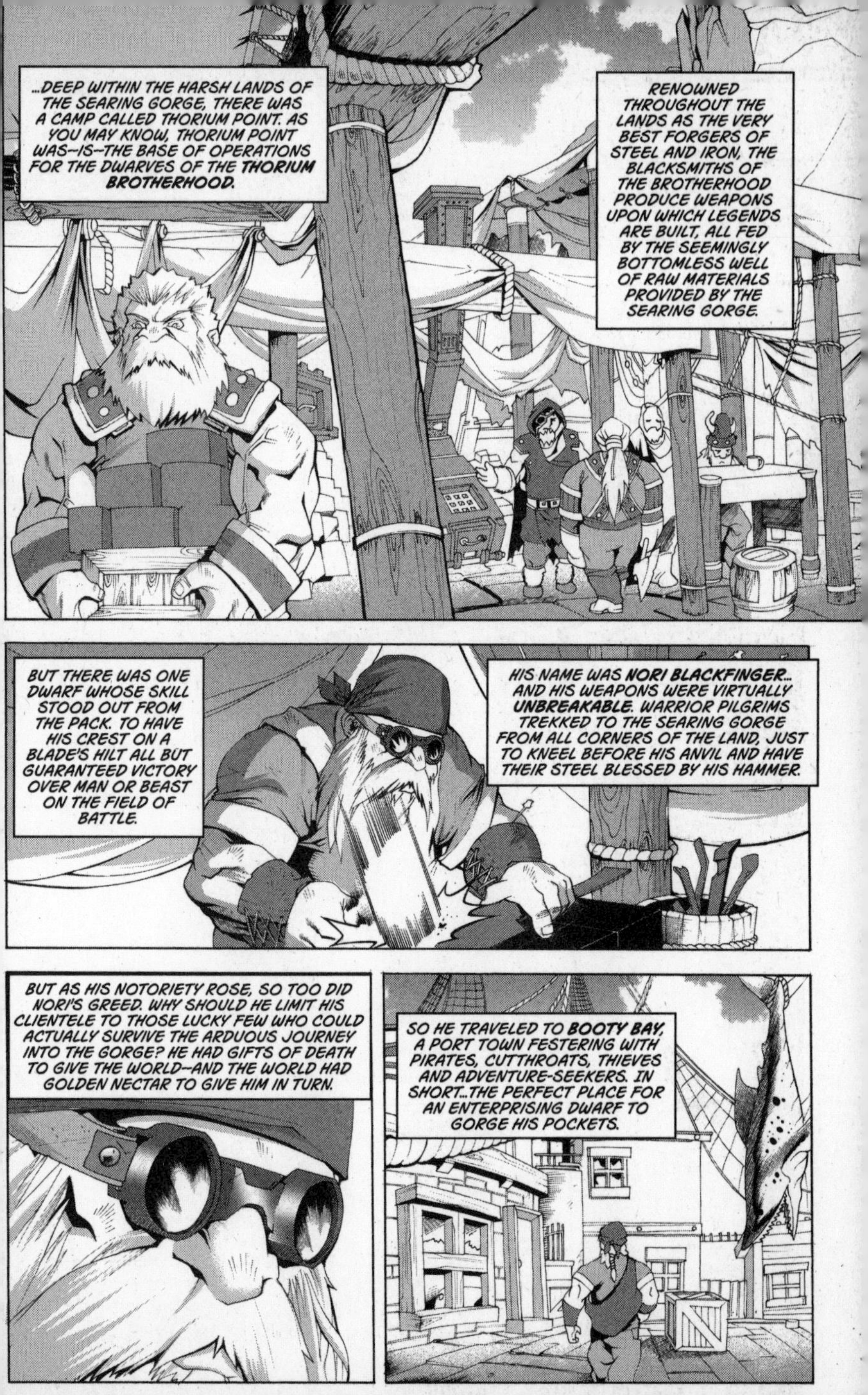
...DEEP WITHIN THE HARSH LANDS OF THE SEARING GORGE, THERE WAS A CAMP CALLED THORIUM POINT. AS YOU MAY KNOW, THORIUM POINT WAS--IS--THE BASE OF OPERATIONS FOR THE DWARVES OF THE THORIUM BROTHERHOOD.
RENOWNED THROUGHOUT THE LANDS AS THE VERY BEST FORGERS OF STEEL AND IRON, THE BLACKSMITHS OF THE BROTHERHOOD PRODUCE WEAPONS UPON WHICH LEGENDS ARE BUILT, ALL FED BY THE SEEMINGLY BOTTOMLESS WELL OF RAW MATERIALS PROVIDED BY THE SEARING GORGE.
BUT THERE WAS ONE DWARF WHOSE SKILL STOOD OUT FROM THE PACK. TO HAVE HIS CREST ON A BLADE'S HILT ALL BUT GUARANTEED VICTORY OVER MAN OR BEAST ON THE FIELD OF BATTLE.
HIS NAME WAS NORI BLACKFINGER... AND HIS WEAPONS WERE VIRTUALLY UNBREAKABLE. WARRIOR PILGRIMS TREKKED TO THE SEARING GORGE FROM ALL CORNERS OF THE LAND, JUST TO KNEEL BEFORE HIS ANVIL AND HAVE THEIR STEEL BLESSED BY HIS HAMMER.
BUT AS HIS NOTORIETY ROSE, SO TOO DID NORI'S GREED. WHY SHOULD HE LIMIT HIS CLIENTELE TO THOSE LUCKY FEW WHO COULD ACTUALLY SURVIVE THE ARDUOUS JOURNEY INTO THE GORGE? HE HAD GIFTS OF DEATH TO GIVE THE WORLD--AND THE WORLD HAD GOLDEN NECTAR TO GIVE HIM IN TURN.
SO HE TRAVELED TO BOOTY BAY, A PORT TOWN FESTERING WITH PIRATES, CUTTHROATS, THIEVES AND ADVENTURE-SEEKERS. IN SHORT...THE PERFECT PLACE FOR AN ENTERPRISING DWARF TO GORGE HIS POCKETS.

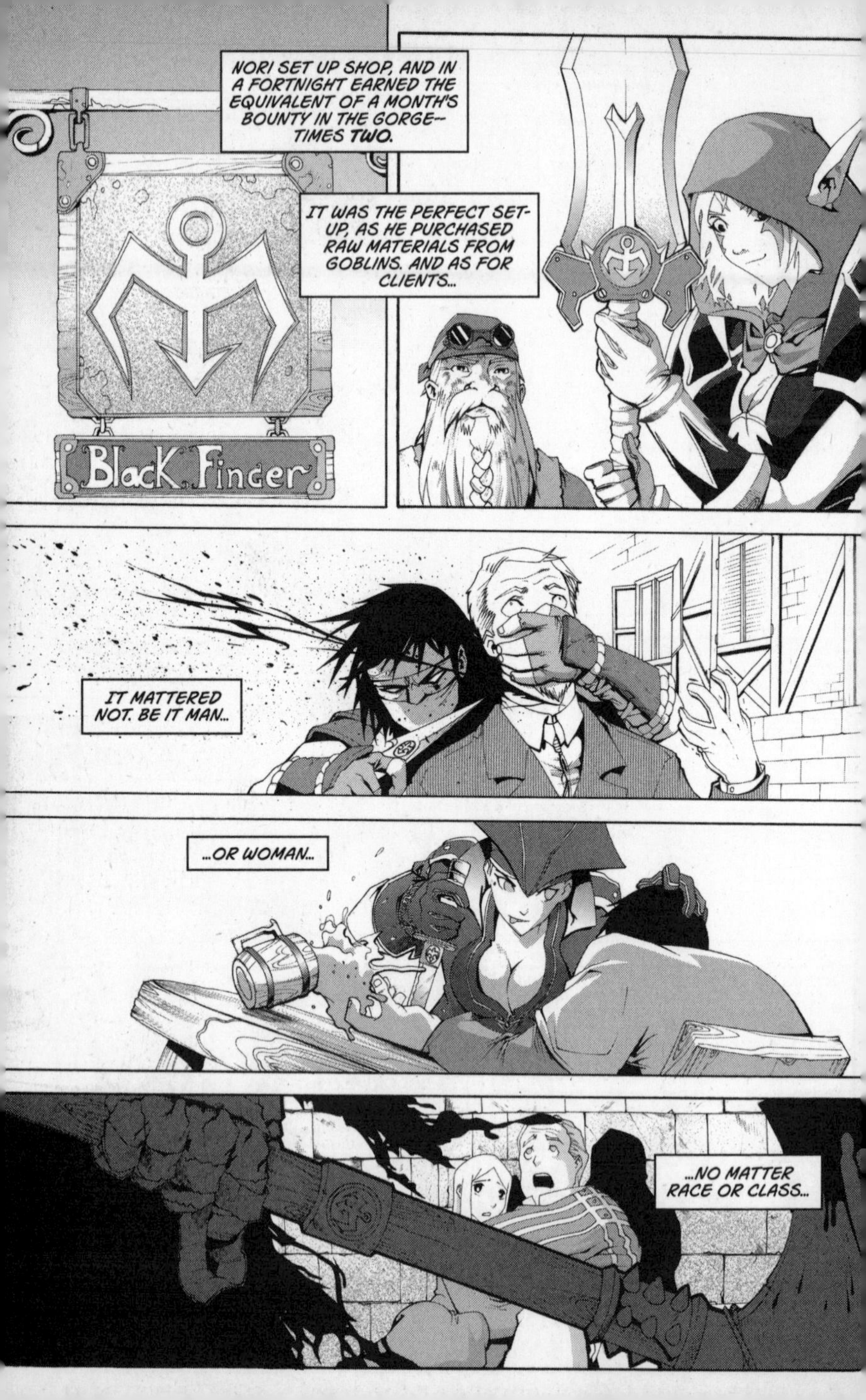
NORI SET UP SHOP, AND IN A FORTNIGHT EARNED THE EQUIVALENT OF A MONTH'S BOUNTY IN THE GORGE-- TIMES **TWO**.
Black Finger
IT WAS THE PERFECT SET-UP, AS HE PURCHASED RAW MATERIALS FROM GOBLINS. AND AS FOR CLIENTS...
IT MATTERED NOT. BE IT MAN...
...OR WOMAN...
...NO MATTER RACE OR CLASS...

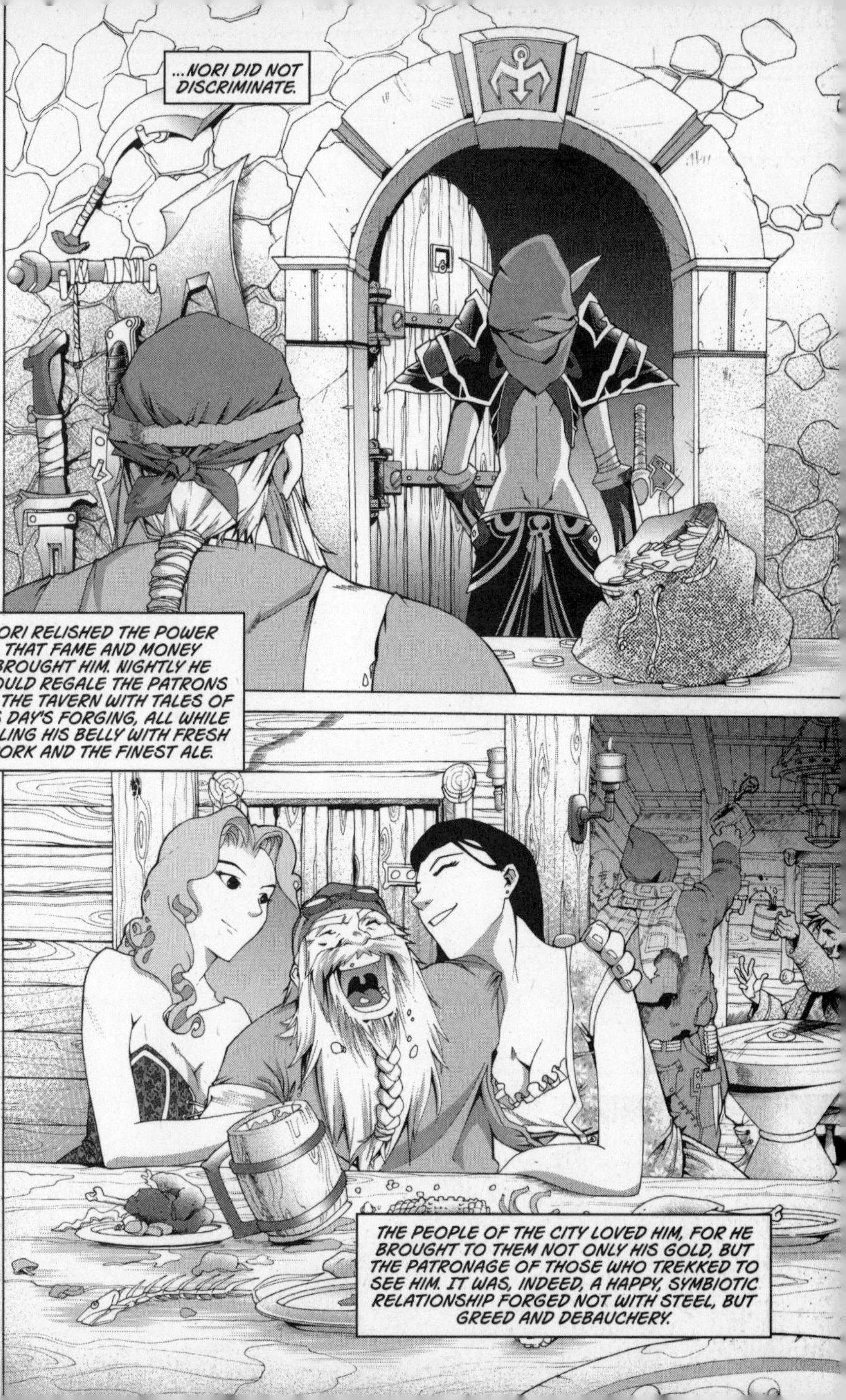
...NORI DID NOT DISCRIMINATE.
NORI RELISHED THE POWER THAT FAME AND MONEY BROUGHT HIM. NIGHTLY HE OULD REGALE THE PATRONS F THE TAVERN WITH TALES OF IS DAY'S FORGING, ALL WHILE ILLING HIS BELLY WITH FRESH PORK AND THE FINEST ALE.
THE PEOPLE OF THE CITY LOVED HIM, FOR HE BROUGHT TO THEM NOT ONLY HIS GOLD, BUT THE PATRONAGE OF THOSE WHO TREKKED TO SEE HIM. IT WAS, INDEED, A HAPPY, SYMBIOTIC RELATIONSHIP FORGED NOT WITH STEEL, BUT GREED AND DEBAUCHERY.

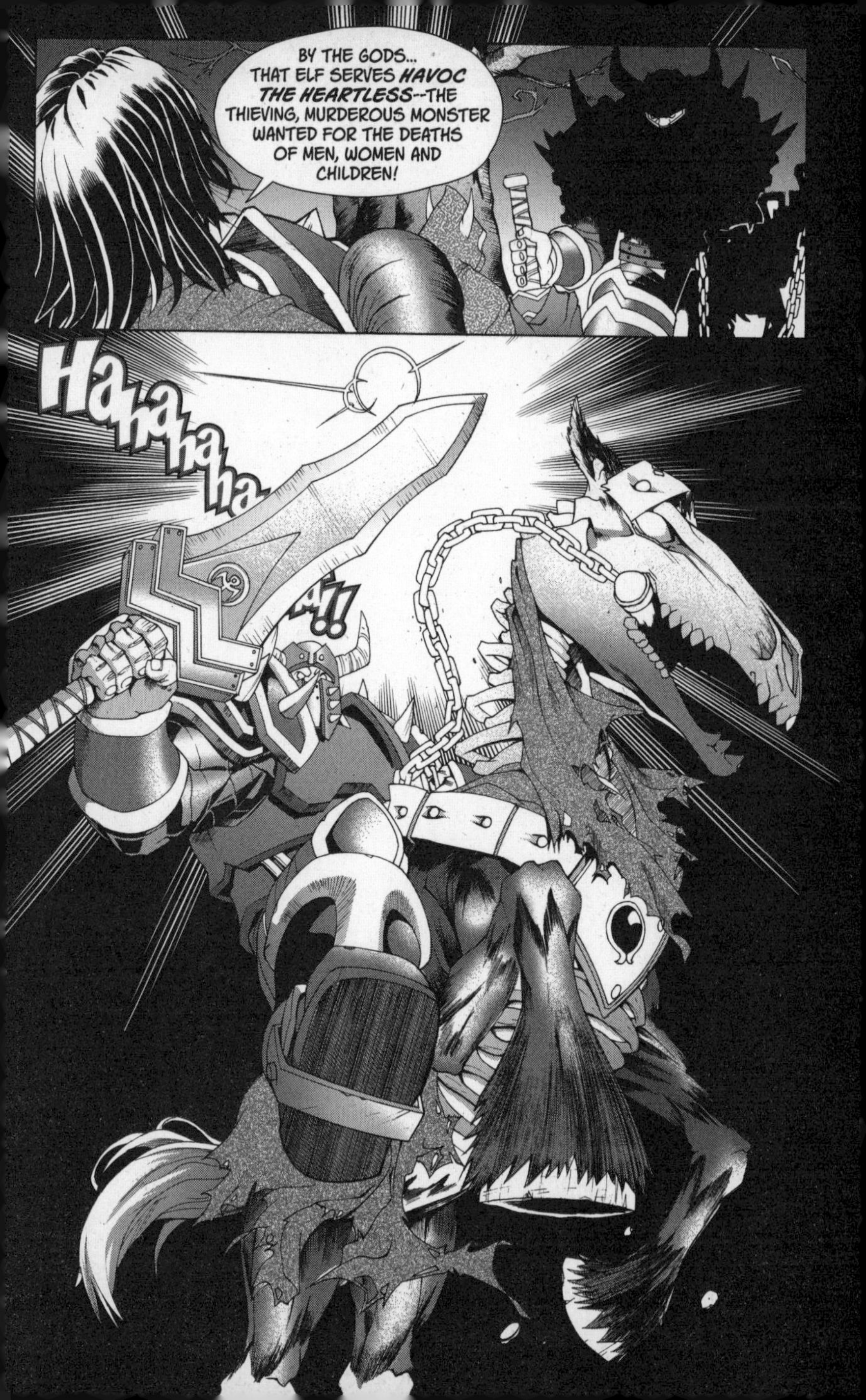
BY THE GODS... THAT ELF SERVES *HAVOC THE HEARTLESS*--THE THIEVING, MURDEROUS MONSTER WANTED FOR THE DEATHS OF MEN, WOMEN AND CHILDREN!
Hahahaha
a!!

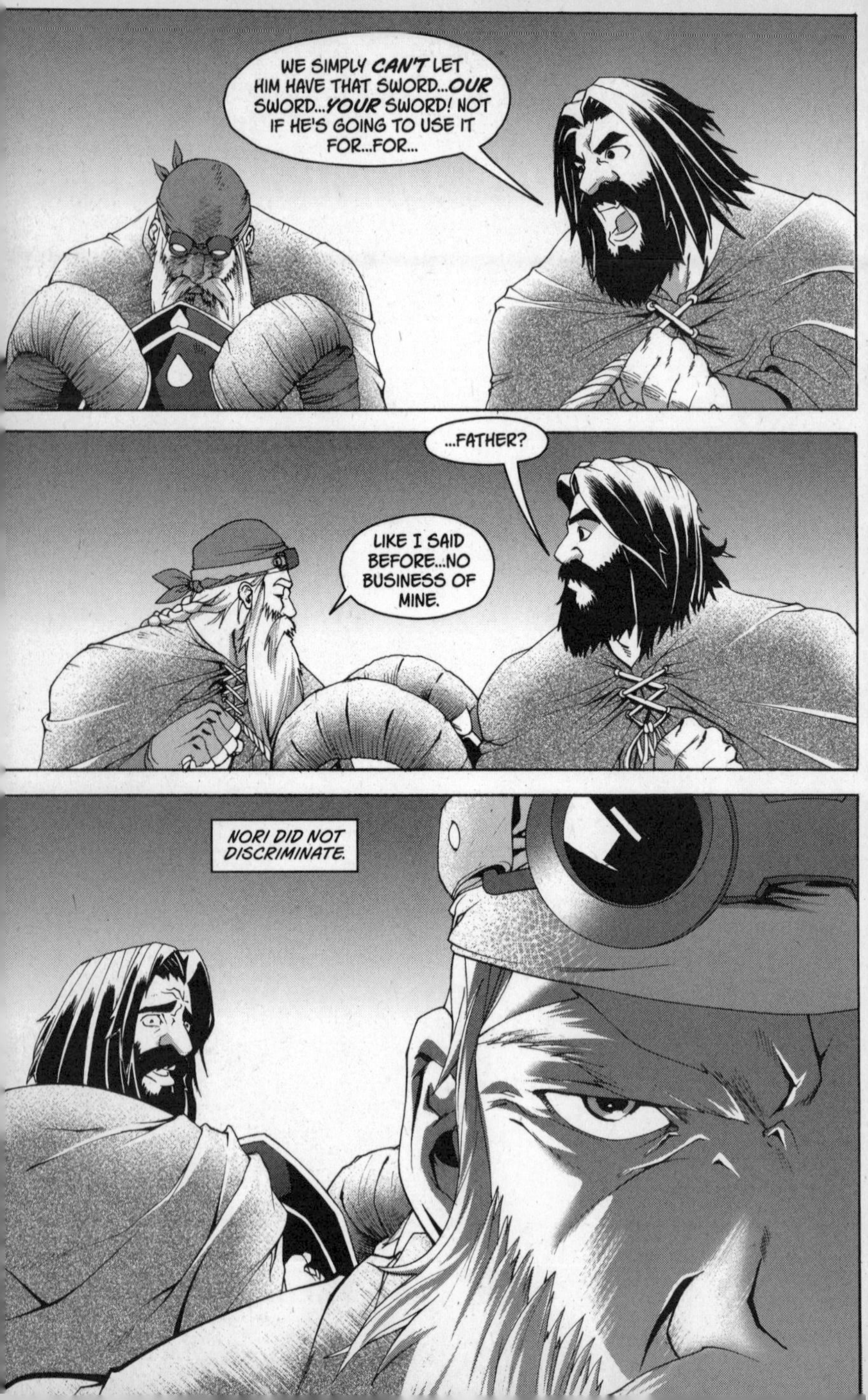
WE SIMPLY **CAN'T** LET HIM HAVE THAT SWORD...**OUR** SWORD...**YOUR** SWORD! NOT IF HE'S GOING TO USE IT FOR...FOR...
...FATHER?
LIKE I SAID BEFORE...NO BUSINESS OF MINE.
NORI DID NOT DISCRIMINATE.

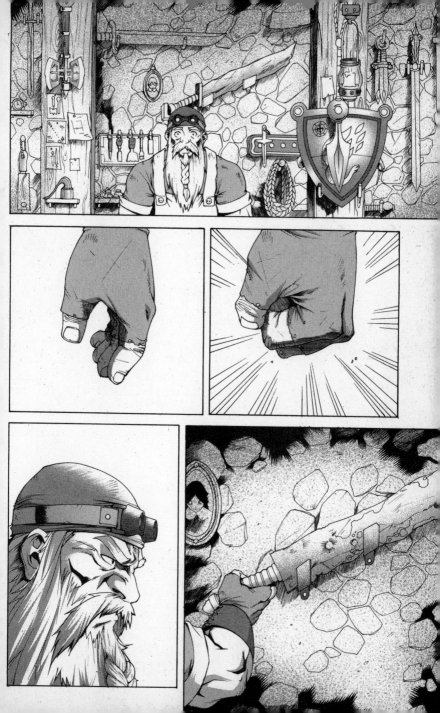

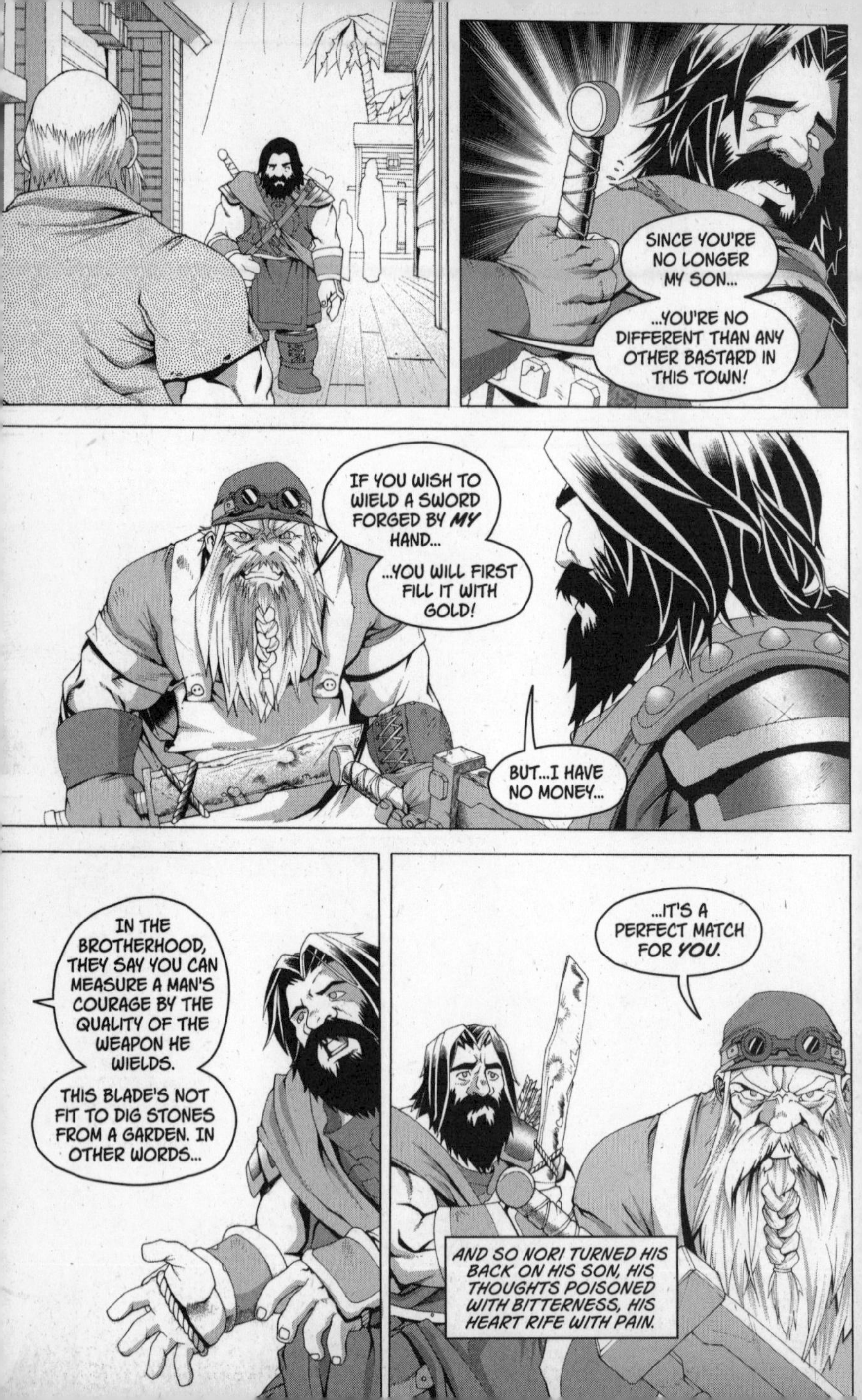
SINCE YOU'RE NO LONGER MY SON...
...YOU'RE NO DIFFERENT THAN ANY OTHER BASTARD IN THIS TOWN!
IF YOU WISH TO WIELD A SWORD FORGED BY *MY* HAND...
...YOU WILL FIRST FILL IT WITH GOLD!
BUT...I HAVE NO MONEY...
IN THE BROTHERHOOD, THEY SAY YOU CAN MEASURE A MAN'S COURAGE BY THE QUALITY OF THE WEAPON HE WIELDS.
THIS BLADE'S NOT FIT TO DIG STONES FROM A GARDEN. IN OTHER WORDS...
...IT'S A PERFECT MATCH FOR *YOU*.
AND SO NORI TURNED HIS BACK ON HIS SON, HIS THOUGHTS POISONED WITH BITTERNESS, HIS HEART RIFE WITH PAIN.

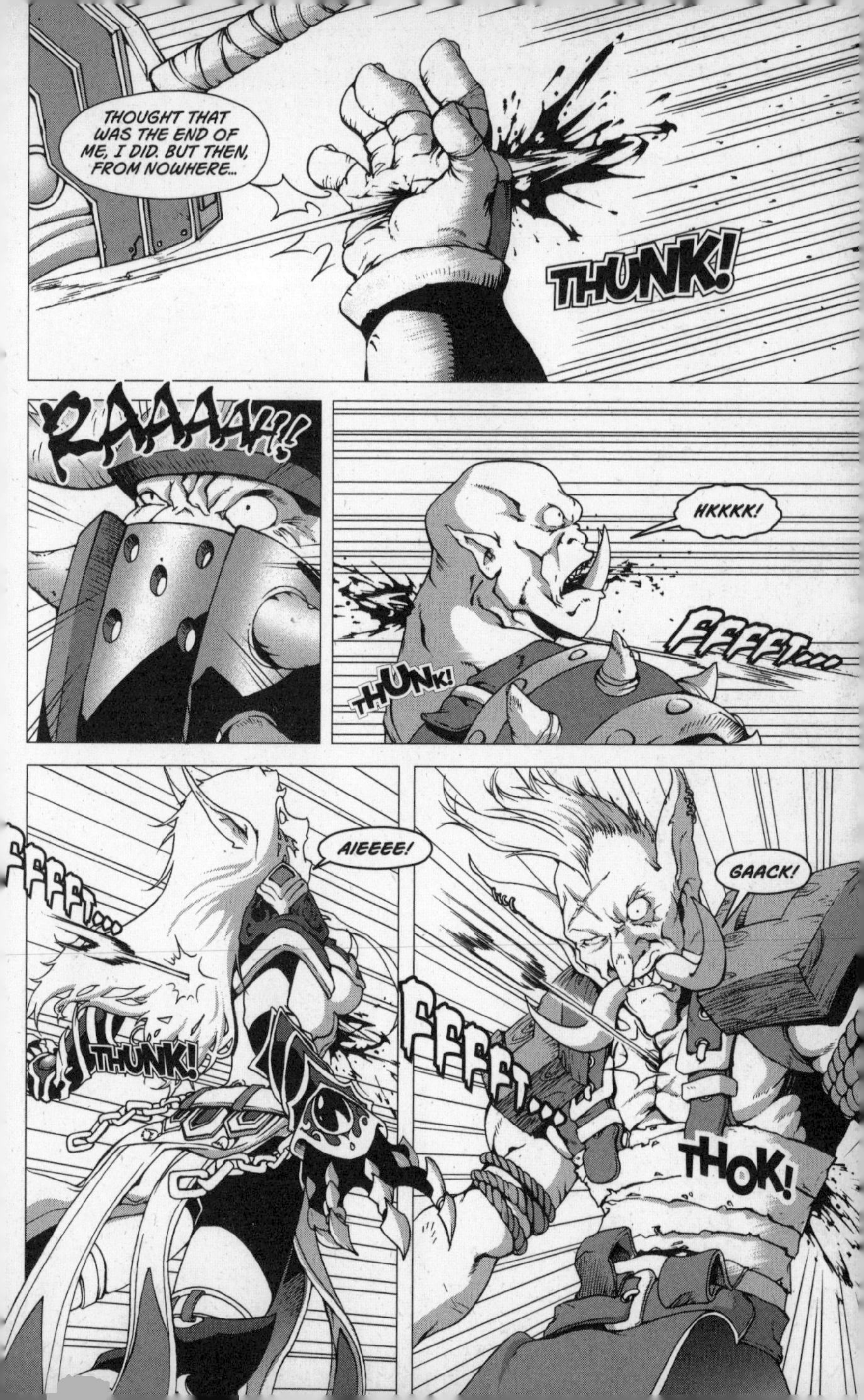
THOUGHT THAT WAS THE END OF ME, I DID. BUT THEN, FROM NOWHERE...
THUNK!
RAAAAH!!
HKKKK!
FFFFT...
THUNK!
FFFFT...
AIEEEE!
THUNK!
GAACK!
FFFFT...
THOK!

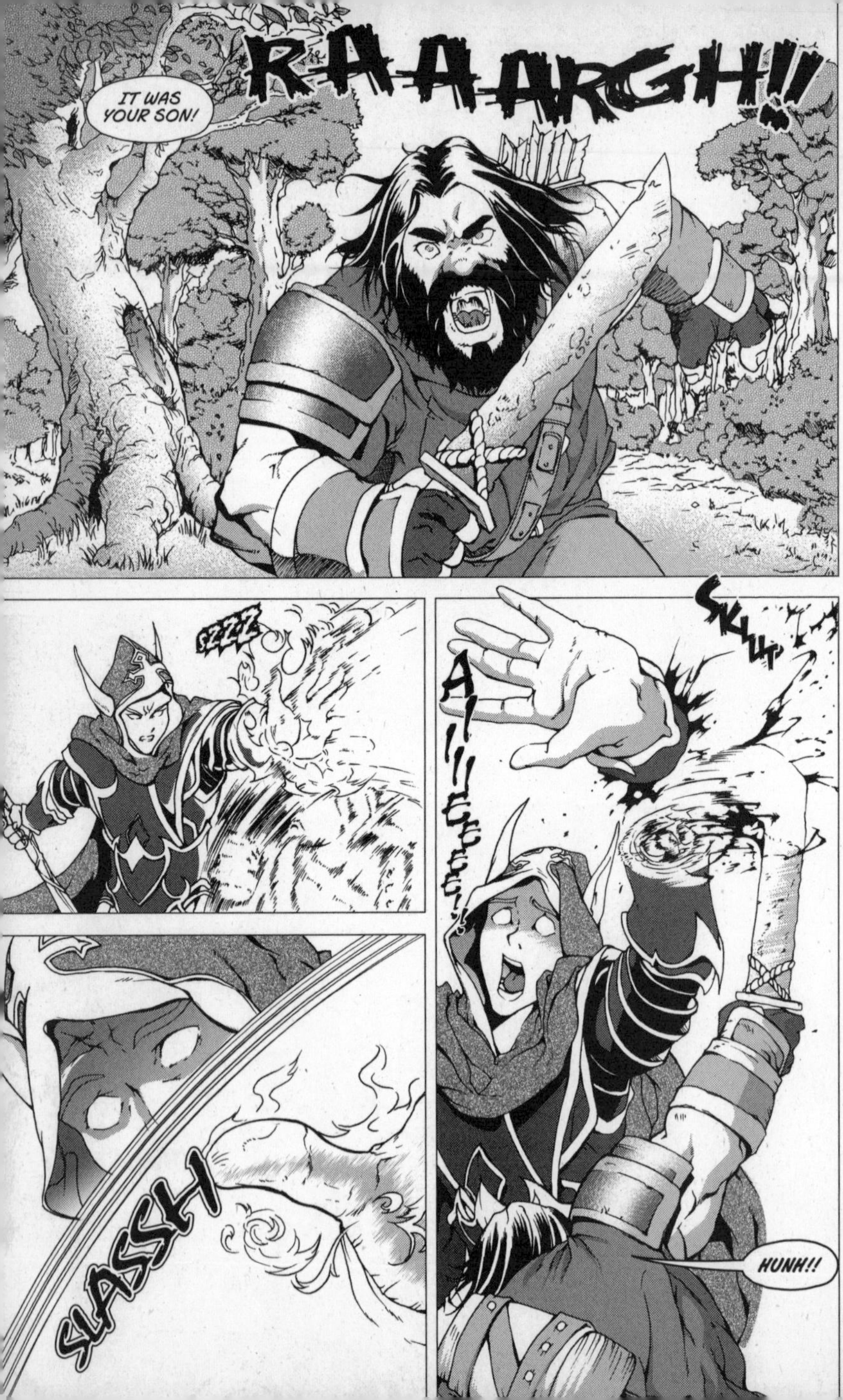
IT WAS YOUR SON!
RAAAARGH!!
SZZZ
SLASSH
SKLUT
AIIIIEEEEEE!!
HUNH!!

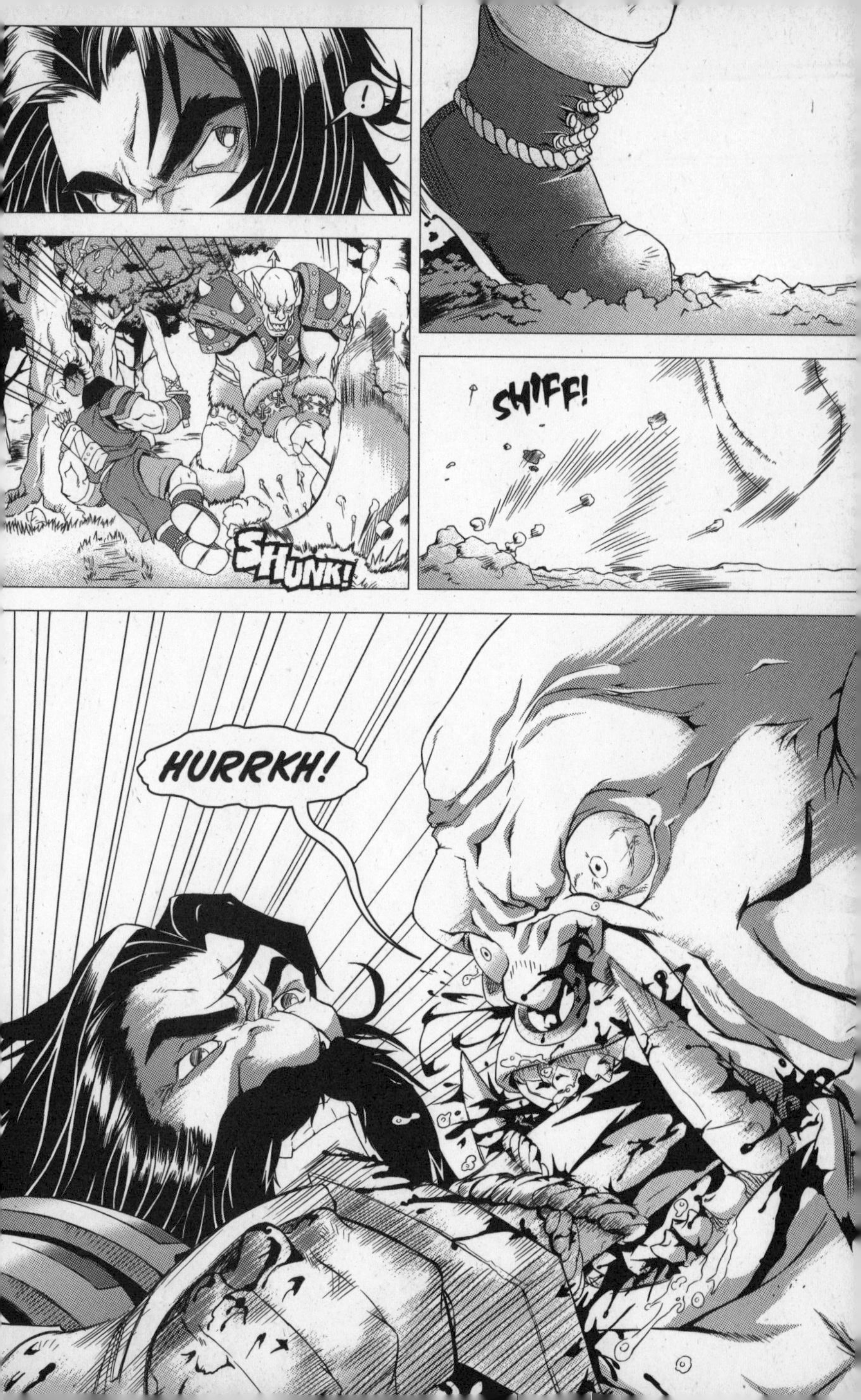
!
SHUNK!
SHIFF!
HURRKH!

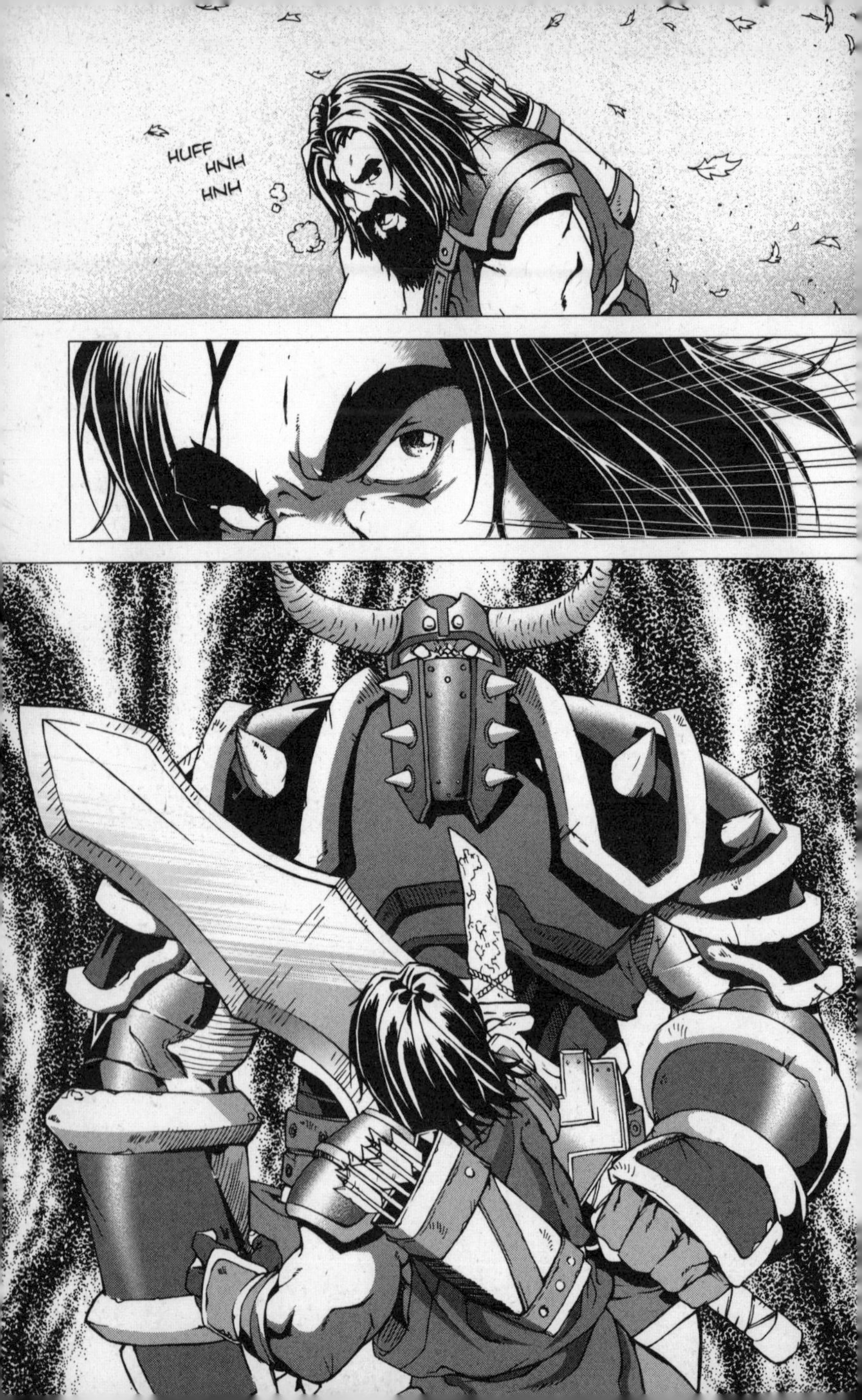
HUFF
HNH
HNH

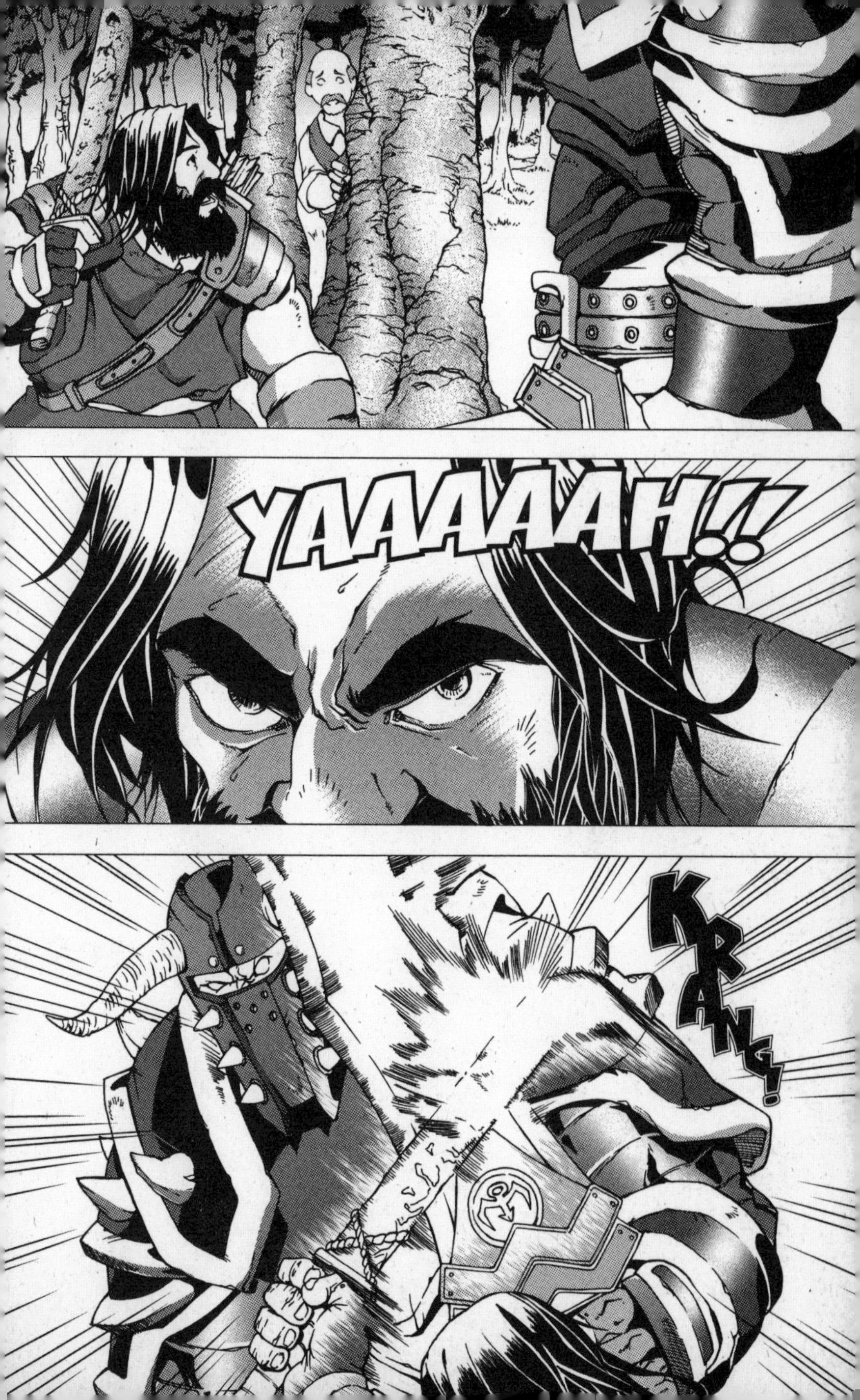
YAAAAAAH!!
KRANG!

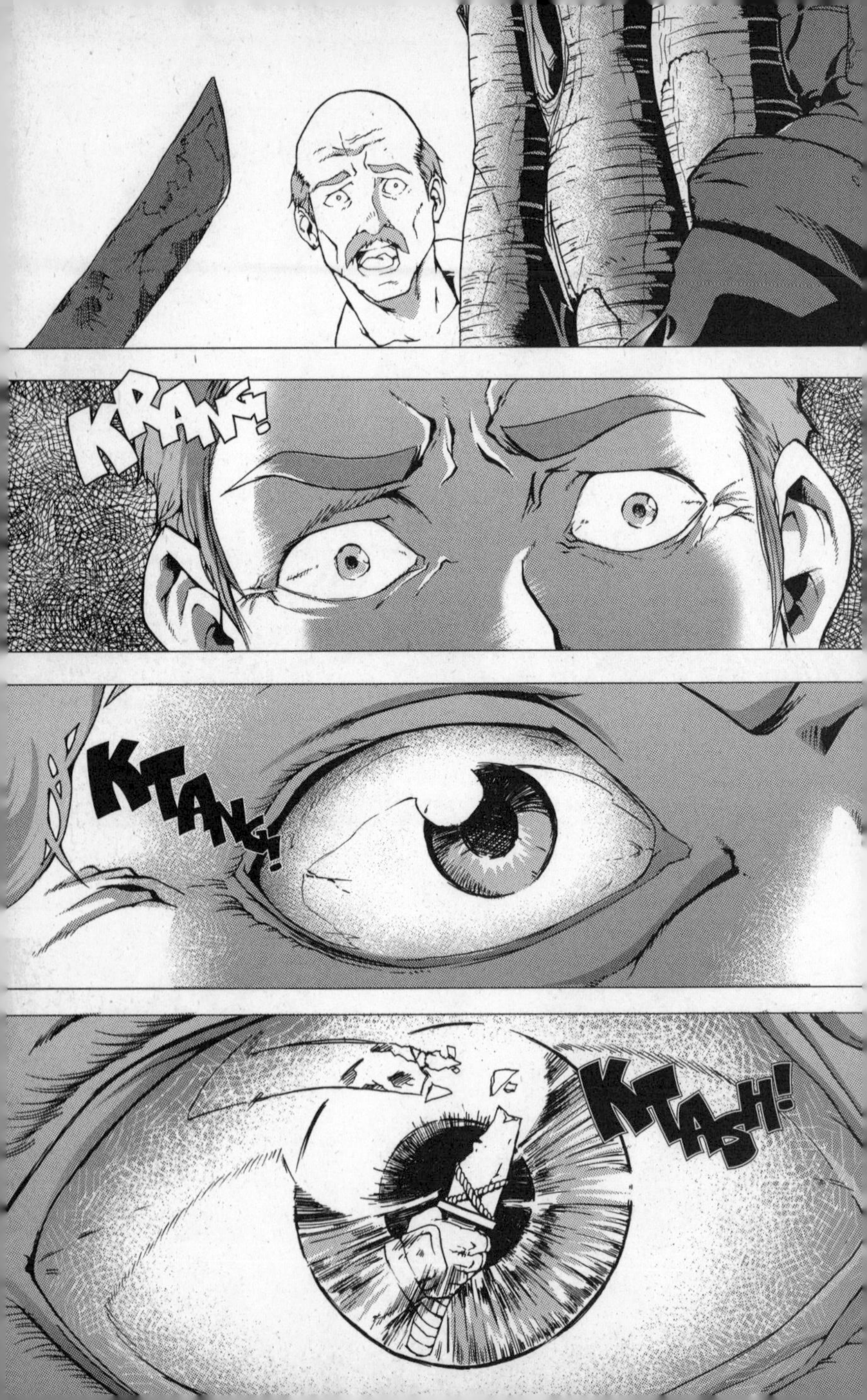
KRANG!
KTANG!
KTASH!

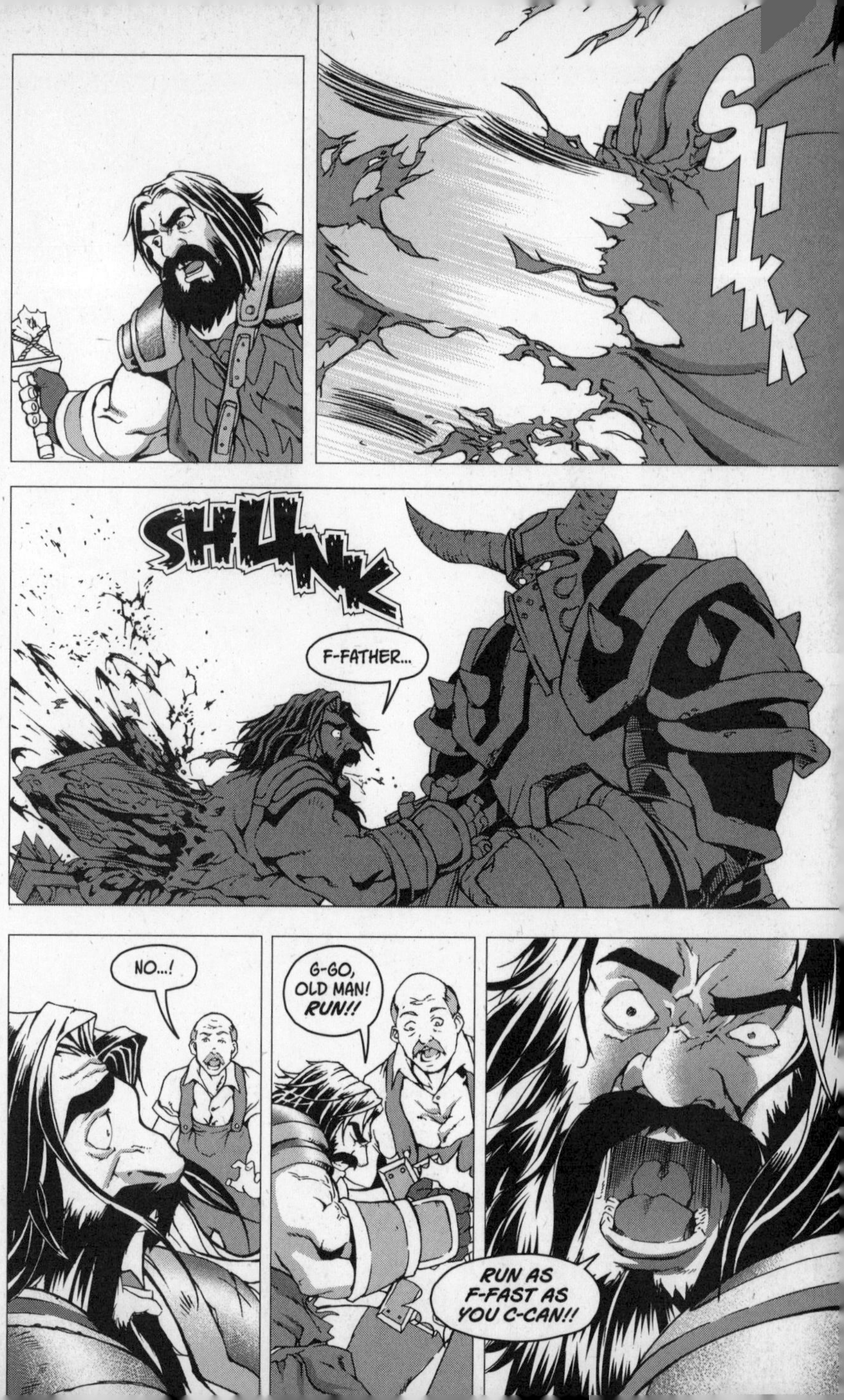
SHUKK
SHUNK
F-FATHER...
NO...!
G-GO, OLD MAN! RUN!!
RUN AS F-FAST AS YOU C-CAN!!

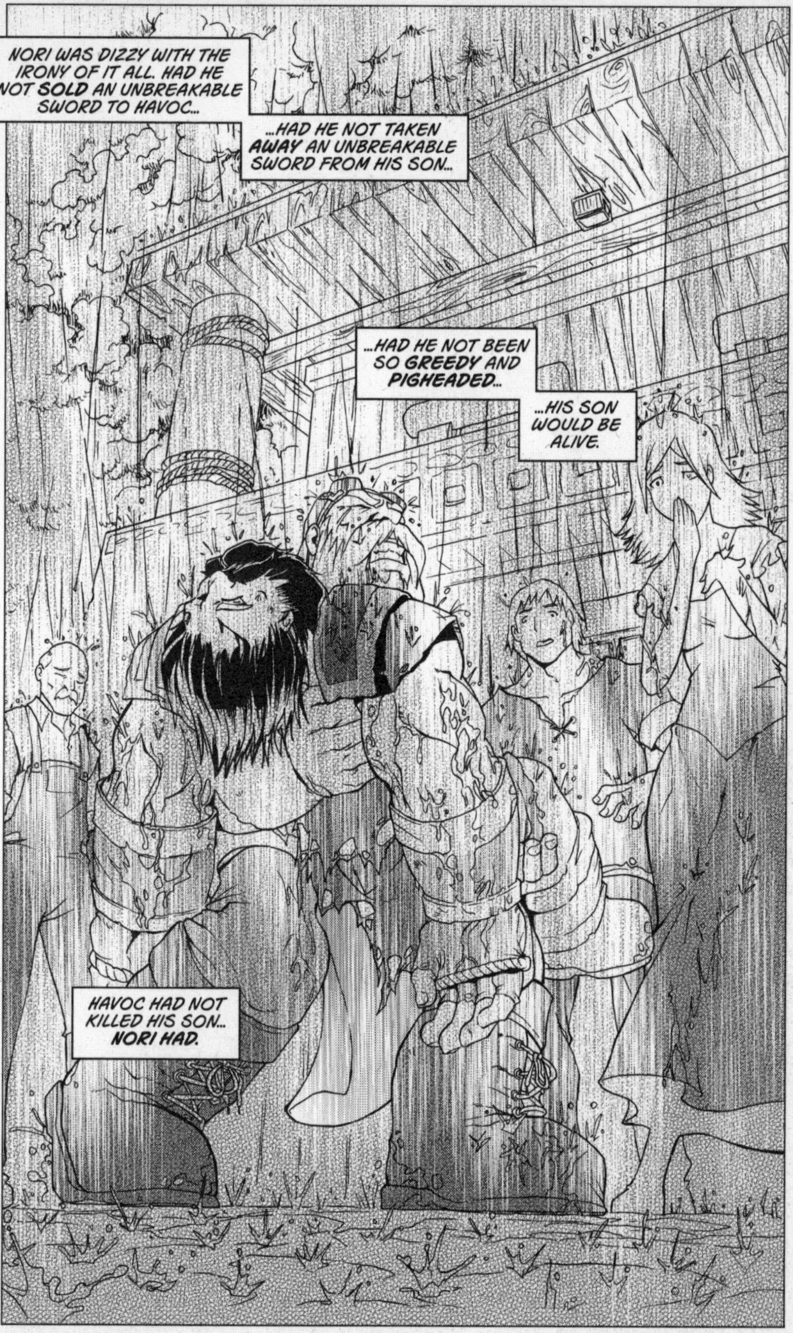
NORI WAS DIZZY WITH THE IRONY OF IT ALL. HAD HE NOT **SOLD** AN UNBREAKABLE SWORD TO HAVOC...
...HAD HE NOT TAKEN **AWAY** AN UNBREAKABLE SWORD FROM HIS SON...
...HAD HE NOT BEEN SO **GREEDY** AND **PIGHEADED**...
...HIS SON WOULD BE ALIVE.
HAVOC HAD NOT KILLED HIS SON... **NORI HAD.**

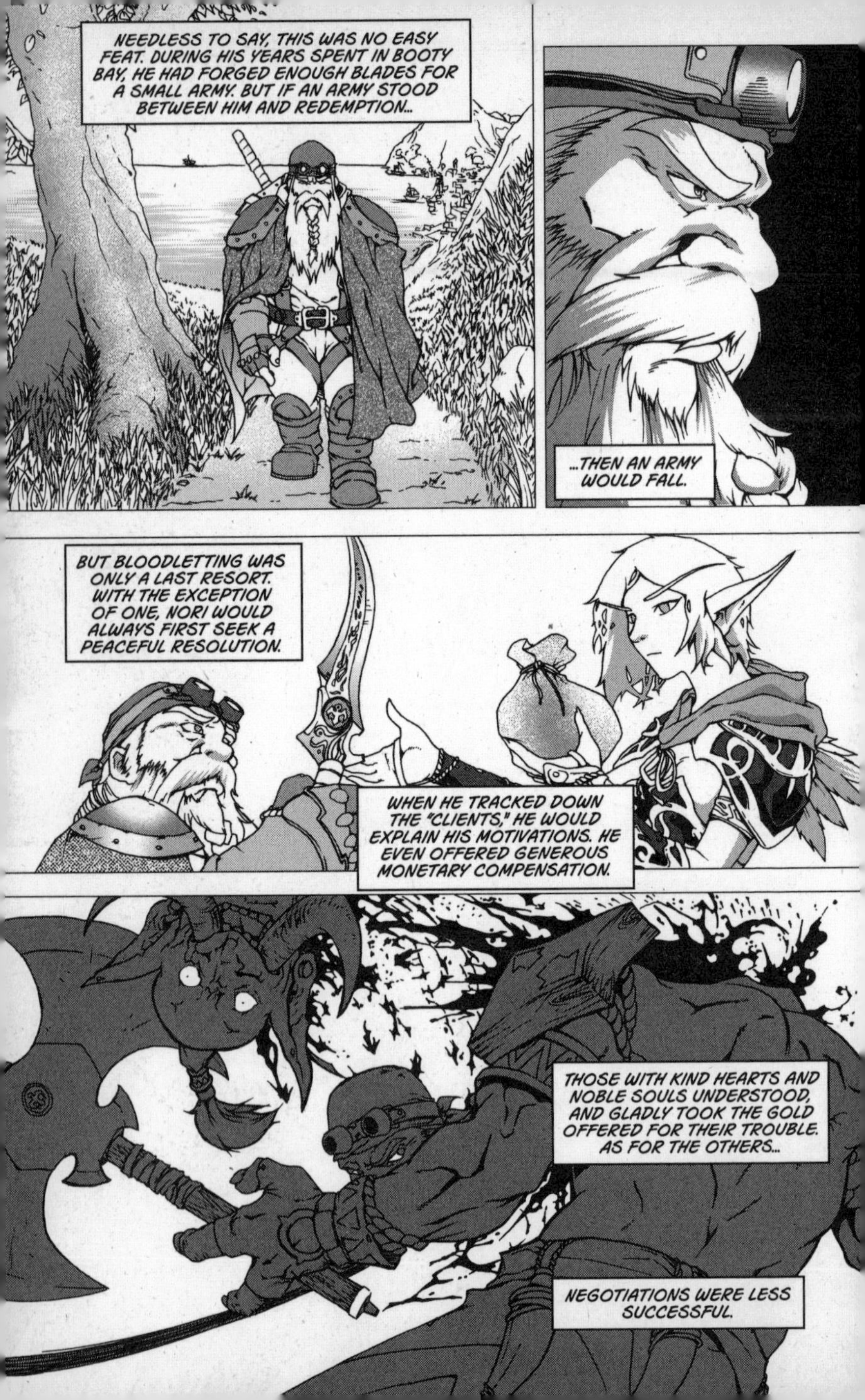
NEEDLESS TO SAY, THIS WAS NO EASY FEAT. DURING HIS YEARS SPENT IN BOOTY BAY, HE HAD FORGED ENOUGH BLADES FOR A SMALL ARMY. BUT IF AN ARMY STOOD BETWEEN HIM AND REDEMPTION...
...THEN AN ARMY WOULD FALL.
BUT BLOODLETTING WAS ONLY A LAST RESORT. WITH THE EXCEPTION OF ONE, NORI WOULD ALWAYS FIRST SEEK A PEACEFUL RESOLUTION.
WHEN HE TRACKED DOWN THE "CLIENTS," HE WOULD EXPLAIN HIS MOTIVATIONS. HE EVEN OFFERED GENEROUS MONETARY COMPENSATION.
THOSE WITH KIND HEARTS AND NOBLE SOULS UNDERSTOOD, AND GLADLY TOOK THE GOLD OFFERED FOR THEIR TROUBLE. AS FOR THE OTHERS...
NEGOTIATIONS WERE LESS SUCCESSFUL.

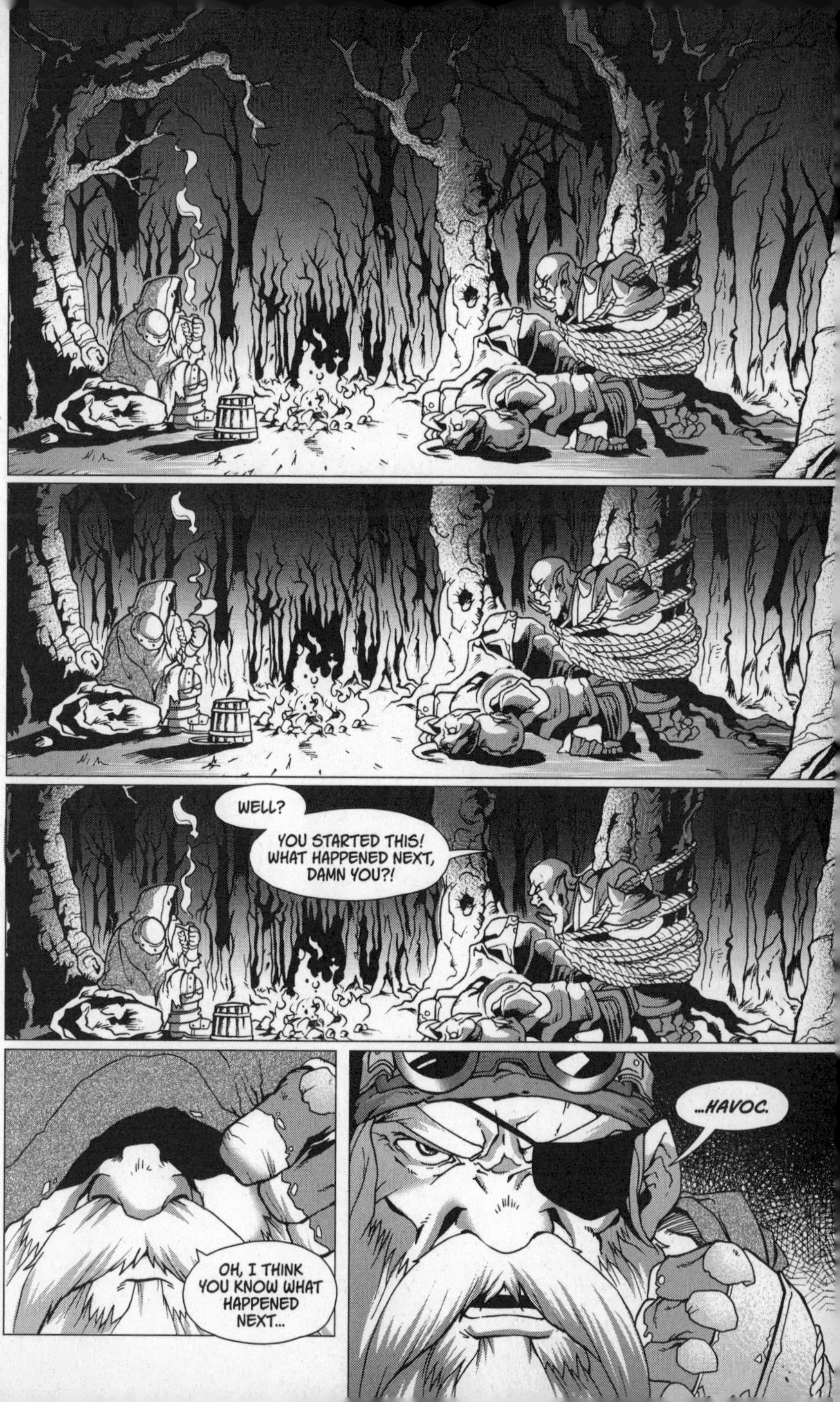
WELL?
YOU STARTED THIS! WHAT HAPPENED NEXT, DAMN YOU?!
OH, I THINK YOU KNOW WHAT HAPPENED NEXT...
...HAVOC.

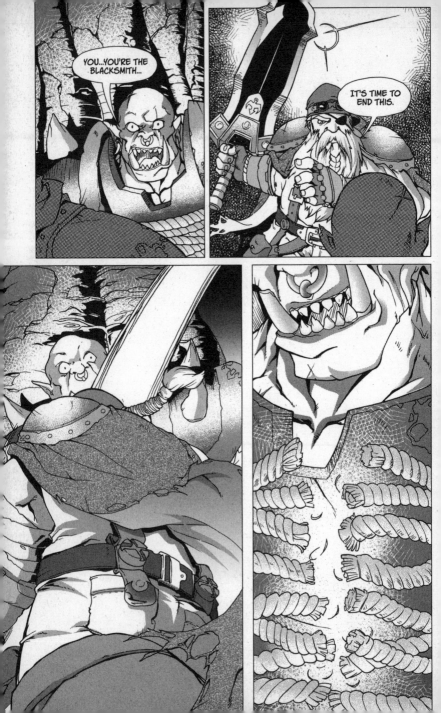

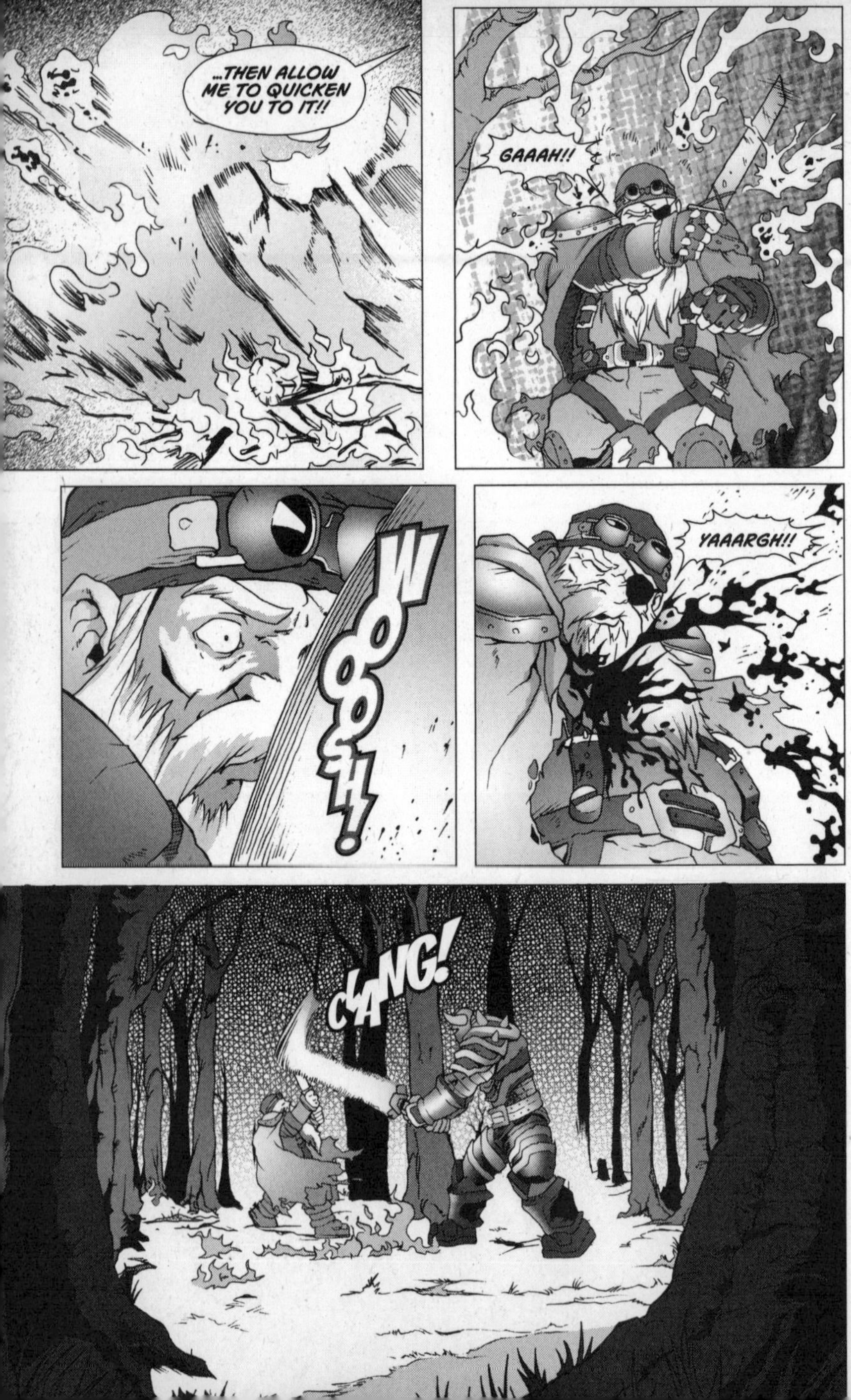
...THEN ALLOW ME TO QUICKEN YOU TO IT!!
GAAAH!!
WOOOOSH!
YAAARGH!!
CLANG!

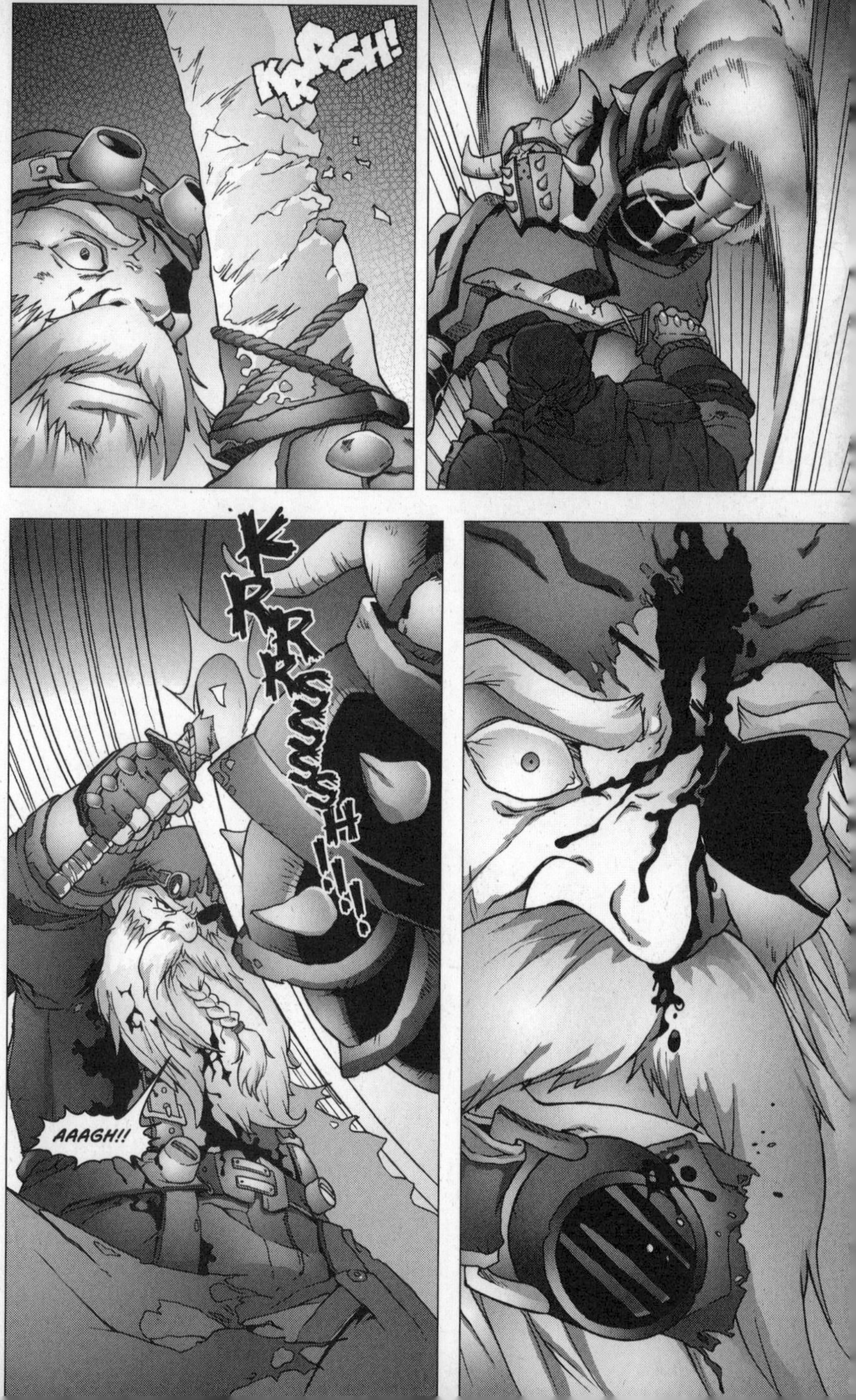
KRRSH!
KRRRSSSHHH!!!
AAAGH!!

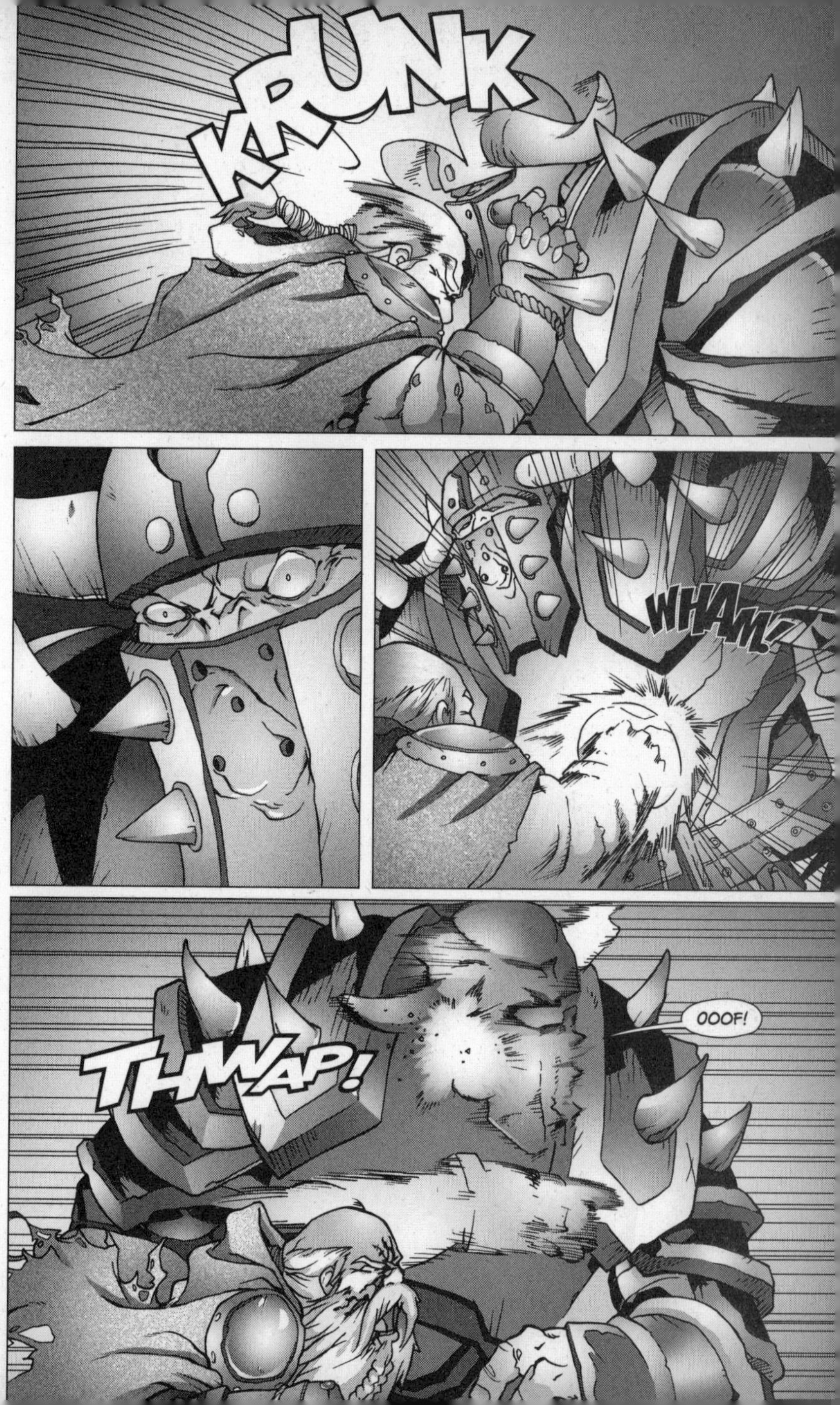
KRUNK
WHAM!
THWAP!
OOOF!

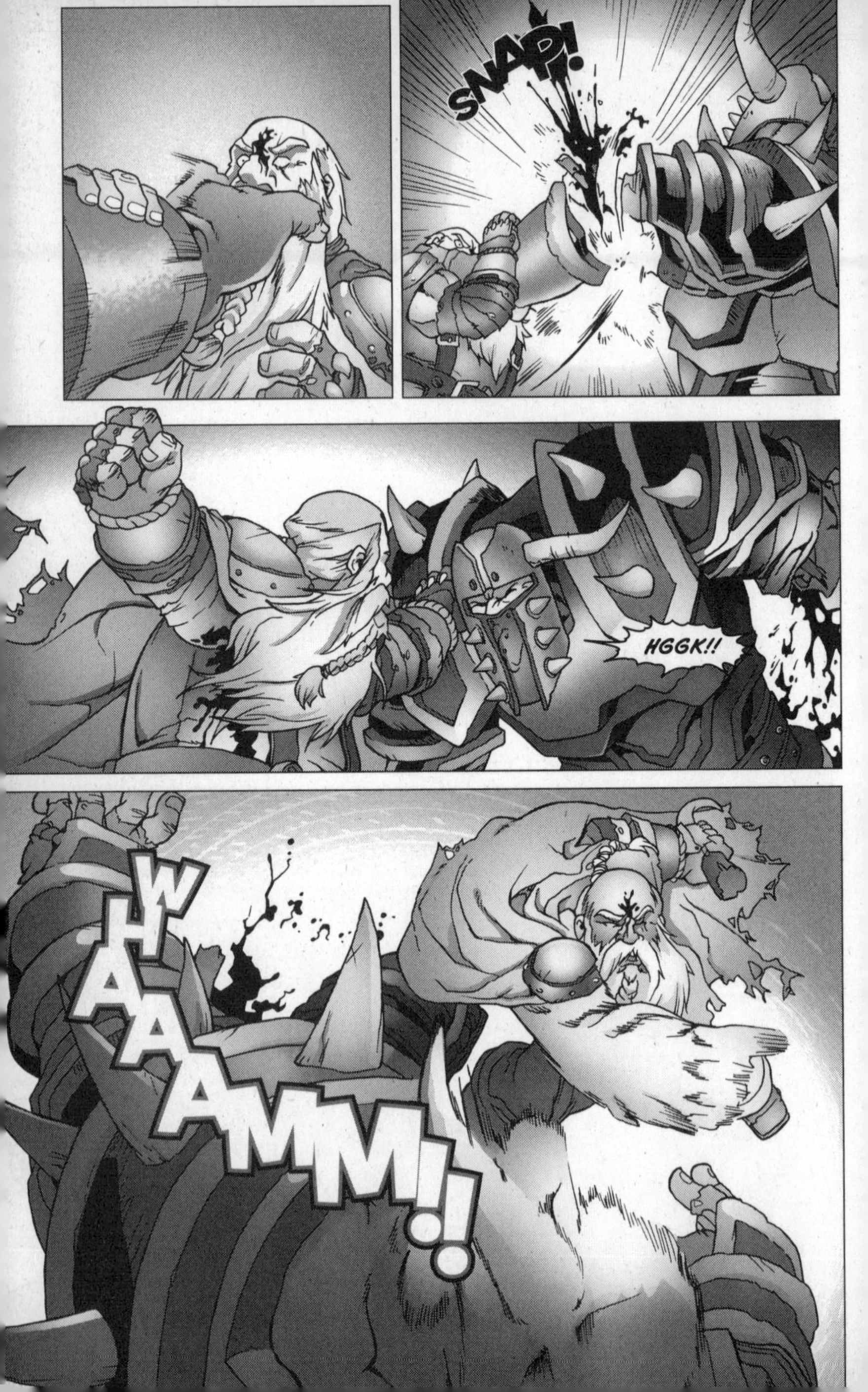
SNAP!
HGGK!!
WHAAAMMM!!

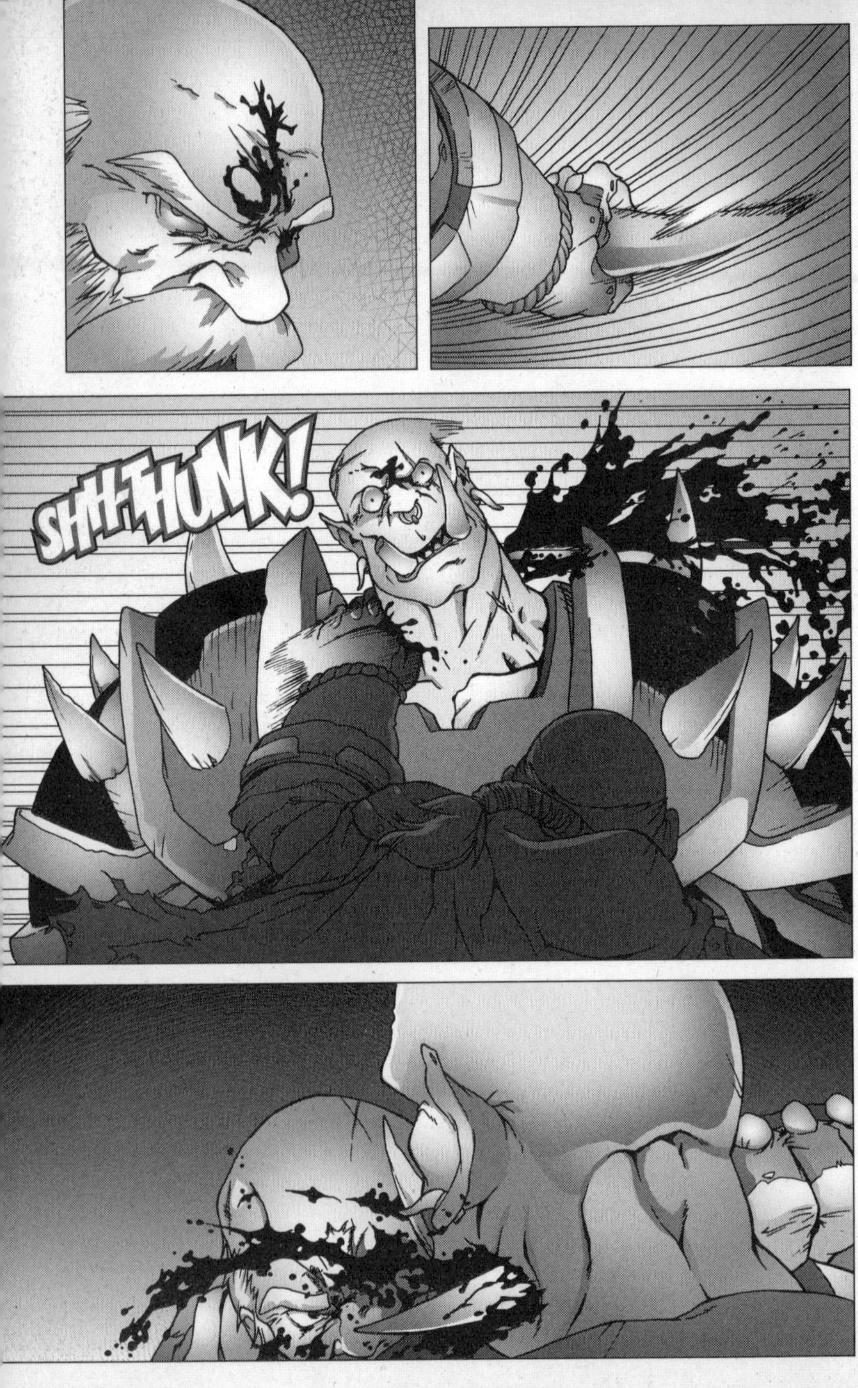
SHHHTHUNK!

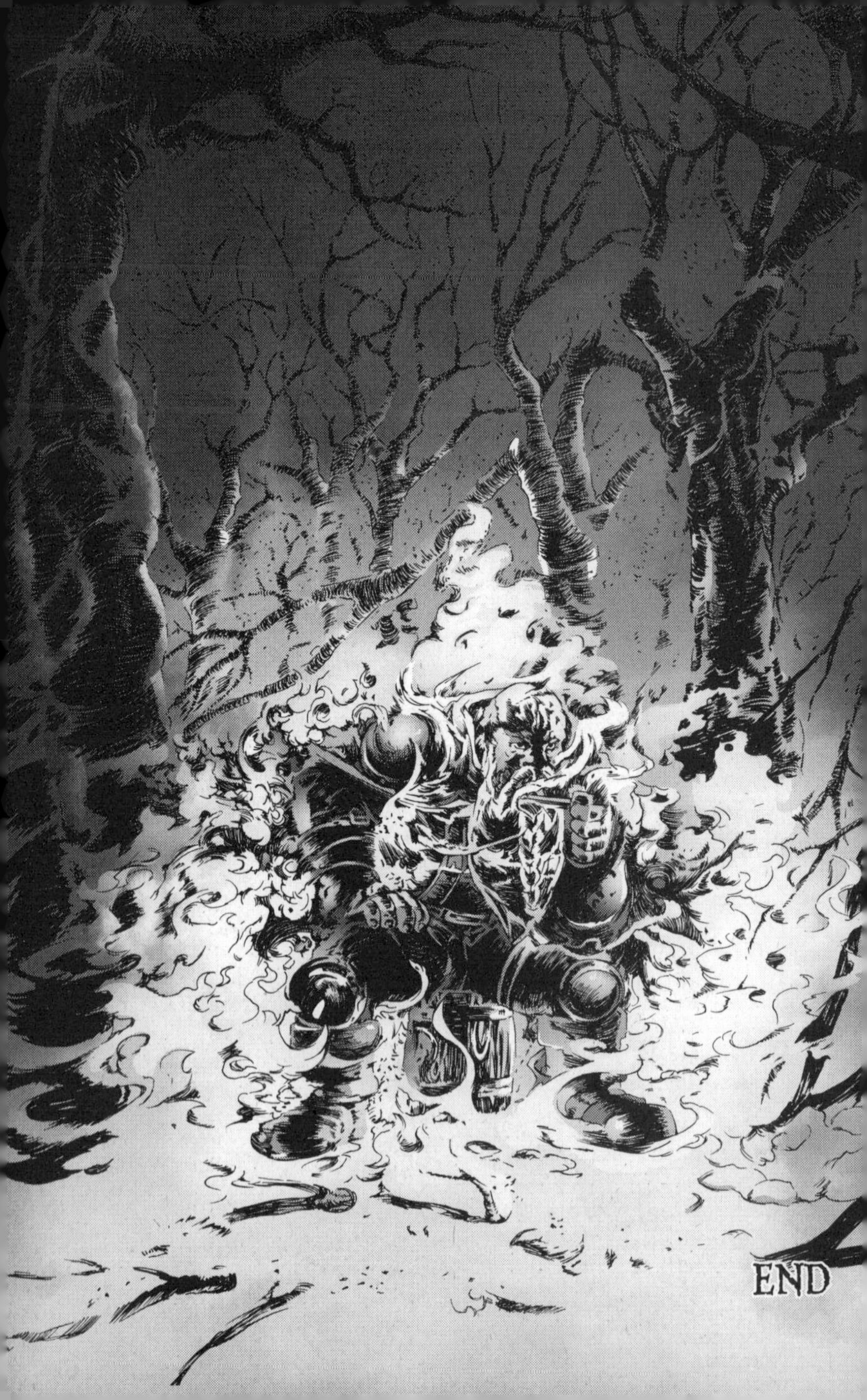
END

ABOUT THE WRITERS

RICHARD A. KNAAK

Richard A. Knaak is the New York Times bestselling fantasy author of 27 novels and over a dozen short pieces, including *The Legend of Huma, Night of Blood* for Dragonlance and the *War of the Ancients* trilogy for Warcraft. In addition to the TOKYOPOP series *Warcraft: The Sunwell Trilogy*, he is the author of its forthcoming sequel trilogy, *Warcraft: Dragons of Outland*. To find out more about Richard's projects, visit his website at www.sff.net/people/knaak.

DAN JOLLEY

Dan Jolley is the author of several books for TOKYOPOP, including the young adult novel, *Alex Unlimited*, and the first trilogy of the bestselling Warriors manga, *Warriors: The Lost Warrior*. Much more information about Dan can be found at his website, www.danjolley.com.

TROY LEWTER

When not donning a loincloth and dreaming of ways to eviscerate innocent farmers, Troy Lewter is a mild-mannered editor at TOKYOPOP. His writing credits include *Mac Afro* and the upcoming TOKYOPOP fantasy manga, *Adomant*, as well as many other unpublished scripts that laugh at him in the dark hours of the night.

MIKE WELLMAN

Mike Wellman was one of the most critically derided bards in all of Andorhal. Despite this, he was able to crank out such cult classics as *Gone South* and *Mac Afro*, as well as his Star Trek short story "The Trial," which appears in TOKYOPOP's *Star Trek: the manga - Kakan ni Shinkou*. Mike is also story consultant and contributing writer for TOKYOPOP's forthcoming *Battlestar Galactica* manga, which will be available in 2009.

ABOUT THE ARTISTS

JAE-HWAN KIM

Born in 1971 in Korea, Jae-Hwan Kim's best-known manga works include *Rainbow*, *Combat Metal HeMoSoo* and *King of Hell*, an ongoing series currently published by TOKYOPOP. Along with being the creator of *War Angels* for TOKYOPOP, Jae-Hwan is also the artist for TOKYOPOP's *Warcraft: The Sunwell Trilogy*, as well as its sequel trilogy, *Warcraft: Dragons of Outland*, which will be available in 2009.

CARLOS OLIVARES

Born in Madrid, Spain, Carlos Olivares published his first comic, *BOUMM*, at age sixteen. He went on to publish many other comics in Spain, as well as a series in France called *Hero Academy*. Along with founding an art school, he has worked in advertising and for Marvel Comics.

NAM KIM

Nam Kim made his manga debut with the TOKYOPOP *Star Trek* short "The Trial," which appeared in TOKYOPOP's *Star Trek: the manga - Kakan ni Shinkou*, and is the creator of TOKYOPOP's upcoming science-fiction/fantasy epic *Adomant*.

MI-YOUNG NO

Born in Korea in 1976, Mi-Young No graduated from Gong-ju College's Department of Manhwa Artistry. In 1998, she entered an amateur manhwa competition, and the attention she got from that catapulted her into the limelight with her first series, *Sal-Le-Top*, which was published in English by TOKYOPOP with the title *Threads of Time*.

Well, here it is! Our first volume of *Warcraft: Legends*, which is the first of fourteen volumes of Warcraft manga that will be coming at you fast and furious over the next three years from TOKYOPOP and Blizzard Entertainment. We hope we've started things off right and that you've enjoyed the four stories in this book. If you did, you're definitely going to want to check out our next volume because, believe us, we're just getting warmed up!

This manga is a product of true collaboration, and it wouldn't exist without the guidance and creativity of the fine folks at Blizzard Entertainment. Particularly, we would like to thank Jason Bischoff, Brian Hsieh, Gina Pippin, Cory Jones, Micky Neilson, and of course, the one-and-only Chris Metzen for their assistance and individual contributions toward making *Warcraft: Legends* a reality and making certain that it pleases the most important people of all: the fans!

Finally, and no less importantly, we'd like to thank all of the writers and artists who devoted their time and talent to this first volume. This extends to not just the guys with their names on the cover, but also the gifted inkers, toners and finishers who helped us in the final stages. Thank you, everyone!

That's it for this volume, but don't forget to pick up the first volume of our other Blizzard series, *StarCraft: Frontline*, available in stores now. (You can check out a preview of it when you turn the page.) And be sure to pick up our second volume of *Warcraft: Legends*, available in October 2008!

Tim Beedle & Troy Lewter
Editors

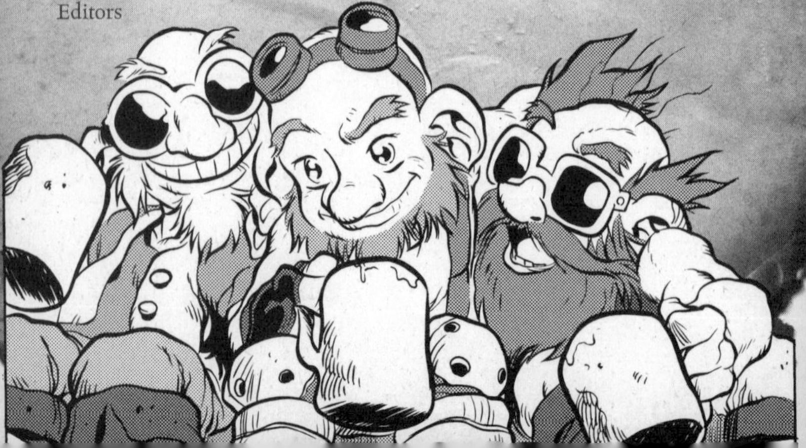

WARCRAFT

LEGENDS

IN THE NEXT VOLUME

You've just read four tales of love, courage, cowardice and revenge...but still you're thirsty for more, eh? Fear not, as this well is brimming with adventures yet to be told...

Trag's journey to Northrend leads to a confrontation with a familiar face...

A tauren shaman's destiny is intertwined with a feisty gnome warrior...

A rebellious orc becomes the unlikely protector of an orphaned draenei girl...

A human girl discovers a young high elf that looks identical to her...

So come back and join us by the fire, as we weave more tales of heroes made, villains defeated...and LEGENDS born.

WARCRAFT: LEGENDS VOLUME 2
COMING OCTOBER 2008

STARCRAFT

FRONTLINE

SNEAK PEEK

WE HOPE THAT YOU ENJOYED READING VOLUME ONE OF *WARCRAFT: LEGENDS!* ARE YOU STILL CRAVING MORE TALES SET IN BLIZZARD'S COMPELLING WORLDS? WELL, LOOK NO FURTHER THAN *STARCRAFT: FRONTLINE!* TOKYOPOP IS PROUD TO PRESENT THIS SERIES OF ANTHOLOGIES BASED ON BLIZZARD'S BESTSELLING STARCRAFT REAL-TIME STRATEGY GAME. TO WHET YOUR APPETITE, HERE'S A SNEAK PEAK AT "WHY WE FIGHT," WHICH APPEARS IN *STARCRAFT: FRONTLINE* VOLUME 1.

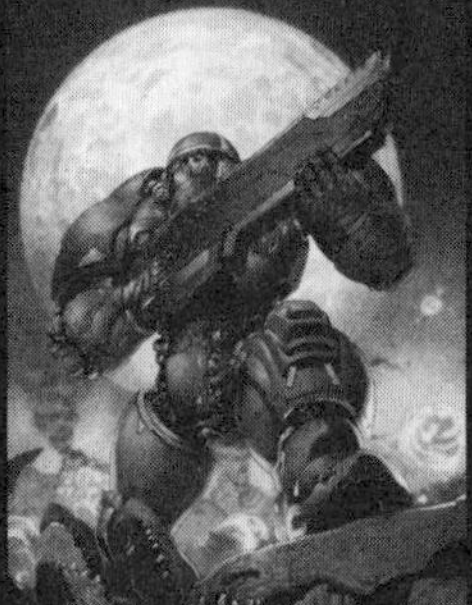

FEATURING AN ACTION-PACKED STORY BY JOSH ELDER AND INCREDIBLY DETAILED ART BY RAMANDA KAMARGA, "WHY WE FIGHT" IS THE PERFECT INTRODUCTION TO THE STARCRAFT UNIVERSE. "WHY WE FIGHT" TELLS THE THREE PARALLEL TALES OF A TERRAN MARINE, A PROTOSS ZEALOT AND A ZERGLING...AND THEIR BRUTAL JOURNEY PROVIDES A MIND-BLOWING LOOK INTO EACH SOCIETY.

STARCRAFT: FRONTLINE VOLUME 1 IS AVAILABLE NOW!

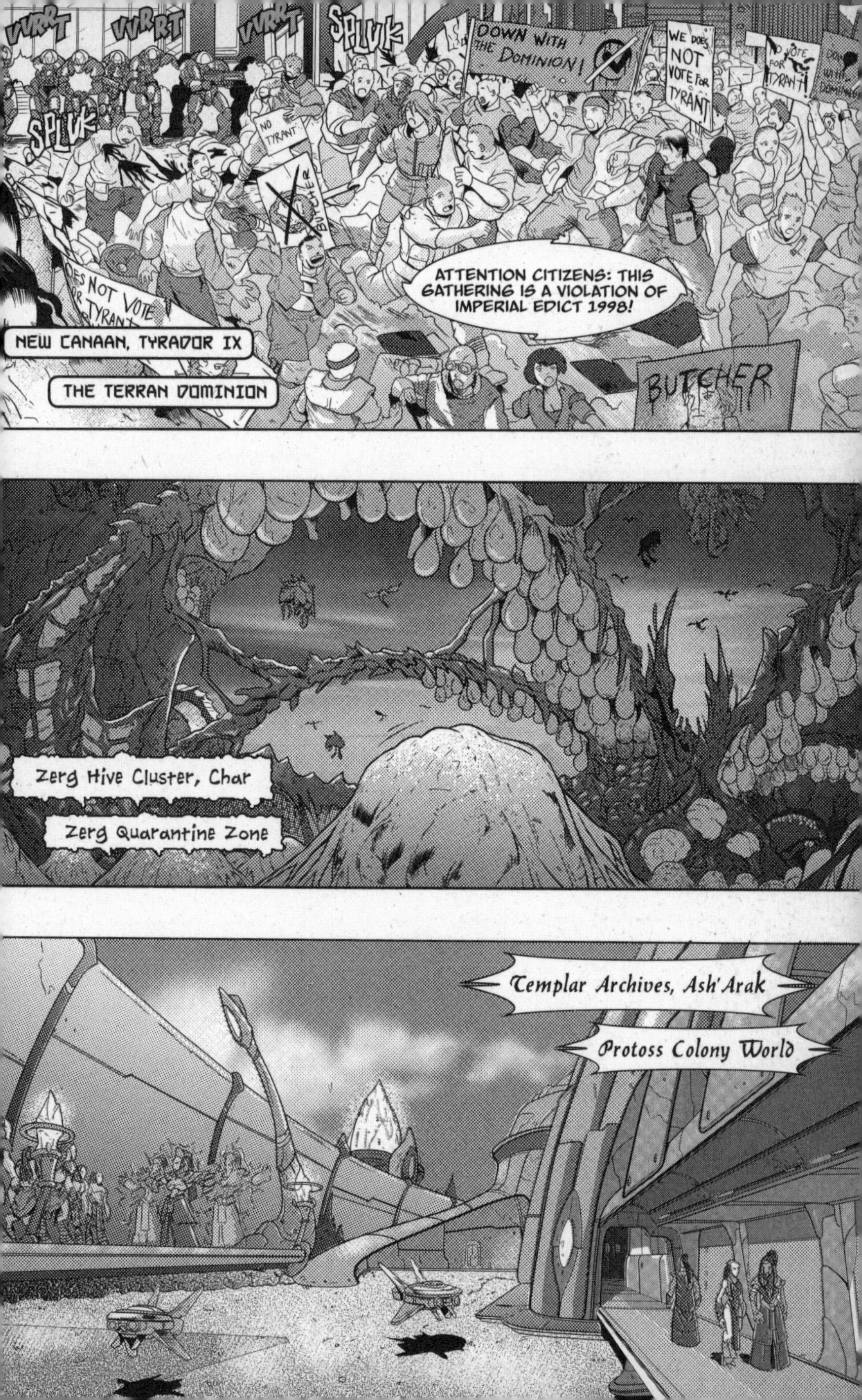
VVRRT
VVRRT
VVRRT
SPLUK
DOWN WITH THE DOMINION!
WE DOES NOT VOTE FOR TYRANT
NO VOTE FOR TYRANT
SPLUK
NO TYRANT
BUTCHER
ATTENTION CITIZENS: THIS GATHERING IS A VIOLATION OF IMPERIAL EDICT 1998!
NEW CANAAN, TYRADOR IX
THE TERRAN DOMINION
BUTCHER
Zerg Hive Cluster, Char
Zerg Quarantine Zone
Templar Archives, Ash'Arak
Protoss Colony World

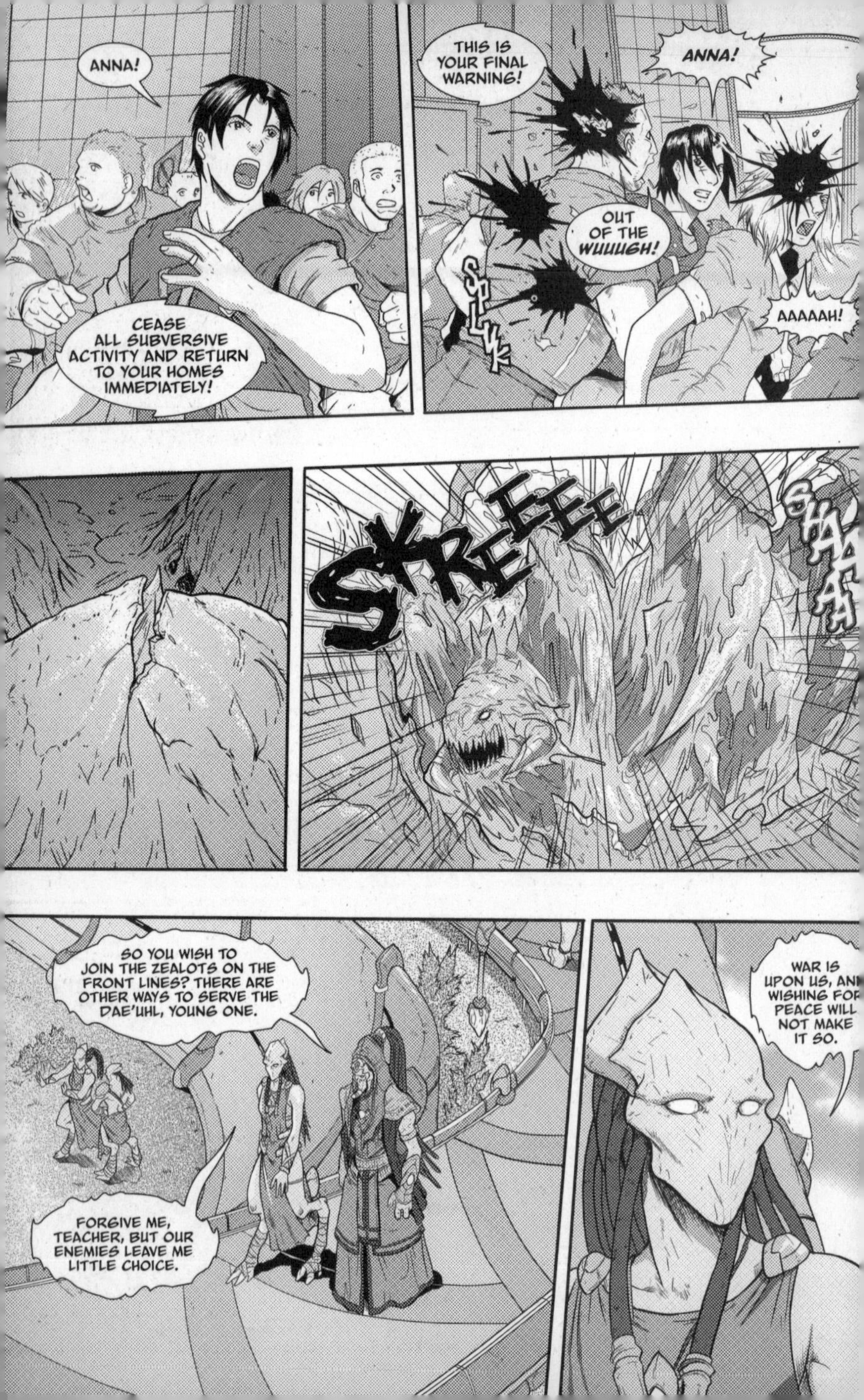
ANNA!
CEASE ALL SUBVERSIVE ACTIVITY AND RETURN TO YOUR HOMES IMMEDIATELY!
THIS IS YOUR FINAL WARNING!
ANNA!
SPLUK
OUT OF THE WUUUGH!
AAAAAH!
SKREEEEE
SO YOU WISH TO JOIN THE ZEALOTS ON THE FRONT LINES? THERE ARE OTHER WAYS TO SERVE THE DAE'UHL, YOUNG ONE.
FORGIVE ME, TEACHER, BUT OUR ENEMIES LEAVE ME LITTLE CHOICE.
WAR IS UPON US, AN WISHING FO PEACE WILL NOT MAKE IT SO.

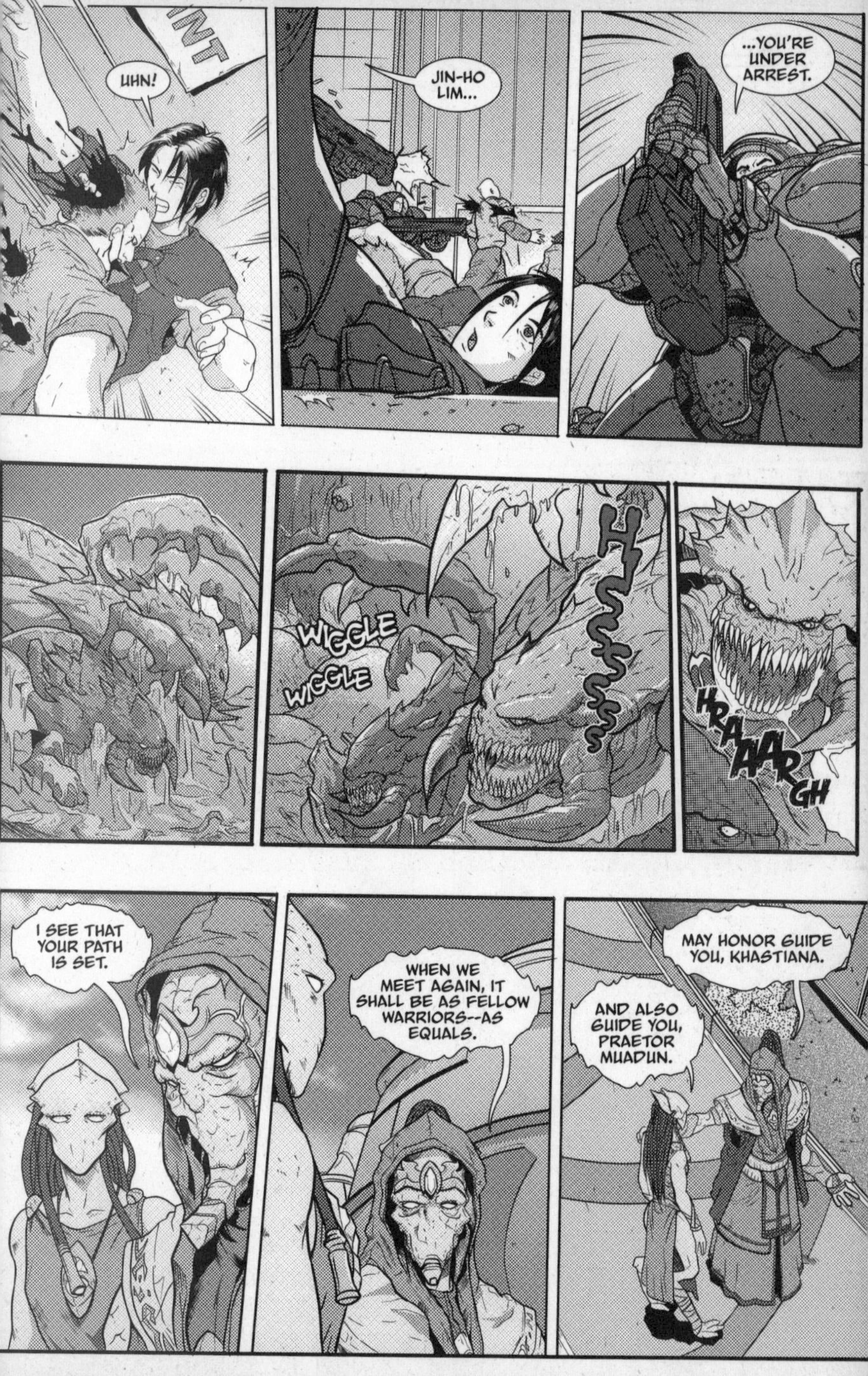
UHN!
JIN-HO LIM...
...YOU'RE UNDER ARREST.
WIGGLE
WIGGLE
HRAAAARGH
I SEE THAT YOUR PATH IS SET.
WHEN WE MEET AGAIN, IT SHALL BE AS FELLOW WARRIORS--AS EQUALS.
MAY HONOR GUIDE YOU, KHASTIANA.
AND ALSO GUIDE YOU, PRAETOR MUADUN.

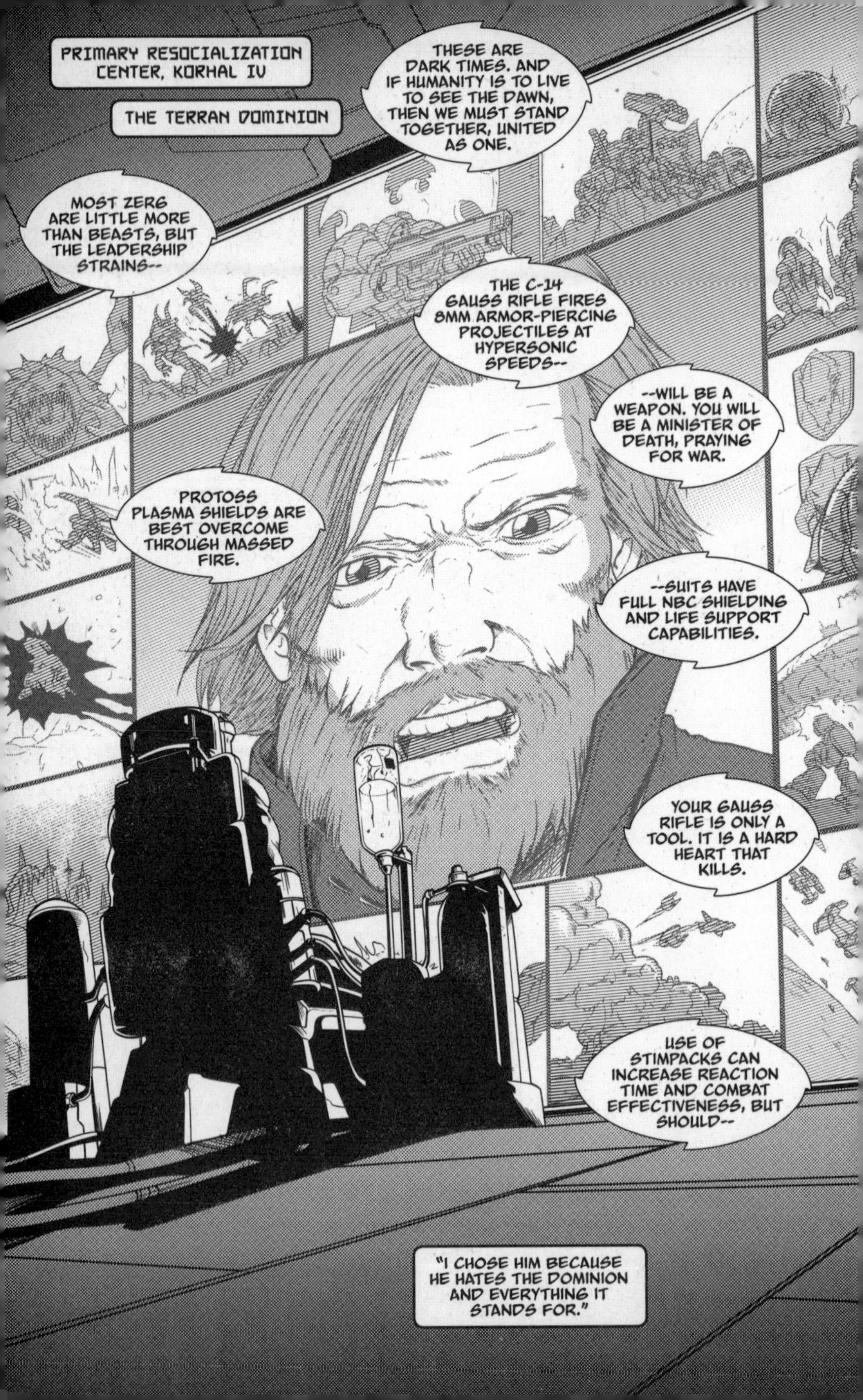
PRIMARY RESOCIALIZATION CENTER, KORHAL IV
THE TERRAN DOMINION
THESE ARE DARK TIMES. AND IF HUMANITY IS TO LIVE TO SEE THE DAWN, THEN WE MUST STAND TOGETHER, UNITED AS ONE.
MOST ZERG ARE LITTLE MORE THAN BEASTS, BUT THE LEADERSHIP STRAINS--
THE C-14 GAUSS RIFLE FIRES 8MM ARMOR-PIERCING PROJECTILES AT HYPERSONIC SPEEDS--
--WILL BE A WEAPON. YOU WILL BE A MINISTER OF DEATH, PRAYING FOR WAR.
PROTOSS PLASMA SHIELDS ARE BEST OVERCOME THROUGH MASSED FIRE.
--SUITS HAVE FULL NBC SHIELDING AND LIFE SUPPORT CAPABILITIES.
YOUR GAUSS RIFLE IS ONLY A TOOL. IT IS A HARD HEART THAT KILLS.
USE OF STIMPACKS CAN INCREASE REACTION TIME AND COMBAT EFFECTIVENESS, BUT SHOULD--
"I CHOSE HIM BECAUSE HE HATES THE DOMINION AND EVERYTHING IT STANDS FOR."

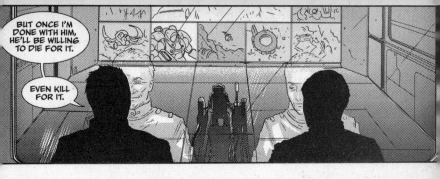

BUT ONCE I'M DONE WITH HIM, HE'LL BE WILLING TO DIE FOR IT.

EVEN KILL FOR IT.

SO WHY NOT JUST USE A RESOC TANK?

A RESOCIALIZATION THIS EXTREME REQUIRES A MORE...INVASIVE TECHNIQUE.

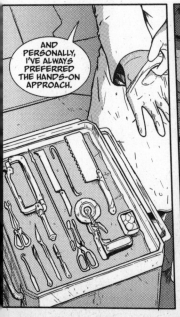

AND PERSONALLY, I'VE ALWAYS PREFERRED THE HANDS-ON APPROACH.

WE ARE ONE PEOPLE. WE HAVE ONE CAUSE. WE FOLLOW ONE LEADER.

--UPGRADE TO U-238 AMMUNITION INCREASES EFFECTIVE RANGE BY 25 PERCENT.

THE RETRACTABLE VISOR CONTAINS A HOLOGRAPHIC HEADS UP DISPLAY OR HUD--

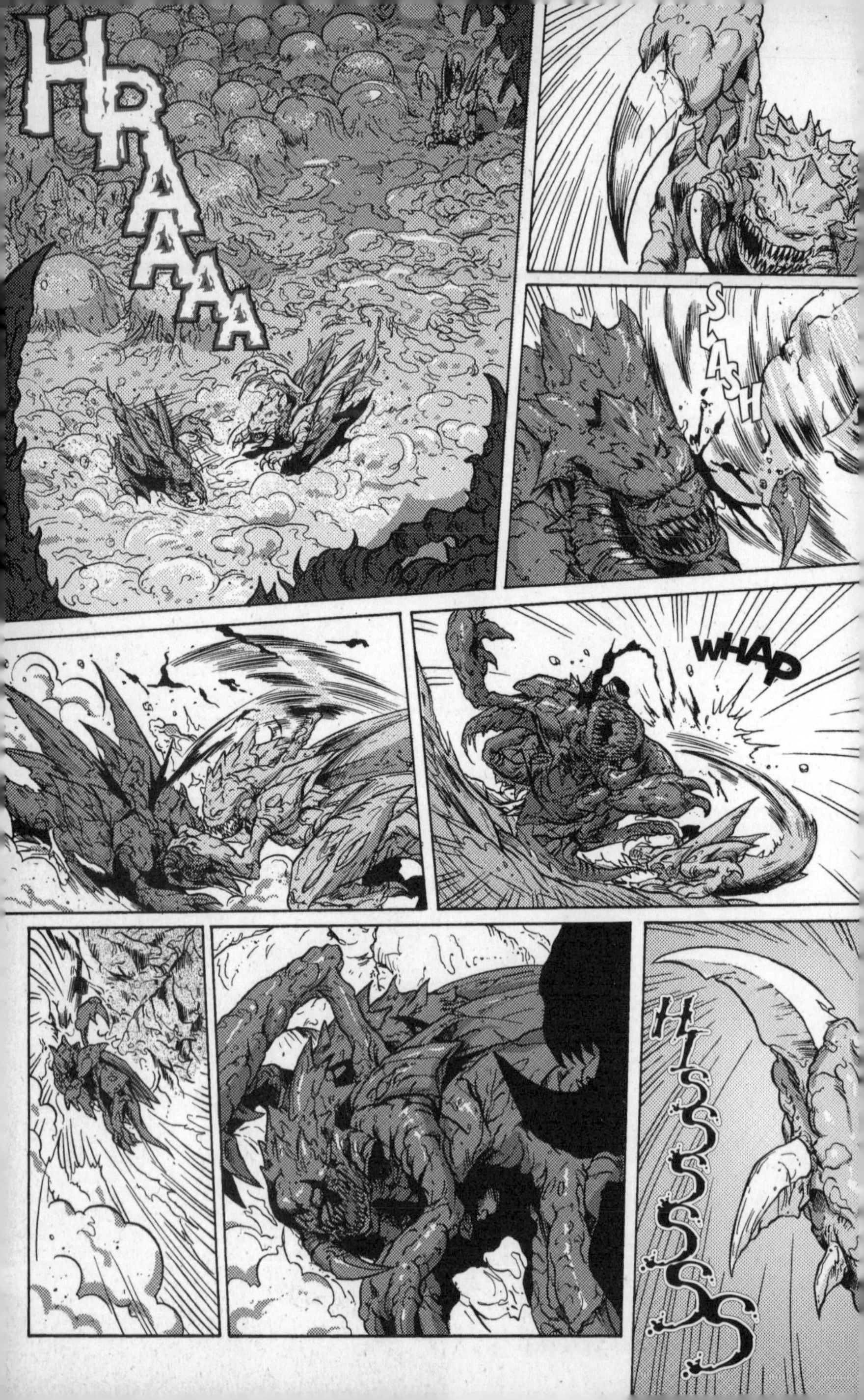
HRAAAAA
SLASH
WHAP
HISSSSS

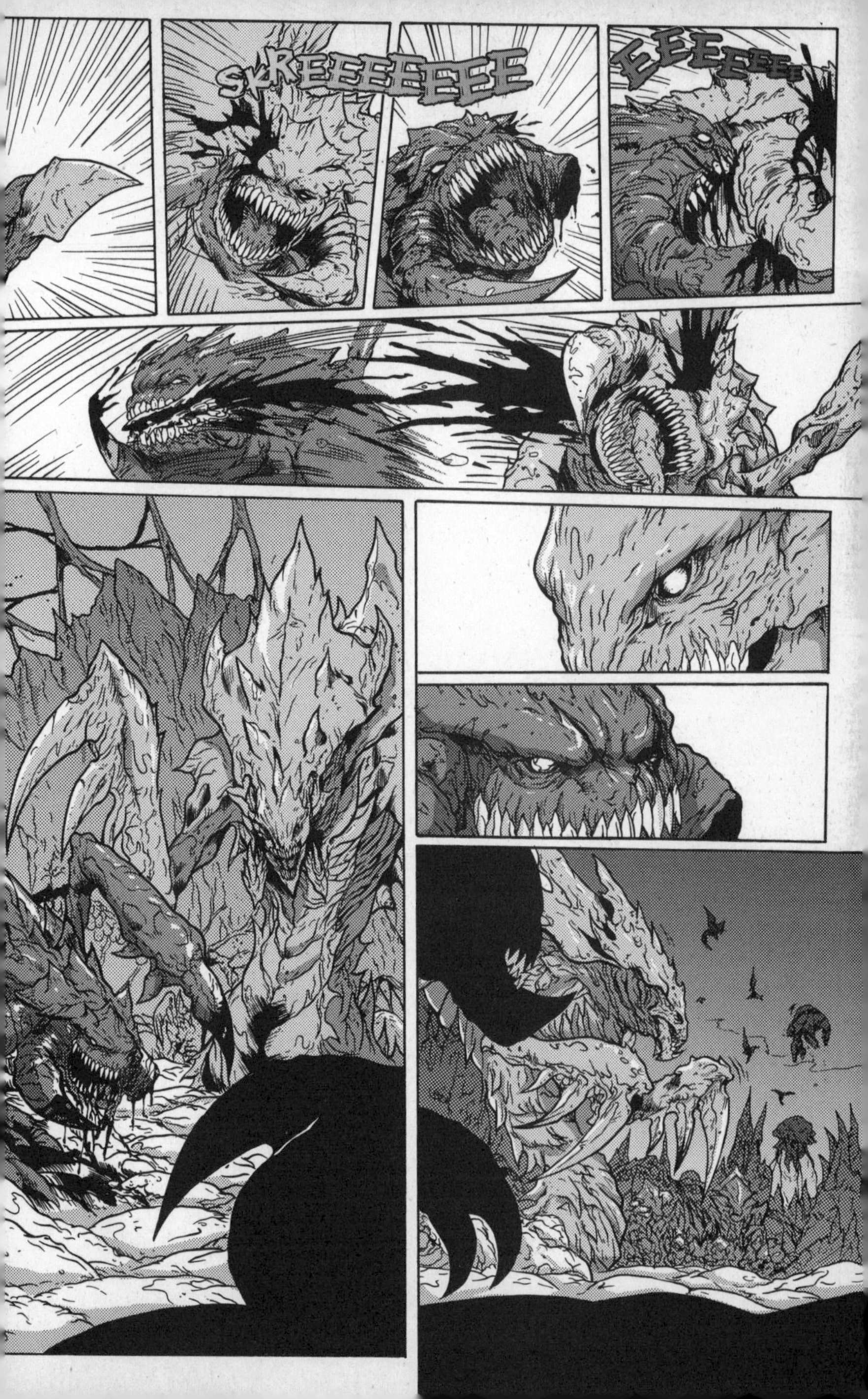
SKREEEEEEEE
EEEEEE

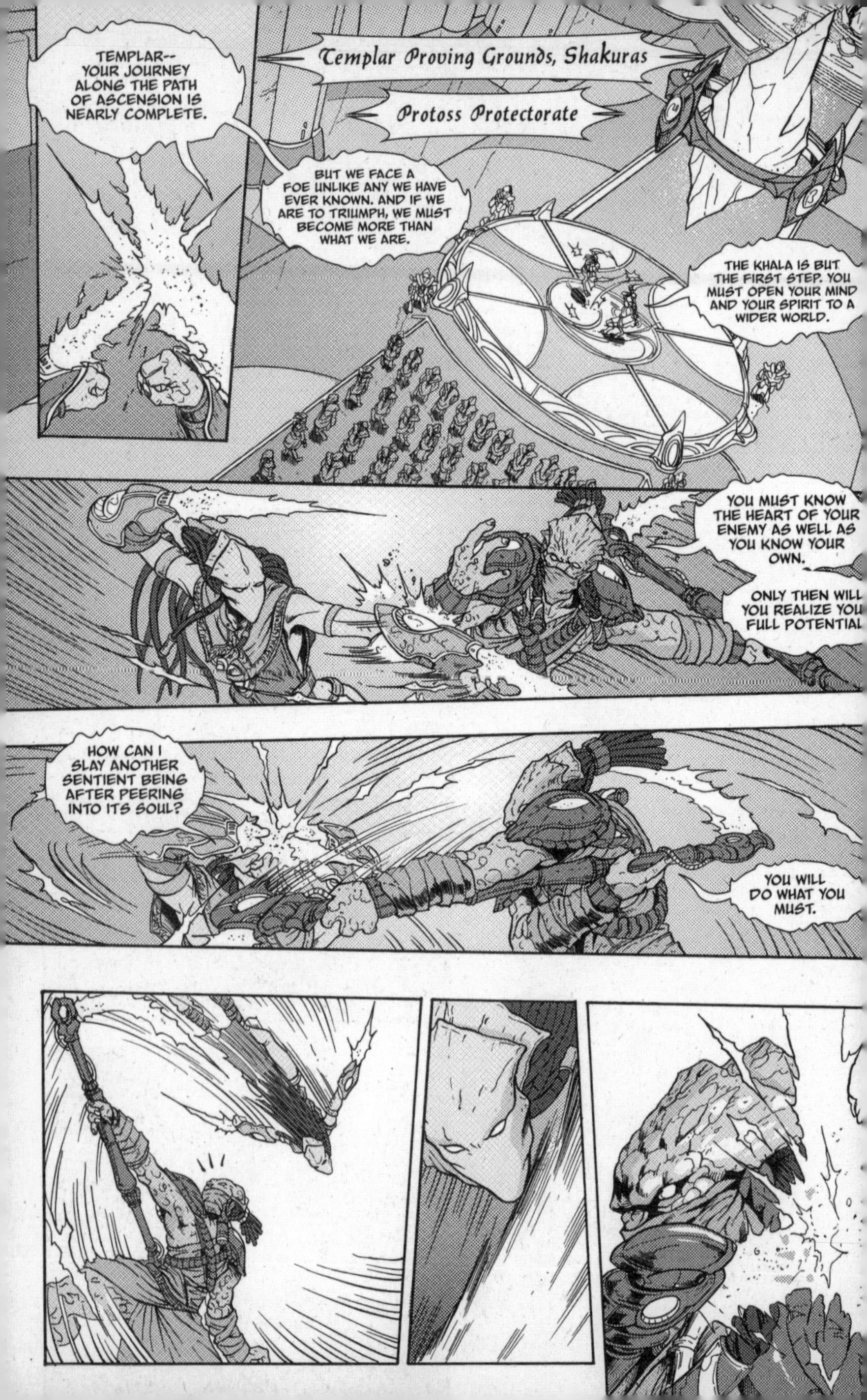
TEMPLAR-- YOUR JOURNEY ALONG THE PATH OF ASCENSION IS NEARLY COMPLETE.
Templar Proving Grounds, Shakuras
Protoss Protectorate
BUT WE FACE A FOE UNLIKE ANY WE HAVE EVER KNOWN. AND IF WE ARE TO TRIUMPH, WE MUST BECOME MORE THAN WHAT WE ARE.
THE KHALA IS BUT THE FIRST STEP. YOU MUST OPEN YOUR MIND AND YOUR SPIRIT TO A WIDER WORLD.
YOU MUST KNOW THE HEART OF YOUR ENEMY AS WELL AS YOU KNOW YOUR OWN.
ONLY THEN WILL YOU REALIZE YOU FULL POTENTIAL
HOW CAN I SLAY ANOTHER SENTIENT BEING AFTER PEERING INTO ITS SOUL?
YOU WILL DO WHAT YOU MUST.

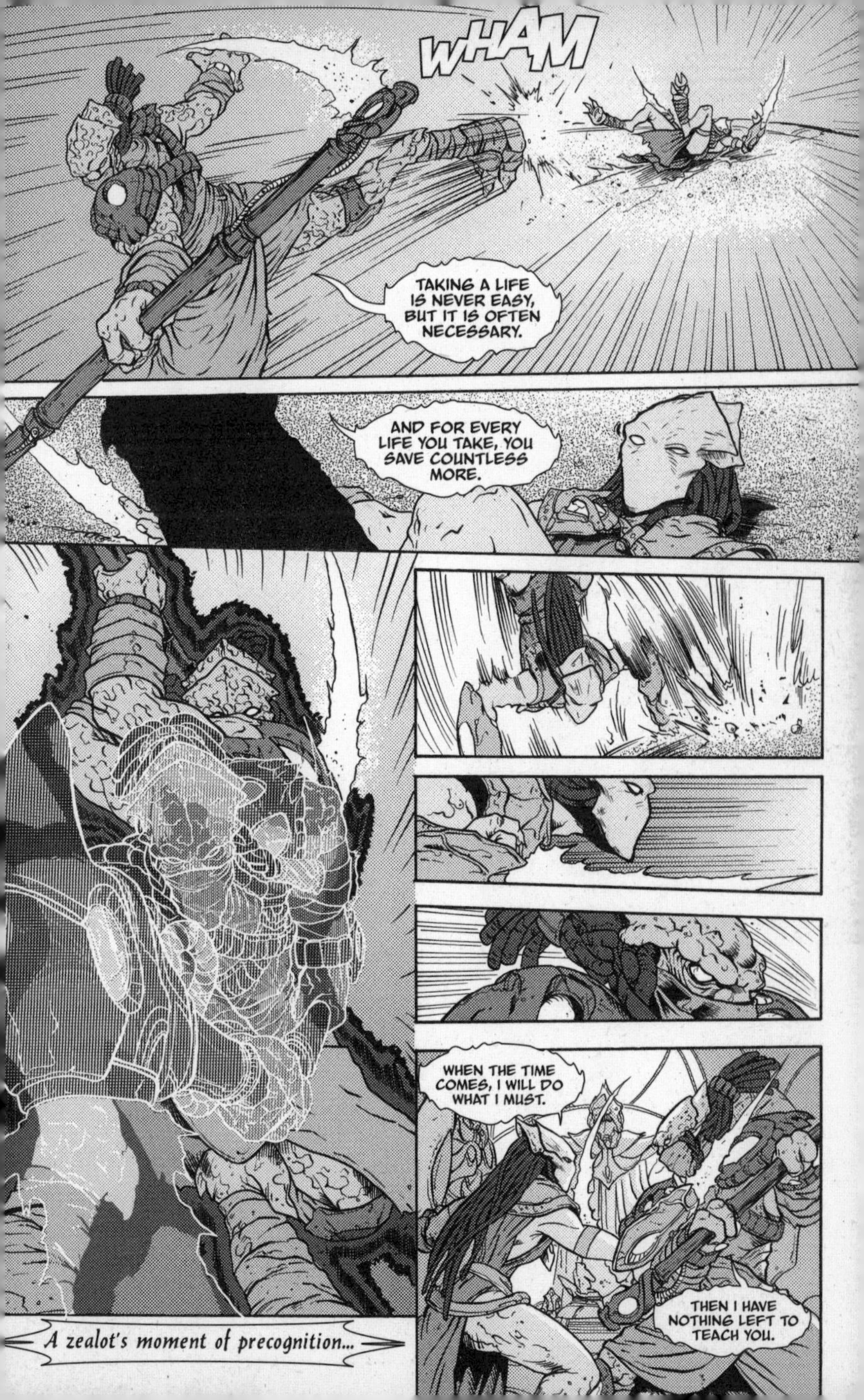
WHAM
TAKING A LIFE IS NEVER EASY, BUT IT IS OFTEN NECESSARY.
AND FOR EVERY LIFE YOU TAKE, YOU SAVE COUNTLESS MORE.
A zealot's moment of precognition...
WHEN THE TIME COMES, I WILL DO WHAT I MUST.
THEN I HAVE NOTHING LEFT TO TEACH YOU.

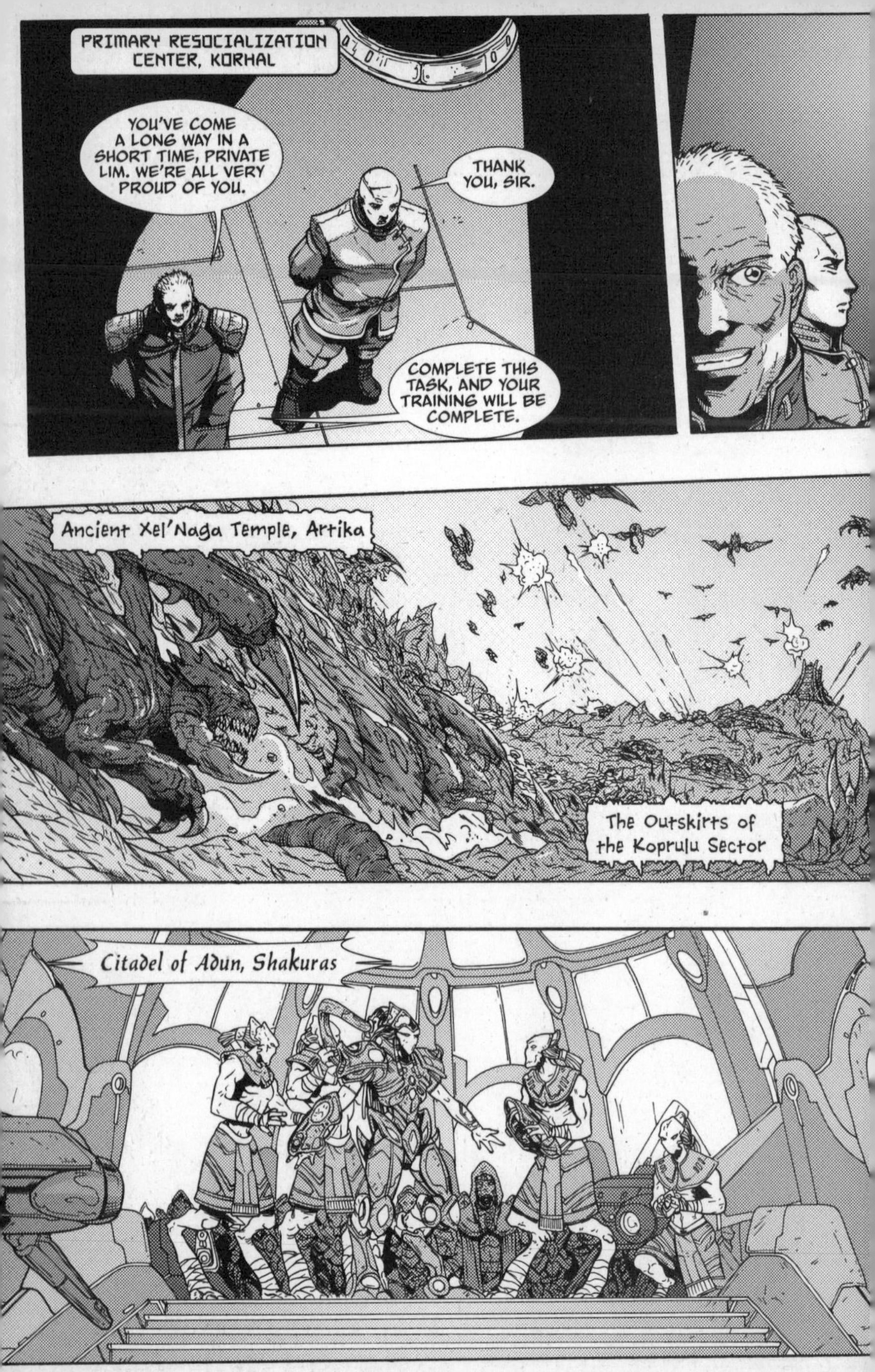
PRIMARY RESOCIALIZATION CENTER, KORHAL
YOU'VE COME A LONG WAY IN A SHORT TIME, PRIVATE LIM. WE'RE ALL VERY PROUD OF YOU.
THANK YOU, SIR.
COMPLETE THIS TASK, AND YOUR TRAINING WILL BE COMPLETE.
Ancient Xel'Naga Temple, Artika
The Outskirts of the Koprulu Sector
Citadel of Adun, Shakuras

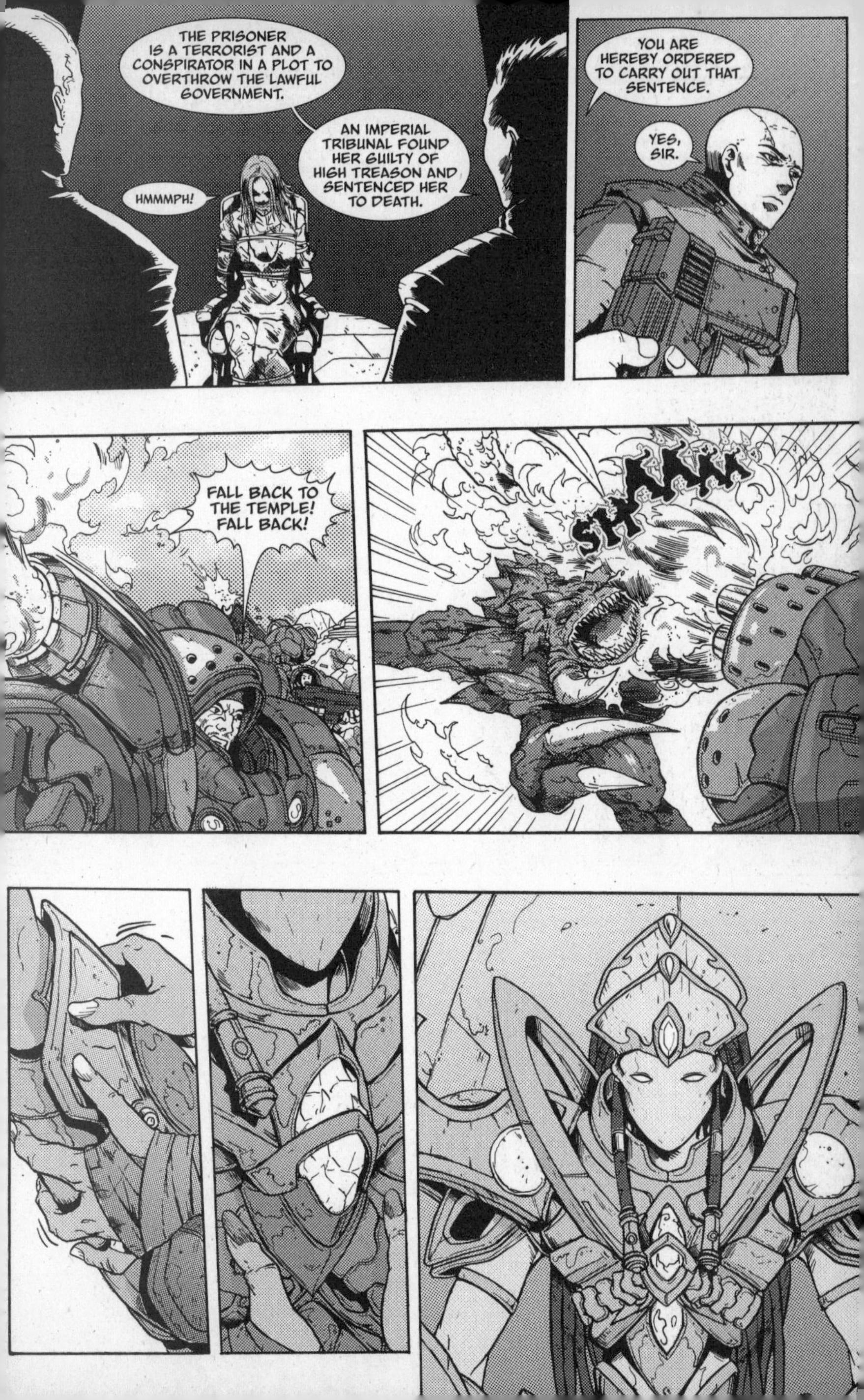
THE PRISONER IS A TERRORIST AND A CONSPIRATOR IN A PLOT TO OVERTHROW THE LAWFUL GOVERNMENT.
AN IMPERIAL TRIBUNAL FOUND HER GUILTY OF HIGH TREASON AND SENTENCED HER TO DEATH.
HMMMPH!
YOU ARE HEREBY ORDERED TO CARRY OUT THAT SENTENCE.
YES, SIR.
FALL BACK TO THE TEMPLE! FALL BACK!
SHAAKK

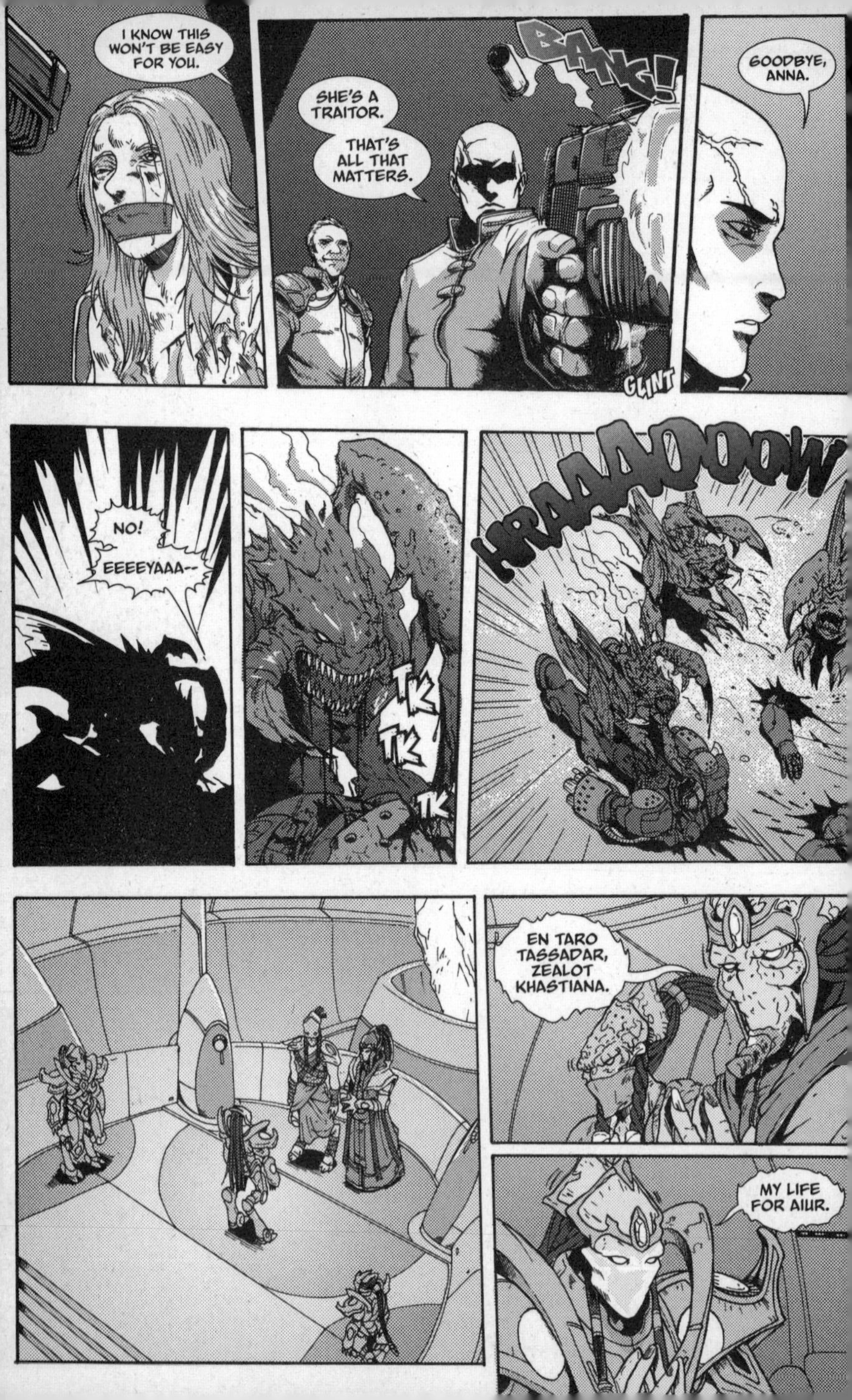
I KNOW THIS WON'T BE EASY FOR YOU.
SHE'S A TRAITOR.
THAT'S ALL THAT MATTERS.
BANG!
GLINT
GOODBYE, ANNA.
NO!
EEEEYAAA--
TK
TK
TK
HRAAAOOOW
EN TARO TASSADAR, ZEALOT KHASTIANA.
MY LIFE FOR AIUR.

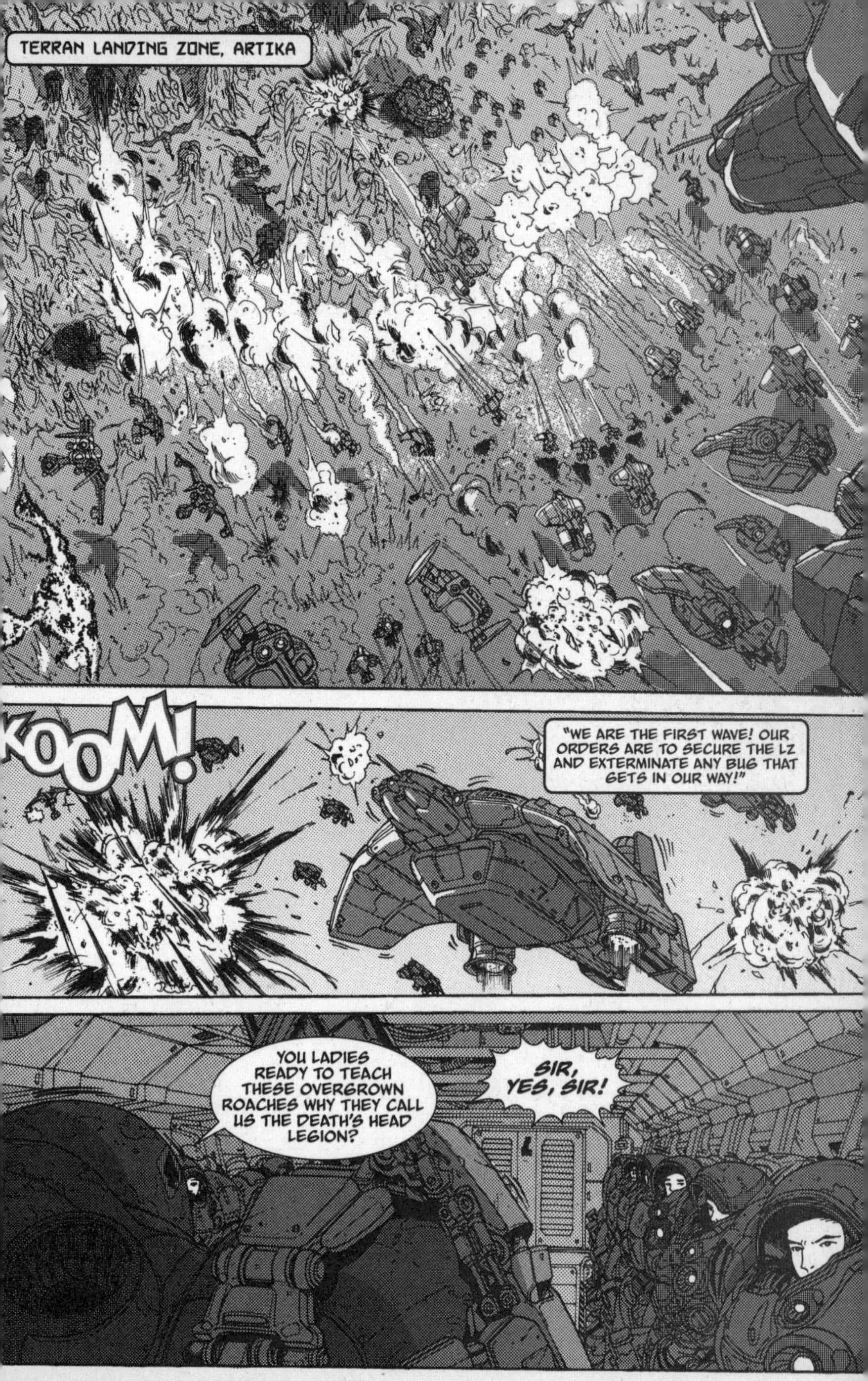
TERRAN LANDING ZONE, ARTIKA
KOOM!
"WE ARE THE FIRST WAVE! OUR ORDERS ARE TO SECURE THE LZ AND EXTERMINATE ANY BUG THAT GETS IN OUR WAY!"
YOU LADIES READY TO TEACH THESE OVERGROWN ROACHES WHY THEY CALL US THE DEATH'S HEAD LEGION?
SIR, YES, SIR!

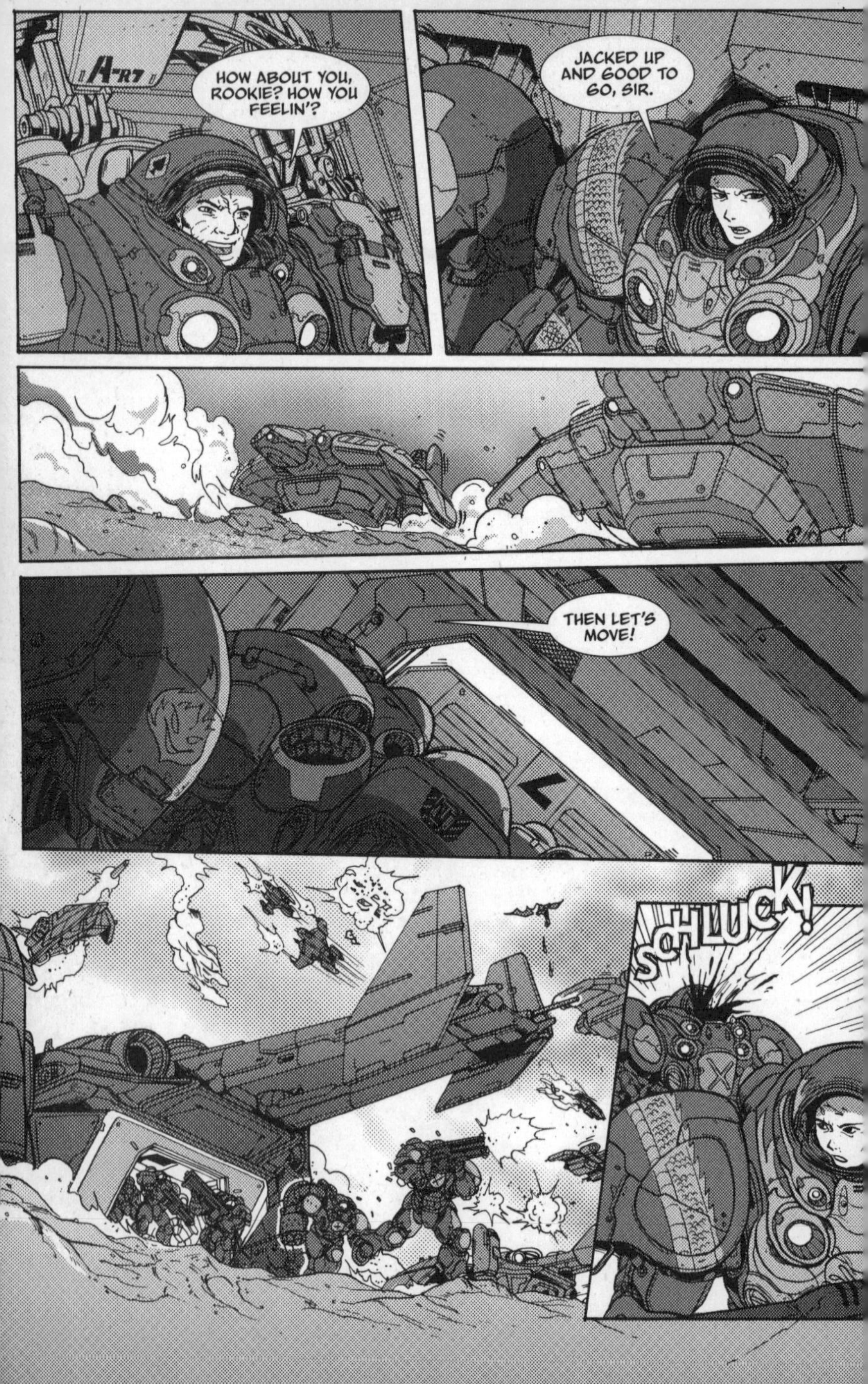
HOW ABOUT YOU, ROOKIE? HOW YOU FEELIN'?
JACKED UP AND GOOD TO GO, SIR.
THEN LET'S MOVE!
SCHLUCK!

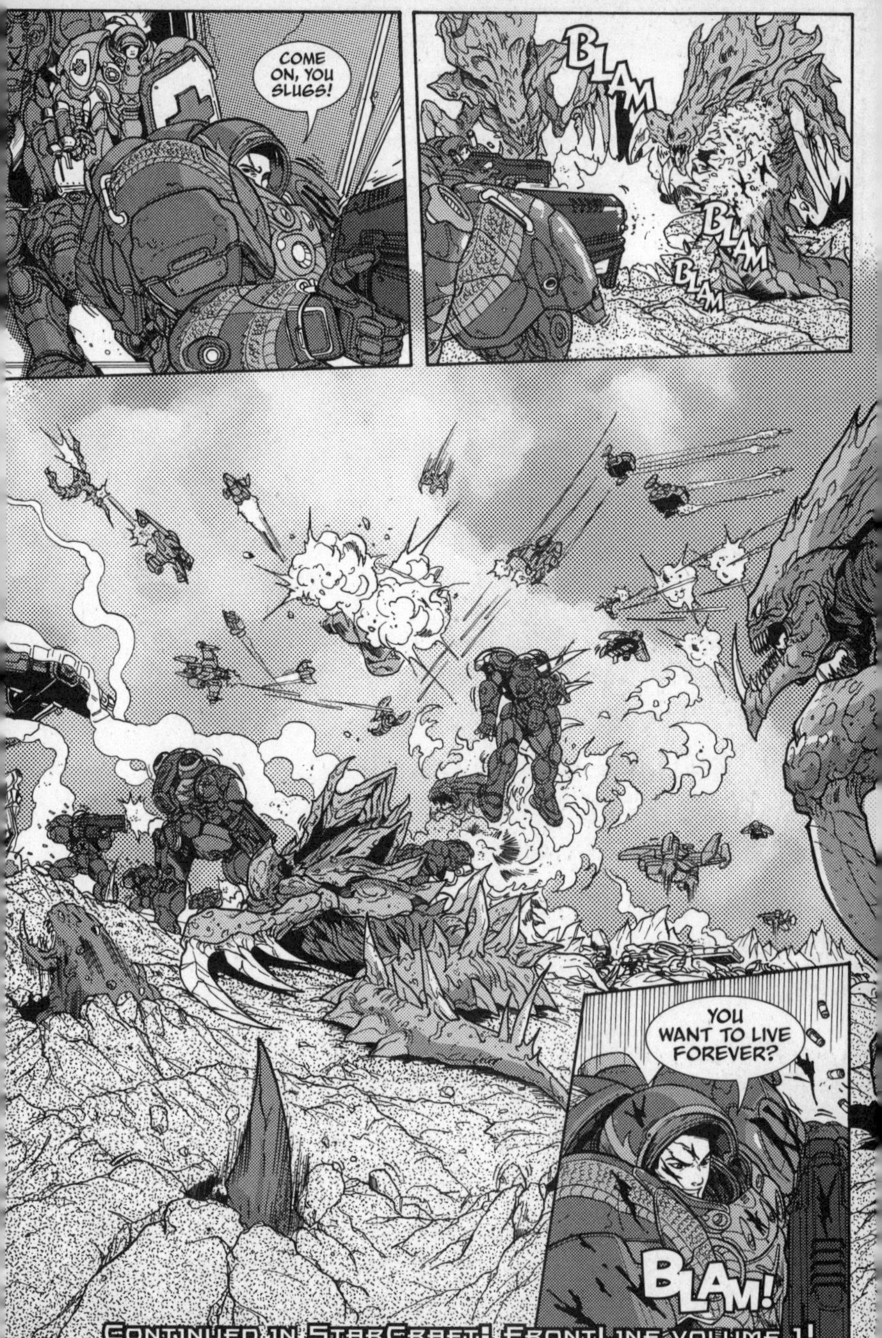
COME ON, YOU SLUGS!
BLAM
BLAM
BLAM
BLAM
YOU WANT TO LIVE FOREVER?
BLAM!
CONTINUED IN STARCRAFT: FRONTLINE VOLUME 1!

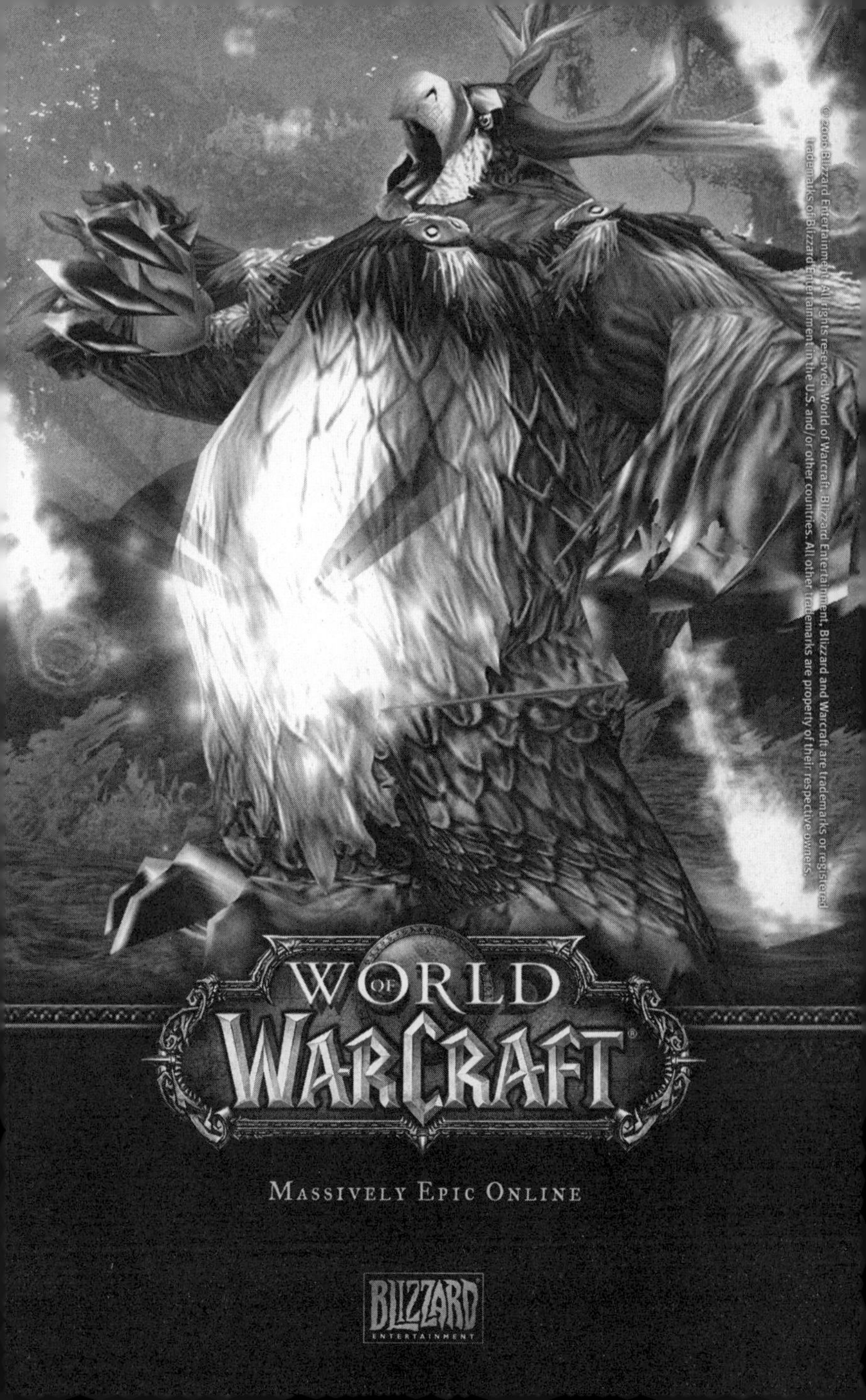

WORLD OF WARCRAFT
MASSIVELY EPIC ONLINE
BLIZZARD ENTERTAINMENT
© 2006 Blizzard Entertainment. All rights reserved. World of Warcraft, Blizzard Entertainment, Blizzard and Warcraft are trademarks or registered trademarks of Blizzard Entertainment in the U.S. and/or other countries. All other trademarks are property of their respective owners.

EPIC BATTLES

IN THE PALM OF YOUR HAND

World of Warcraft® Collectible Miniatures Gam[e]

- Premium miniatures with detailed paints designed by Studio Mc[...]
- Standard and deluxe starter sets plus three-figure boosters
- Innovative game play utilizing the unique detachable UBase

Coming Fall 2008!

For more information, visit

WOWMINIS.COM

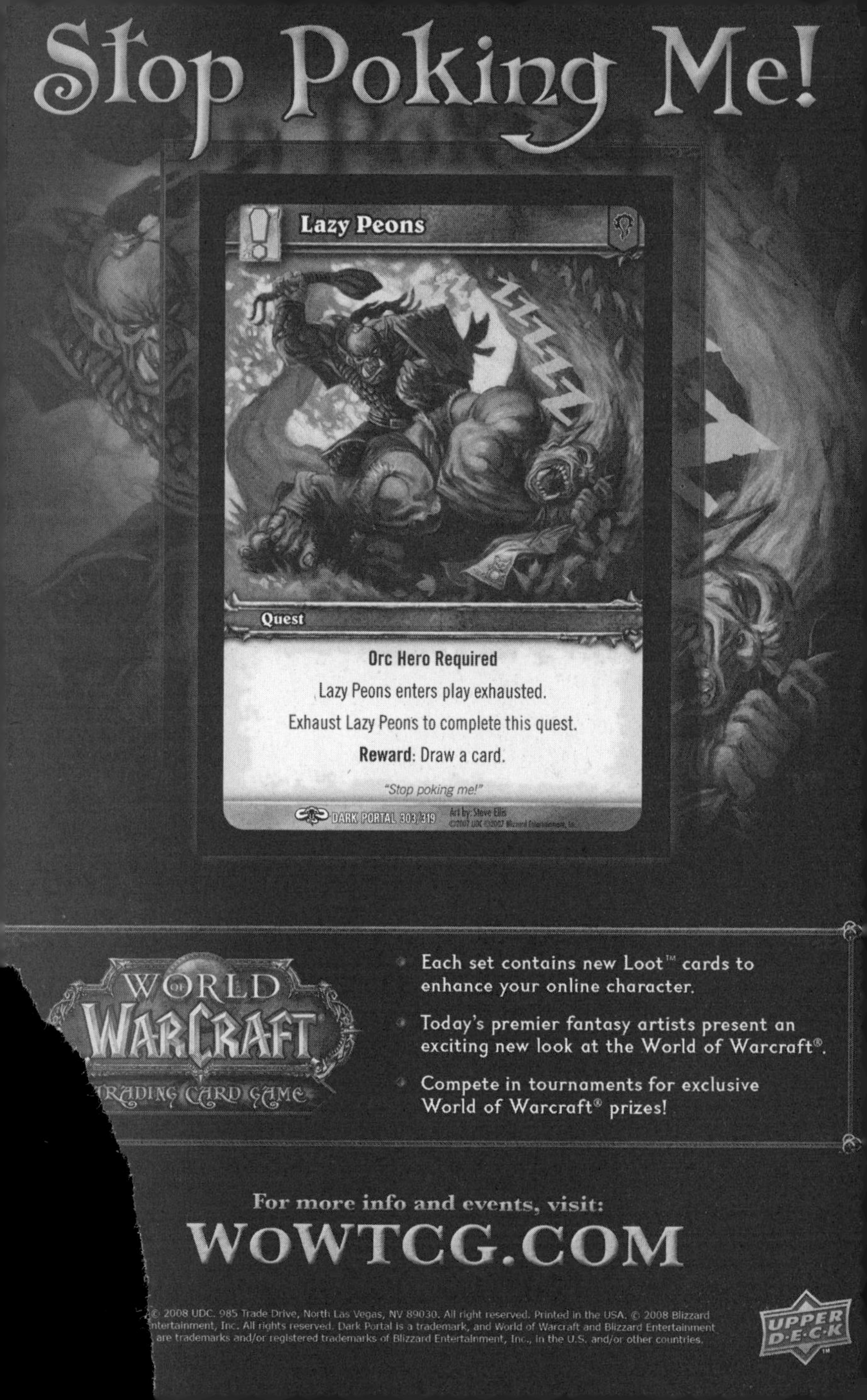
Stop Poking Me!
Lazy Peons
Quest
Orc Hero Required
Lazy Peons enters play exhausted.
Exhaust Lazy Peons to complete this quest.
Reward: Draw a card.
"Stop poking me!"
DARK PORTAL 303/319
Art by: Steve Ellis
WORLD OF WARCRAFT
RADING CARD GAME
Each set contains new Loot™ cards to enhance your online character.
Today's premier fantasy artists present an exciting new look at the World of Warcraft®.
Compete in tournaments for exclusive World of Warcraft® prizes!
For more info and events, visit:
WOWTCG.COM
© 2008 UDC. 985 Trade Drive, North Las Vegas, NV 89030. All right reserved. Printed in the USA. © 2008 Blizzard
ntertainment, Inc. All rights reserved. Dark Portal is a trademark, and World of Warcraft and Blizzard Entertainment
are trademarks and/or registered trademarks of Blizzard Entertainment, Inc., in the U.S. and/or other countries.
UPPER DECK

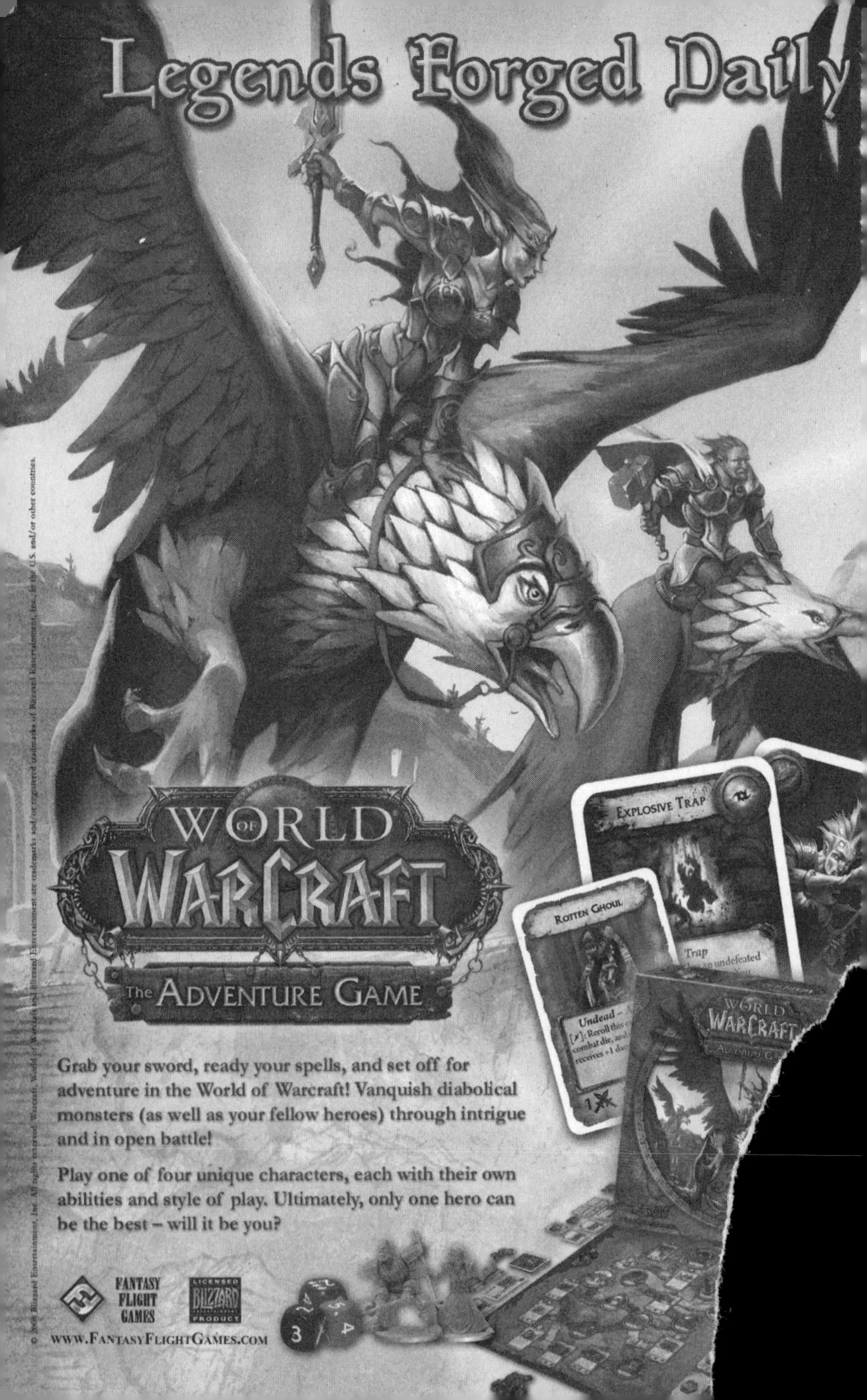
Legends Forged Daily
WORLD OF WARCRAFT
The ADVENTURE GAME
Explosive Trap
Rotten Ghoul
Undead
Grab your sword, ready your spells, and set off for adventure in the World of Warcraft! Vanquish diabolical monsters (as well as your fellow heroes) through intrigue and in open battle!
Play one of four unique characters, each with their own abilities and style of play. Ultimately, only one hero can be the best – will it be you?
FANTASY FLIGHT GAMES
LICENSED BLIZZARD PRODUCT
www.FantasyFlightGames.com
© 2008 Blizzard Entertainment, Inc. All rights reserved. Warcraft, World of Warcraft and Blizzard Entertainment are trademarks and/or registered trademarks of Blizzard Entertainment, Inc., in the U.S. and/or other countries.